PERFECT ROSE CRACKED VASE

PAMELA L. REYNOLDS

© 2019 **Pamela L. Reynolds**
All rights reserved.

No part of this book may be reproduced in any form without permission of the author and publisher with the exception of brief quotations embodied in reviews and other non-commercial use as permitted by copyright law.

For information about this title or to order other books and/or electronic media, contact the publisher:

Highland Publishing LLC
PO Box 452, Gilbert, Arizona 85299

Illustration: Tanya L. Reynolds • TLReynolds712@gmail.com

Printed in the United States of America

ISBN: 978-0-9982209-0-1 (print)
        978-0-9982209-1-8 (eBook)

This is a fictional memoir. The events are portrayed to the best of the author's memory. While all the stories in this book are true, some names and identifying details have been changed to protect the privacy of the people involved. She has endeavored to recreate events, locations, and conversations from her memories of them. She may have changed some identifying characteristics and details such as physical properties, occupations, conversations, and places of residence.

In memory of my parents.
Roger and Jaqueline Shelton
They left a legacy of love by their example and sacrifice.
Thank you, Mom and Dad,
for loving me unconditionally.
I love you always and forever.

CONTENTS

CHAPTER 1	Past and Present 1
CHAPTER 2	Around My Neck. 9
CHAPTER 3	Miss Mary Mack. 13
CHAPTER 4	Gigi. 23
CHAPTER 5	Life as I Knew It. 29
CHAPTER 6	Changes 35
CHAPTER 7	Wish on a Star. 41
CHAPTER 8	Wet White Pants 45
CHAPTER 9	Wishy-Washy 49
CHAPTER 10	Crush or Not to Crush 55
CHAPTER 11	Bike Ride. 59
CHAPTER 12	Dad's Magic Polisher 69
CHAPTER 13	Best Friends. 73
CHAPTER 14	Christmas Eve 81
CHAPTER 15	French Toast 89
CHAPTER 16	Date 95
CHAPTER 17	Second Go-Around 99
CHAPTER 18	Rejection. 103

CHAPTER 19	Liberty Box	109
CHAPTER 20	ROTC Ball	113
CHAPTER 21	Summertime	117
CHAPTER 22	Cowboy Dallas	125
CHAPTER 23	Truth or Lie	139
CHAPTER 24	Girl's Camp	145
CHAPTER 25	Haunted or Not	149
CHAPTER 26	Camp Letters	155
CHAPTER 27	Blindfold	171
CHAPTER 28	Thanksgiving Thanks	175
CHAPTER 29	Guillain Barre	183
CHAPTER 30	Grandmother's Visit	191
CHAPTER 31	Washington, DC	195
CHAPTER 32	Prom Night	201
CHAPTER 33	Yearbook Signing	205
CHAPTER 34	Test	209
CHAPTER 35	Moving On	219
CHAPTER 36	Mom's Wonderful Trick	231
CHAPTER 37	Tattered Bag—Tattered Heart	247
CHAPTER 38	Letter of Love	249
CHAPTER 39	Graduation	257
CHAPTER 40	Camp Geronimo	261
CHAPTER 41	Dance, Dance, Dance	277
CHAPTER 42	Blind Love	281
CHAPTER 43	Circle of Survival	287

1
PAST AND PRESENT
June 17, 2006
Don't let trivial things poison your happiness.

I scooted to the edge of the recliner and focused on Mom's papers on my living room floor. Her hidden secret papers, which captured her emotions, had been stashed in my garage. My memories awoke from their slumber of when her glassy eyes glared into mine when I was eleven. A framed picture of her on the end table, with her drooped head and oxygen tube in her nose, displayed the sixty-seven years of distress. Her light-red lips released a small grin that, at that moment, I wished could speak. Mom loved me as much as Grandmother hated Mom. The years Mom attempted suicide numbered fewer than the times my classmates called me the "one-eyed freak." I sank back in the recliner and began to read the papers that were meant only for her one-eyed-freak daughter to see.

"My eighteen-year-old daughter, Rose, came bounding through the door; her blond hair, glistening in the sun, flowed behind, and her soft blue eyes looked with wonder at me.

Was the phone for me? Who called? I must eat quickly and take a shower before my meeting. I will need a ride to the Saturday night dance. Kahuna and Dax will be there. What dress do you think would look nice? Maybe I can borrow Sophie's shoes.

Typical chatter of a young teenage girl. All parents go through it as their sons and daughters reach teen years.

No one would ever believe that the beautiful girl, wholesome, Christian, pure, morally straight, never on drugs or alcohol, had once been given up on by doctors, who thought that her highest quality of life would be only that of a vegetable.

In my fourth or fifth week of pregnancy, I contracted the German measles from the Girl Scout troop that I was a leader for. My boys were three and five years and went with me to the meetings. I wanted a little girl, and, not having any, enjoyed working with these Girl Scouts. The girls all came down with the German measles. I did not think anything about it. When I became ill, I was very ill for three days. I still did not worry. Then, as if the world had been waiting for this to happen to me, I read an article about German measles and how it affected the fetus in the first months of pregnancy. When I realized I was pregnant and had been pregnant when I contracted the measles, a chill went through me as I read more articles in magazines and newspapers. *Oh, no! My unborn child could be born blind, deaf, mentally handicapped, or have a heart defect.* Clutching my stomach for what might come to be, I never dreamed of abortion and never would—even if given the option by the doctor.

During my pregnancy, I read everything I could find about German measles. I have since learned that there was an epidemic of babies born with rubella syndrome at the time. The doctor cautioned me on what could happen when my baby was born. I listened, but I already knew. I had lost a baby previously by miscarriage. Every time I did not feel the baby move, I would lie on my stomach and pray that I could feel its little body. *Don't let the baby die,* I pleaded to the Lord. I knew what might lie ahead, yet I longed to hold the baby in my arms. I knew I would never have any more children. My pregnancy—as far as my own health was concerned—was okay. I was fine after my three days of measles. I never got sick again.

One night, my husband, who was a member of The Church of Jesus Christ of Latter-Day Saints, came home from work. *"I have talked to the Bishop in our ward. He is going to send home teachers."*

A gentle, humble man came to our home. It seems to me he came alone, and he brought such love into our home. He sent the missionaries. They were two older, widowed women. Their motherly kindness was so appreciated. They shared the gospel with me. The bishop would come over, and I was encouraged to go to the church on Sunday. My husband worked on Sunday and could not attend church. I had been attending the local Baptist church with the boys.

I sat Sunday night in Sacrament meeting at The Church of Jesus Christ of Latter-Day Saints, listening to a young returned missionary speak of his mission in Mexico. My ears could not listen hard enough for my brain to register all he said. I wished he would repeat his talk. He said that a man in Mexico, very sick, about to die, wanted to be baptized. He would have to be baptized in a local river. The weather was cold, and the doctors said that, if he were baptized, he would get chilled and die. Yet, he had faith. He told the missionary, *"Baptize me."* He was baptized. The old man never got any worse. In fact, his health improved. This was it. This was the message to me. The Lord was talking to me through that missionary. I longed to shake his hand and question him more. Yet, I couldn't. It was as if the realization given to me was to be a secret. I must be baptized while I carried this child.

I went to the Bishop. *"Please baptize me during the next baptism time,"* I pleaded.

I was eight and a half months pregnant and very, very heavy.

The bishop touched my shoulder. *"Let's wait until after your delivery."*

I did not want to wait. I could not tell him what I had been inspired to know. It was my secret, and I held it close within my heart. My heart sang. The Lord could heal the little life within me. I could help the baby to be born well and normal. For the first time in a long time, I sang a song in my mind that sang of joy. The Bishop okayed my baptism. Our humble home teacher baptized me (my husband was not an Elder). I was so large that two other men assisted. I went into the water to not only bury my sins and arise new in the Lord, but to give new life to my unborn child. I became a member of The Church of Jesus Christ of Latter-Day Saints and was given the gift of the Holy Ghost. I had such a blessing, to be a member of Christ's church, to know that my baby's body was made whole. I didn't worry for the rest of my pregnancy. Several weeks later, on a Friday night, I delivered. It was a girl. My own little girl.

Horror upon horror, what was wrong? She was not breathing. I could not see what the doctors were doing, yet I knew they were working feverishly to get her to breathe. I watched the clock. Although only seconds had passed, it felt like hours. At long last, I heard her first faint cry, her first breath. They carried her over to me on the delivery table. They laid her in my arms. Something was wrong. Her frail body was blue. She was not well. I could tell they believed she may not live. They placed her in an incubator and wheeled her out with me. How like a little sparrow she looked, one who had fallen out of the nest. I was so proud of my little daughter. Oh, I was thrilled to have a girl. Yet, what about the promise I had from the Lord? He had not told me the truth. It was all a lie. I felt anger at God. How could He have lied to me? My husband and I clasped hands as I was wheeled out of the delivery room with fear for the life of our daughter in both our minds and hearts. Neither one spoke of it, but I knew the doctor had told my husband she might not live through the night. Both of us, being new in the church and not realizing about the priesthood or blessings, we did not call the Bishop or our home teacher. In the recovery room, I dreamed of the dresses I would put on my new little girl. I would not accept the fact that the doctor said she may not live through the night.

She lived through the night; the second crisis passed. There were problems that night and the next day, but she passed through each one miraculously. I nursed this tiny, frail life and again gave life through my body. The doctors said very little, but I could sense their concern and knew they were trying to hide something from me. Still being a babe in the church, I did not call upon the priesthood. I stayed angry at God; I could not pray to Him. Several times, they could not bring her in to eat, as she was ill. Each crisis she passed miraculously.

Monday, I was due to go home. I got out the little outfit made so lovely by her grandmother. The other babies were brought to their mothers. When they had gone home and my husband came for me, they still had not brought me my baby. Finally, my husband and I, together, tried to question the nurse.

The nurse told us, "You must leave your daughter. She is not well. We want a specialist to see her."

I ran to the window and looked out. *"Oh, God, why? Why did You lie?"* I could not cry. I could not feel. "Leave her? Leave my precious little girl? I'm breast feeding her—what about that?" The nurse put her arm around me. "If you take her home, she might die. Here, we can watch her and have doctors to call in an emergency. Don't you think it would be better to leave her here?"

I was wheeled out in a wheelchair, my arms empty and her little clothes in my hands. An OB doctor rode the elevator down with us. He looked at the floor. I knew he could think of nothing to say. My husband called the Bishop that evening. As I was breast feeding, I would have to go to the hospital several times a day. The women in our church arranged care for my boys.

Months had passed, and the specialist could not find anything seriously wrong with my daughter. Another miracle. They called us and told us we could take her home.

We drove quickly to the hospital. I dressed her in her special clothes and carried her in my arms. On the way out, the pediatric specialist stopped me. "I want to tell you," he said, "that the best thing you could do is put this child in a home. Don't get attached to her. She will never be normal, and she could still die."

Endless tears flowed as I stacked the 5 × 7 pages in order. Now at the age of forty-two, I'd discovered this story buried at the bottom of a box of papers. I was a frail sparrow that had fallen from a nest. If only Mom could have read my journals and love letters, she would have known the truth about her fragile sparrow.

I might have been a miracle to Mom, but I have never felt like a miracle, even though I was among the few to have survived Congenital Rubella Syndrome (CRS). Yet, is survival enough? I'm still damaged goods, questioning whether I was at all normal. The only way I was the same as others was in my desires. Or was I? Did others wonder to the point of anguish: *Am I pretty? Do I look out of place? Do I give the impression that I'm not capable?*

Sorrow resurfaced at the thought of Dad taking his last breath eleven months before Mom died. My hands shook. I had to erase those gloomy memories, so I imagined Dad wearing his fluorescent orange hat I had given him decorated with a black marker with all the grandkids' names, and struggling to push the old, deteriorated lawnmower across the front yard. First, warmth filled my chest, and then a smile stretched across my face with thoughts of Dad, until I remembered he'd never come back. Then the warmth gave way, and I realized that I would never hear him say, "No money in the world could replace being sealed to your mother in the temple."

I sobbed, vacant inside, because I believed they had prematurely deserted me, their one-eyed-freak daughter who was their miracle. Unable to focus,

I needed to review my past I had hidden in my journals and love letters. My life sat concealed in a brown trunk nestled in the stairway closet, holding untold stories of painful family secrets.

Unsure how to stop myself, I stared at the trunk, worked up the courage, and opened it. Memories circled me with a life I never wished for, and a musty odor of books escaped. Unsteady hands uncovered my collection. Some were embossed with my name. I ran my fingers across the gold letters, "Journal," written in cursive on a light-blue, padded three-ring binder. It brought memories of grandparents, parents, and Kahuna (Kah-*HOO*-nah). I sat near the light, rested against the family-room wall, thumbed through my journals, and read.

2
AROUND MY NECK
August 1974

When you break the heart, you crush the soul.

I stood in front of my closet and stared at my small selection of shoes. I grabbed my white sandals that made me feel pretty, slipped the strap between my toes, and buckled the band that went around my ankle.

I closed the closet doors and pictured Mom and Dad's delight to have bought a new house under the "two thirty-five" plan when I was seven. I wasn't sure what that meant, but it was the only way they were able to qualify for a home. Several times a week, we made the one-mile trip from our rental house to the construction site to see the progress on our home. It fascinated me to watch it rise from foundation to roof in the poor part of the city in a new subdivision.

Our house had unfashionable, donated, mismatched furniture. Carpet was not beneficial to Dad's asthma, so we had linoleum flooring throughout the house.

The saving grace to our home was the two large red-brick arches and two mulberry trees that produced tons of berries. Dad developed a passion for the front yard, which cost little to maintain. Almost daily, he sat in the front yard and directed the hose with an attached powerful sprinkler. I believed it gave him solace.

Air went through my sandals, cooling my feet, as I leisurely strolled to the bathroom to brush my teeth. I stared at the water descending into the basin and listened to its own musical song. Each swoosh of my brush over my teeth made me think of my mother and how we were as different as two people could possibly be. She wore dentures, and I had perfectly straight teeth. Where my mom was pessimistic and passive, I was always active and tried to think positively about life, even though I feared what others thought of me and could do to me. She was frightened to venture out at times, and I wanted to be a part of it all. Our physical features were completely different, too. I had light-blond straight hair and blue eyes; she had curly, brown short hair and hazel eyes.

I entered my parents' room, and Mom wasn't on her bed.

I called, and she responded, "In here."

I followed her voice to the master bathroom. She stood unmoving.

"Mom, I'm walking to the church building."

She gave a defiant stare, a vicious glare of despair. She didn't say a word but swiftly clutched her hands around my throat and squeezed. I wanted to pull her hands away. I looked at her with disbelief and hoped my face displayed fear and a plea for her to stop. I couldn't move my head but moved my eyes to stare in the mirror at her. Did she know I couldn't breathe? She released her hands and pushed me away. I gasped for air and looked at the floor. Silence was around us, and I left without a word. I ran out the front door in tears. My hands trembled, and I couldn't comprehend why my mom wanted to hurt me.

"Was this common—for a mother to do that to her daughter?" I asked that question out loud and hoped no one had heard me.

I hated depression, I hated life, and I hated who my mother had become. I tried to tell myself with each step I took that she didn't mean to harm me. I tried to wipe those few seconds in her bathroom out of my mind, but it was difficult because I had the sensation that her hands were around my swollen neck. Fear set in about how I would deal with what had happened.

My dad was, as always, on his truck route, unable to protect me. If I told him, it could cause more pain and stress. The sun beat down on me, and my pores released sweat. The common drive-by shootings by gang members didn't seem to be an issue for me right now. Even though, in times past, I ran when a low rider came by with music blasting, today, it was the least of my worries. I decided, with each step I took, I would never tell a soul that she'd tried to strangle me. I walked two blocks, and my mouth craved water; I was glad I had only one more block to go.

The doors to the church were inviting, offering peace and safety, and when I went inside, the cool air surrounded me. I froze near the doors, licked my dried lips, and stared at the drinking fountain. Voices from others in the building echoed down the hallway. I darted to the restroom before anyone saw me. I stood in front of the large mirror and leaned my head back, just enough so I could see if there were noticeable marks. Luckily, the marks were faint and blended well with my red face. I arranged my long blond hair to conceal my neck. I hoped no one would notice.

All during the activity, which was making dolls out of cornhusks, I couldn't get my mom's glassy eyes out of my mind. I knew when I returned home, it would be awkward for both of us. I was terrified, but I believed Mom wouldn't try it again.

When I returned home, Mom and I were the only ones there. I went into my bedroom to be alone. Down in my heart, I was frightened. I knew Mom's body lived in my home, but her mind seemed to be in another world. Just like the two arches in our front yard, I wished we had an arch of communication that was secure, engaging, and normal. I would dream for now.

I rested against my door, closed my eyes, and envisioned our front yard, where Dad worked to make it appealing from the street. Often people would congratulate him on how inviting the green St. Augustine grass yard was. No one knew, but, to me, home was far from warm and pleasurable. He left an impression that he was capable of anything.

The house was not a refuge, because Mother had slipped into a world beyond my understanding, a world of no protection.

Perfect Rose Cracked Vase

My room was somewhat of a sanctuary, but the rest of the house seemed chilly, and it wasn't because of the cold, linoleum floor. I needed my mother to provide a warm blanket of protection, but for some reason, she couldn't give it to me. I curled up on my bed with my dog Gigi and hid from her, with covers over my head. Deep in my soul, I knew my mother didn't like herself, and I was convinced my grandmother had possessed long-lasting control of Mom's mind, soul, and life. My grandmother seized any life my mother could have had and held Mom captive. Just like the Congenital Rubella Syndrome held me captive.

3
MISS MARY MACK
September 1974

My outer appearance is deceiving to many, including me.

In fifth grade, most days were the same, but sometimes I was the student and other times the main attraction at a freak show. Why, you ask? Because of my classmates' glares at my deformities. To pass time, I stared at the clock mounted on the wall and listened to its distinct click. Most of the time, when I focused on it, it blocked the noises of the other students and of my teacher, Miss Mayer. It gave me a few moments to daydream about my bedroom—a safe place—and it softened my anxiety about a girl named Tasha, who was six inches taller and whose skin was darker than mine. Thinking about her made me antsy, wishing I could slink off my chair and crawl away without being seen.

Miss Mayer was short, only an inch or two taller than her students, and she had hideous gray hair like an old man's. Did she wear a wig? Her monotone voice made me believe she was a robot with mechanical parts. Around eleven o'clock each day, Miss Mayer stood by the door with a wooden, twelve-inch ruler in her hand. She randomly called out our names in the order we were to sit in the cafeteria.

Fear stirred in me when Miss Mayer called the kids individually to the lunch line. I studied Miss Mayer's wrinkled face and hoped she'd notice how anxious I was about being near Tasha. I knew Miss Mayer was older than my grandmother, and she certainly was wiser and not as hateful.

Barry, who was a twin, sat in the desk behind me, and he constantly played with my long, light-blond hair. Sometimes, when Miss Mayer called me to the line, I couldn't move because Barry had stuck a handful of my hair in between his desk and my chair. It hurt to move.

Did Miss Mayer notice his antics? She said nothing, other than, "Rose, when I call your name, you come to the line."

The way to keep Barry from touching my hair was to gather it together and tuck it under my chin. I loved it when Barry wasn't at school; it made my days pleasurable.

On the way to the cafeteria, we walked single file. Miss Mayer walked in the front of the line, the engine to the train of misbehaving kids. My classmates watched for Miss Mayer and, when she wasn't looking, they ran out of the line and then back to their same spot, just to be funny. I didn't find it humorous, especially since Tasha took it a step further. Even with five or more classmates behind or in front of me in line, she would run and push or hit me.

We arrived at the cafeteria, and Miss Mayer reminded us to wash our hands under the faucets, which I believed never shut off. A large silver rectangular basin mounted to the brick wall captured the water and drowned out Miss Mayer's monotone voice. We entered the cafeteria and stood in an assembly line, where there were different foods to choose from. My skinny, long arms strained to carry the tray with the heavy ceramic plate and silver utensils. I looked for certain foods every day, hoping they would serve something that was familiar from home. Spinach was my favorite, and all the students around me gave me theirs. Each bite of the spinach stirred comforting memories of Dad and me as we sat at the kitchen table and ate canned spinach as our only course for dinner. Teachers walked between the long rows of tables. Sometimes they stopped and listened to our conversations. Daily, I worried they might notice the other children dumping their spinach on my plate. After I ate, I took my tray to the counter, where some old ladies dressed in white uniforms washed the trays and dishes.

When lunch was over, my daily routine would continue. Every day, I would walk toward the exit doors, hoping someone wanted to play catch or kickball with me. I'd pass some girls playing hopscotch or jacks near the cream-colored brick wall, wishing they would call my name and extend an invitation. I would take the same, slow steps along the sidewalk, contemplating whether I was confident enough to go out onto the playground or to join with the girls near the building who were playing clapping games and singing:

> *Miss Mary Mack, Mack, Mack*
> *All dressed in black, black, black*
> *With silver buttons, buttons, buttons*
> *All down her back, back, back.*
> *She asked her mother, mother, mother*
> *For fifty cents, cents, cents*
> *To see the elephants, elephants, elephants*
> *Jump over the fence, fence, fence.*
> *They jumped so high, high, high*
> *They reached the sky, sky, sky*
> *They never came back, back, back*
> *Till the 4th of July, ly, ly!*

One day, durable me walked past the girls to the top steps of the playground and paused for a few moments. I inspected all areas of the field, with diverse groups of kids playing kickball or softball. The playground was deep in the ground, and the steps were like being on a hillside. I scanned the areas to see where Tasha was before I walked down the twenty-plus cement stairs to the playground.

Each step down diminished my confidence and brought back the negative thoughts that no one would want to play with me. Alone, all alone, when I tottered onto the playground with its dried grass beneath my feet,

I shook. I reminded myself to be courageous like a soldier out to battle, even though I had no combatant with me.

It never failed that, when I got far enough out on the field, to where the teachers couldn't see, Tasha appeared out of nowhere. I did have friends, but with Tasha on my back, they stayed away from me so they wouldn't get hit or beat up, too.

That day, I stood dead center in the middle of the field and tried to figure out if I wanted to join the kickball or softball game. I was pleased when Tasha wasn't at either game. I made the choice to play kickball and ran in that direction. Moments later, Tasha was running toward me. I gathered the strength to run faster than ever, hoping to get far enough away from her. Yet, each move was the wrong one.

Her group of dark-skinned friends yelled out, "Stop, Rose."

Terror echoed in me as I clenched my stomach and ran for my life. The playground was endless and filled with potholes and weeds with prickly thorns connected to them. I looked back one more time and then looked forward again, just as my right foot slipped into a pothole. I lost my balance and hit the dead grass so hard my face burned. I rolled over and saw Tasha right above me. I tried to stand, but as I pushed my hands against the thorny weeds, Tasha punched me in the stomach.

Her friends gathered around and yelled at me, but I couldn't quite focus on what they were saying. Then Tasha yelled over her friends' voices.

"Why is your eye like that?"

I didn't know how to respond. The question seemed completely out of context; it puzzled me that she would ask me such a question. I didn't comprehend why my right eye was such an issue. To me, it was no different from anyone else's. Tasha bent down and looked at me, "You are useless, and you are a one-eyed freak. You better watch out because I'm going to beat you up after school." I was glad the teacher blew the whistle. I lay there and watched Tasha leisurely walk away, as though she owned me. Why didn't the teachers who were supposed to protect me ever come to my rescue? I got up and removed the weed thorns off my pink dress.

After lunch recess came Physical Education class. The coach divided us into two groups after he'd picked two team leaders. I stood with my head down, feet close together. I knew the team leaders wouldn't want me on their team. I couldn't gauge when to kick or hit the ball with a bat. All the kids knew I couldn't score a point for the team. While I listened to the team captains choose their teams, I alternated, standing first on one leg and then the other and rubbed the red sole of my black-and-white saddle shoe over the grass. At least I didn't have metal braces on my legs anymore, just hideous corrective shoes. I hoped I wouldn't be the last one chosen and placed on the losers' team.

Joe, with his large-framed body and his huge confidence to match, was always a team captain.

"I pick Sharon and John."

Becky, the other captain, looked at me and then looked away.

"I pick Tasha and Curtis."

Joe had ten people left to pick from.

"I pick David and Karl."

Joe had picked two guys, so I hoped Becky would pick two girls.

"I pick Gina and Lisa."

My head dropped after three more rounds of picking.

Joe spoke. "I pick Terry and Barry."

Becky pointed at Chris. "I pick Chris and Rose."

When PE was finished, Miss Mayer led us to the restrooms and water fountains. When it was my turn to get a drink, I pointed to each spout, lined up like Christmas lights on a long, silver pipe and sang a song: "Coffee, tea, soda pop, pee." When other students got a drink out of the one named "pee," my friend Brenda and I laughed. Once everyone used the restrooms and had a drink, we walked, single file, back to class.

When we entered the classroom, a smell of sweat penetrated the room. Miss Mayer walked to the front of the class and yelled so loud that I'm sure the teachers down the hallway heard her.

"Take your pencils out, and complete the math sheet on your desk."

I glanced at Tasha. She gave me a nasty look. How she convinced kids to be cruel to me was a big mystery. When Miss Mayer wasn't looking, Tasha did what she'd done countless times before. She came to my desk, grabbed my pencil, broke it, and called me a name I would never repeat. As usual, it was a name I'd never heard before, and it was delivered with an ugly sneer. She never got caught—or did she?

Miss Mayer was afraid of Tasha, too, because she must have known about Tasha's brother, who was in ninth grade, like my brother Bobby. The story blared out on the news and was talked about at recess how he'd killed a cashier down at the local grocery store by stabbing him in the chest with a knife. It made me queasy even to think about it.

Seconds after the long hand on the clock reached the three, I darted out the classroom door and ran. My fragile, skinny legs struggled with every step to pull my heavy saddle shoes toward home. I didn't want to repeat what had happened weeks before. I ran and pictured those kids around me as they had pushed me into their circle. One kid pulled my hair and left a tender spot. The pain of Tasha's fist punching me in the stomach gave me the energy to lift my feet high enough to run faster. Who knows what would have happened last time if it hadn't been for Tasha's twin sister, Zora. She was my only saving grace. I loved how she yelled, "Leave Rose alone." If Tasha hadn't listened to Zora, I would have had a swollen black eye. Now, thinking about last time, I tried to stay focused as I ran, but that event weeks ago played in my mind, and I could still hear the kids yell, "Hit her. Give her a black eye to match her ugly eye."

I remember how I had cried and tried to hold back the pain of rejection. This time, as I ran, Zora was absent and not able to help. I was so grateful that Zora had been there before and had caught Tasha and stopped her, which started a fight. Zora saved me when she pushed me into the ditch while she fought Tasha. This time I had no one to defend me, so I sprinted and kept focused.

I ran down the narrow dirt path that paralleled an irrigation ditch on one side and Encanto Street on the other. I darted in between kids to get additional distance from Tasha. I didn't take the time to look back to see her behind me. I knew that, if I did, it would slow me down. Terrified, I continued to run fast, even though my legs were sore. She bellowed my name.

I reached the church building and glanced over at it, wishing someone were inside to rescue me. I took my chances and jumped down into the irrigation ditch. Though it was half full, I thought it was better to have wet saddle shoes than a black eye. I slogged through, dug my fingers into the muddy walls of the ditch, and climbed out the other side. I entered the wheat field with relief, even though I knew I might get disoriented further in.

Exhausted, I tried to stop from falling. I couldn't let Tasha beat me. I knew if she caught me that's what she would do, and all the while she was hitting me, she would remind me that the next day she'd give me a fat lip. I panicked and pushed the tall wheatgrass away from my face. I contemplated which way to go and stopped to scratch where the wheatgrass had touched my legs and arms. I looked at the sky and asked God to guide me home.

I sighed when I stepped out of the field. Without delay, I looked both directions down the alley for the neighborhood kids who lived across the street from me. They were as mean to me as Tasha. Did they pick on me because I was so fair skinned? I sensed someone near and heard footsteps. I dared not look back.

Then, out of nowhere, Deena, who was my age, jumped in front of me. Her large stature made me quiver.

"Don't you dare say a word or move one inch."

Her friends grabbed and pulled me in two different directions. Deena's eyes got big when she pulled my hair.

I had to be strong, as she yelled, "You are in for it."

Her friends dragged me to an ant hill and laughed.

I wiggled and begged them, "Please, let me go."

Deena kicked me, and her friends held my arms tight while army ants crawled on my legs. When they thought they had tortured me for a sufficient amount of time, they released me and walked away laughing. I ran in the opposite direction and dropped to the ground to remove my shoes and white knee-high socks.

I tried not to give in to the tears that freely came.

Perfect Rose Cracked Vase

I rubbed the red ant bites and spoke out loud, "Do I need to go home or to the foster family?"

I arrived on my street to find an ambulance in front of my home. I ran, although my head ached, and my legs turned into an inferno. I walked up the driveway; paramedics were pushing my mother on a gurney with her hands and legs strapped down.

I ran to her. "Mom, where are you going?"

"I'll be back home soon, Rosie; you be a good girl."

The tall, skinny paramedic looked at me. "You need to move so we can wheel your mother down the walkway."

The pain in my heart overshadowed the constant ache my blind eye had from the glaucoma. I never understood why it hurt, because I had two eyes like everyone else.

The paramedics lifted her into the ambulance. A tap on my shoulder startled me, and I turned to see who it was. A woman with short red hair was holding a brown paper bag. It reminded me of when she held out a bowl of hominy, lima beans, and zucchini for dinner the last time I stayed at her home and told me if I didn't eat dinner, I couldn't go to my ballet class. One positive thing I had was that my Dad had attended high school with my dance instructor, who let me attend ballet for half price and sometimes free.

"Rose, you need to put a week's worth of clothes in this bag."

Tears cascaded down my face. "I want my mom. Why did they take her away from me?"

The lady put the bag closer to me. "Your mom needs help, and you can't stay here by yourself."

Did the lady notice the red marks on my legs?

I took the bag and said, "I want my dad, then."

She spoke with a calm voice. "Your dad is at work and won't be home until after dark."

I rubbed my legs. "Then I will wait here for my brother," I said.

"Rose, please get your clothes, and come with me."

Confused at all the commotion, with the paramedics locking the ambulance doors with my mother inside, who would put my glaucoma medication in my eye morning and night? With my brown bag in hand, I looked for clues as to why they'd taken my mother from me. I needed to tell her about Tasha and the neighborhood kids. With each piece of clothing I placed in the bag came one more emotional punch from Tasha. Instead of leaving my own home, I wanted to sit with Dad and eat canned spinach. Ugh! I hated the thought of one more night sleeping in someone else's home without my two brothers, father, or mother to be my guard against a world I simply couldn't comprehend.

4
GIGI

January 1975

Loss of life strangles time, memories, and untold stories.

After months of living in a foster home, I was relieved I could go home after school and be greeted by Mom and our dog, Gigi—it never failed when I arrived home. I dashed to the restroom. When I got off the toilet and turned to flush, I caught out of the corner of my left eye my small black poodle lying still on her side in the bathtub.

I couldn't produce any sound, not even a gasp. Finally, I called her name.

The silence reminded me of the soundproof rooms where I had to go for frequent hearing tests. I hated those rooms and how the door made a vacuum sound when it closed. Those rooms made me feel isolated.

I wanted to leave the bathroom, but my body froze in front of the toilet. Time stopped; my body stopped; Gigi's life had stopped.

I forced myself to face the mirror. Tears fell.

With my hands under the faucet, I hoped Gigi would bark. After washing my hands, I looked at Gigi's lifeless body. My sweet, loving dog had been taken from me.

The bathroom door squealed as I opened it. Even though our hallway walls were white, gloom swept over me with each step toward my mom's bedroom. Her cry became more intense, and she mumbled, "I had to do it."

I peeked through the small opening in the door and saw her sitting on the edge of the bed, rocking back and forth. Tears were streaming down her red face.

Her flowered yellow pajamas looked wet. The usual smell of baby powder wasn't present—instead, the smell of wet dog. The telephone was next to her on the bed. She must have called someone.

I tried to piece together what had happened, to make sense of any of it.

I pushed open the door, and words came out of Mom's lips.

"Rose, go to your room."

I stood there, a confused, frightened, little girl. My legs shook. Her face held the same expression as when she'd curled her hands around my neck. I wanted to run but, instead, took a deep breath.

I ran to my room and shut my bedroom door. I leaned against it, slid down, and dropped to the floor.

How would I survive, unable to catch a breath? Nightmares resurfaced to haunt me.

For months, I had dreadful dreams of men with long, shabby hair and mountainous moles on their faces, who lived underneath my bed and in my closet—with a desire to attack me with their sharp knives.

I was lucky Mom and Dad let me sleep with my ceramic doll lamp on that kept strangers out of my room.

To push those daunting nights away, I recalled Mom's words about when I was two and a half and from the doctor putting a patch over my good eye to see if my blind eye would function. She said, "Rosie, you played on the porch for hours and rubbed your hands over each Fisher Price figure and called them by the names you gave them."

And, yes, I still call them by those names. Lanie was my favorite.

How did I cope with being blind? Even though I don't remember details, I can still sense the emptiness.

I peeked underneath the bedroom door.

"She is in here, so bring the gurney."

It had to be the state hospital workers coming again to take my mom. She must have called the hospital before I got home from school. I hoped this time I wouldn't have to stay with a foster family. The gurney wheels squealed, and I imagined the stretcher outside my bedroom door with Mom on it.

I looked under the door and prayed Dad would rescue me.

My walls darkened with strange shadows. I couldn't move from the spot where I had dropped, hours before.

My fear multiplied as darkness crept into my room. I was there, alone in the house with my dead dog, Gigi. The dog I had loved. In the bathtub.

I squeezed my hands tight and tried to capture some type of light, but there wasn't even the tiniest ray to be found. Trapped in the darkness, with four walls holding me hostage. My body tingled at the thought that a bug could crawl on me. The seconds ticked on, and each second seemed to drag into hours. Bleakness became my new best friend.

I leaned against the door and thought of my visits to my ophthalmologist. What was the big idea for him to examine my blind eye for what seemed hours? I wished at that moment, in the blackness of my room, that I was in the dark examination room; at least I had some form of light. It was comical the way he would point his flashlight over to the wall and then tell me: "Okay, Rose—you need to look at the wall over there."

He wore a silver band around his head with a flashlight attached. That beam of light made my eyes burn. Next, he put on these weird magnifying glasses. With his head two inches in front of my face, I couldn't see the place where he told me to look. He talked as he looked into my eyes so the nurse in the corner of the room could write down notes. He said numbers, like "negative two," or things like, "Her right eye is floating upwards."

When he was finished, he asked the nurse to turn on the light and would tell my parents: "I need to dilate her eyes to see them better." *Here come the yellow drops that make their way to my shirt instead of my eyes.*

My memories were interrupted when the doorbell rang. There was no sound of Gigi's bark to give warning. I kept still and listened and heard feet shuffling down the hallway.

I pushed my body against the door and thought about the last time Gigi, my black poodle, scratched my door, begging to come into my room. The big dark eyes connected with mine as she wagged her tail. I called her, and she climbed in bed and curled up next to me. What happy energy she brought to our home. Her bark was never a nuisance, and she was a furry alarm who kept watch over our home. I loved how she stood at the dinner table next to my chair with sad eyes of hunger. I always gave her one bite of my dinner. She even liked spinach. When we said her name, she'd come and roll over onto her back. Mom loved that Gigi slept at the foot of her bed. Grandmother did one thing right—she gave Mom Gigi. With each stroke over her black curly hair, my eyes got heavy, and I slipped into a comfortable world.

The memories of Gigi vanished when someone pushed on my door to open it.

"Rose, are you in there?"

"Yes."

"This is Mrs. Nottingham from church. I have come to get you."

"Who called you, Mrs. Nottingham?"

"Your mom had a doctor call me."

I moved away from the door so she could open it all the way.

She turned on my bedroom light and handed me a brown paper bag.

"I need you to put clothes in the bag."

I didn't want her snooping in my dresser drawers, but, at the same time, I didn't want to be alone.

I glanced at her kind face and asked, "How many days of clothes do you think I will need?"

"Enough to get you through this week."

I looked in my bag. "I think I have enough clothes."

"Let's go, Rose."

I followed her down the hallway and looked at the bathroom door. *Did she know Gigi was dead in the bathtub?*

Right before we walked out the front door, the phone rang. My heart ached to answer it, and I hoped it was my mother. I knew it couldn't be my father, because of his truck route.

"Shouldn't I get the phone, Mrs. Nottingham?"

"No. Let's get going, Rose."

When I got into the back seat, I tightened my grip on the brown bag that contained memories of my life at home—a shirt Mom had bought or the lacy panties she believed were appropriate for me to wear.

When we drove away, I knew, again, that my loving home would be erased in someone else's bed that night. My mind unfolded the events of the day into the coldest of blankets . . . a nightmare.

Tears moistened my pillow. I wished Dad would come home from work and save me.

5
LIFE AS I KNEW IT

May 1977

A daughter should be worthy of her mother's love.

Dad's smile didn't seem authentic when we were in the hospital elevator. Three floors up and a hundred feet to the right would be mother's hospital bed in the corner of a huge room with other mentally ill people in their respective beds.

Mom's illnesses came in cycles, like the orbits of the moon around the earth, and it gave different appearances. My favorite type of moon is either a full moon or a half moon. I had heard a new moon, also called the "dark moon," when shadowed from the sun, can either be invisible or have a slender crescent. On this visit, Mom was invisible and in the dark moon cycle, which made it impossible for her to be a part of our family or my life.

We stepped off the elevator, and I found her across the room with her uncombed hair. She was sitting on the edge of her bed, with her light-blue hospital gown displaying the outline of her large breasts. With each step I took, I examined Mom's right leg, bouncing with a constant rhythm. I was familiar with this habit of hers. I sat next to her, rubbed her arm, and hoped she would escape from this world that held her captive.

She rocked back and forth, making a continual hum under her breath. She didn't move her arm or respond to my touch, but her leg continually bounced. My heart ached to have any kind of love and attention from my mother. I searched her face. There was no smile, no twinkle in her eyes, and I sensed bottomless pain, deeper than any ocean and taller than any mountain, unending in either direction.

Dad sat on the other side of Mom and tenderly touched her back.

I leisurely looked around at other patients in the same state as my mother. Some yelled, some banged their hands against the wall, and a small, old lady pulled her hair for gratification.

I repeated to myself the word, "Courage." I needed to show courage to be strong for Mom, bravery not to be afraid of the people who surrounded me. My hands trembled. I clasped them and hoped no one noticed. I watched as a worker stopped at the bed of each patient. He pushed a cart with small, clear cups on a tray and a water pitcher with individual medication containers.

Mom usually wasn't on the third floor, but, for some odd reason, she had taken a setback emotionally. I liked our visits on the second floor better, because she was verbal.

When my hands stopped shaking, I touched my mother's hand. *Does she remember holding Gigi's head under the bath water or when she squeezed them around my neck?*

I hoped she could abandon the ugly memories from her past locked inside her. My dad told me that the twenty-one electroshock therapies during these last two years had helped some of the past vanish. I personally hated the electroshock, because it made her vacant inside, with no emotion. It made her become a robot.

I grabbed my ponytail and stroked it, trying to think of the words I could say that would persuade her to come home. Now that I was thirteen, I needed her. I needed her to teach me how to style my hair. My friends talked at school about shaving their legs, wearing a bra. I needed guidance. Mom needed to teach me about what my friends had learned.

"Mom, when are you coming home?"

I waited for her response, and, while I waited, I watched a woman across the room who yelled nonstop. When Mom spoke, I ignored the woman and listened to my mom.

"I am not sure, Rose."

I breathed in through my nose and smelled the odor of sour milk. I began to get sick to my stomach. I exhaled and bent forward so I could see my dad on the other side of my mother. Amidst all the people, Dad and I were the only ordinary ones in the room. This time, my brothers didn't come; I wished they had.

A clock on the far north wall made a distinct click. I looked at the clock. Did Mom know what day and time it was? Did Mom hear the clock?

Moments before we left, I wrapped my arms around her and whispered into her ear, "I love you, Mom."

I then walked over to the elevator and waited while Dad talked privately with Mom. She glanced away as he spoke.

I took a picture in my mind of my parents and captured it in my heart with a prayer; someday we'd be a normal family, under the same roof again.

Dad drove me back to the Nottinghams' and parked in front of their house. I wished he would have driven me home instead.

Dad squeezed my shoulder. "Rose, we are here."

I moved my body nearer to him and hugged him.

"I love you, Dad. Can you please take me home with you?"

Dad rubbed his hand over his mouth.

"Oh, honey, I wish you could come home. Let's have faith that it will be soon. Look, they are waiting for you at the door."

I didn't want to let go, but I had to. I staggered to the Nottinghams' front door and kept the warmth of my father's love with each step I took.

That night, I lay back on the bed they had provided me and held a letter I had written to my mother. I stared out the window thinking about an experience I'd had with my dad, when he drove me around town in his semi-truck, delivering orange juice, lemon juice, pickled onions, plus other foods to bars, stores, and restaurants. Happiness came when I was with my dad, even though I had to ride in the trailer, which was basically a large refrigerator on wheels, with crates stacked and tied from floor to ceiling. Either go with Dad on his delivery route or be put back in a foster home. Mom was unable to be a mother, so Dad kept me safe. When I climbed into the trailer, the arctic breeze circled around me—a bonus after being in hundred-plus degree weather. My dad turned a crate upside down so I could sit on it.

Dad smiled at me. "Are you okay there? I wish you could ride in the cab with me, but if my boss found out, he'd fire me."

I smiled and sat down. "Yup," I said.

He grinned as he closed the doors of the trailer, and darkness surrounded me. The door latch shut, and then I counted how long it took for Dad to climb into the cab to start the engine. I envisioned his short, stocky legs as they reached to the steps. Even though the trailer was cold, I trusted that Dad would let me out. When Dad turned a corner, the crate I was sitting on slid across the trailer. I gripped my fingers tightly in the crate holes and prayed it wouldn't tip over.

A knock on the bedroom door broke that safe feeling, as if I were there, not just in thought, in the back of Dad's truck and on my way home. Oh, how I wished I could go back to my best friend, Tyli's, like I had last summer, even though her brother Floy teased me.

Before falling asleep in my new bedroom that they had let me use, I read what I wrote to my mother.

Dear Mom,

> *Mom how are you doing at the hospital? I wish you would get better than what you are. Why don't you write me and some other people like Dad, Kevin, and Bobby?*

My schooling is doing all right here, and Dad is still eating his waffles. This note was done on Sunday night. Please come home and be my mom.

Please tell everyone I said, "Hi," OK?

Smiles beats a mile, Mother.

Love, Rose

6
CHANGES

May 1978

**When life slips to a different rhythm,
find a way to catch the beat.**

It was the last day of eighth grade when I plopped down on my usual seat on the small bus and took one last look at the school I had attended for the past three years. It's where I learned how to dive from Lloyd Bridges and volunteered as a ball girl for the school fundraiser tennis tournament. Never again would I socialize with celebrities named Farrah Fawcett, Barbi Benton, Linda Carter, Dick Van Patten, and Jamie Farr, who called me "Tomato Face" because of my sunburn. I'm glad he never looked at me as a one-eyed freak.

The school was magical, because when I first attended Devereux Day School, I moved back home and lived with my family. No more Sundays at church peering over at my brother, who sat with his foster family, and then over at my dad, who sat alone. I'd watch my dad smooth the back of his hair; then he would bend forward as though he were going to drop to the floor. It was as if an invisible barrier were cemented firmly, preventing me from being with my family. I often tried to read my brother's facial expression and figure out what he was thinking. We both wanted to be with our beloved, lonely father, who was lost in an upside-down world he'd never asked for, and neither had I or my brothers. I dreamed of leaning my head on Dad's shoulder and listening to the speakers. Someday we would have a normal family, like the ones I lived with. I took a sigh of relief after being in foster care on and off for four years. The school was also where I had my first boyfriend, and it was where I found stability from the drama of watching my mother cope with her own mental illness and with the abuse she continued to receive from my grandmother.

Before the bus pulled away, I focused in on my teacher, Ms. Humble, who was standing on the curb near the bus, and I thought of how I desired to take her home with me. She had done so much more than teach me in class, and I wanted to have her continue to teach me cooking skills, how to apply makeup, and the proper way to act in the ways a young lady should.

I studied Ms. Humble's hands as they elegantly held books. I pictured her small hands holding a head of lettuce and showing us girls how to properly remove the inner core. It was remarkable how the core had slipped right out after she banged it on the edge of the counter. That field trip to her house is where I learned about cooking skills, and I thought about other times she had reached out to me. The warmth of her smile brought comfort to me on days I believed the world was going to end.

So, that day, with the bus pulling away from the curb, I had to capture her smile one last time. She helped me see the potential I had to be successful, even with—and in spite of—my learning disabilities. No more feeling like a one-eyed freak.

Still, my reflection in the window reminded me that I didn't like who I was. And, yet, for some reason, my classmates had chosen me as homecoming queen. My eyes watered at the thought.

The bus engine rumbled, and the bus door made a *swoosh* sound when the driver closed it. I stood over the other kids' heads and glanced one more time at the pool. I pictured Lloyd Bridges with his arms up, telling me to dive with my legs close together. He was another person who made me feel I mattered. Like my dad, he had a jolly spirit and, when he visited our school, he took me and my classmates out for lunch in his limo Rolls-Royce.

The force of the bus moving forward made me fall back into my seat. When the tires of the bus made their last roll around the curve and out of the parking lot, I knew my title as student body council president would vanish forever. Such opportunities and successes were possible only because Devereux was a very small school—a private school that I'd been privileged to attend, thanks to help from the district by paying my tuition.

My body sank down in the seat. How would I convince my parents that I couldn't attend a public high school, when Devereux was my refuge?

I held tight to the ceramic Holly Hobbie doll I'd made in art class, and I observed the others on the bus. The bus rides were long and drawn out, but when the kids on the bus acted like circus clowns, it didn't seem that long of a ride. I thought it was kind of comical that we went through more bus drivers in one month than there are months in a year. The pranks the kids pulled sent them over the edge. I'll never forget when the high school boys, who were four years older than me, opened the emergency door and had everyone jump out and run around the bus several times in the middle of an intersection. The poor bus driver was too large to walk down the aisle of the bus, and he yelled out the window during three light changes. "You kids get back in the bus, now." That bus driver never knew that the teenage boys drank vodka on the bus.

I didn't want to take part in what the kids were doing, but, if I didn't join in, they would touch me inappropriately. Like I was a cookie jar at their disposal; any time they wanted a cookie, they would reach in and grab. My body was slim, small, and not much to it, so why did they want to touch me? Oh, how this made me want to jump out the bus window.

Dawn's blond hair danced with the wind. Did she like who she was? She missed her best friend, Owen, who would use his hands as though they were puppets while he talked like a ventriloquist. Dawn, who, that particular day, was sitting in front of me in the bus, asked me, "Why did Owen get hit by a car and die?"

I told Dawn I didn't know why. Then, we argued about who would die first, she or I. Sad to say, three years later, she died while sitting in a truck bed that jackknifed.

I overheard the teenage boys behind me bragging about how they are going to get drunk with a large bottle of vodka to celebrate summer break. My lower lip began to tremble, and I tried to hold back the tears. Life was changing quicker than I wanted it to, and it brought tears of frustration, regret, and other emotions all mixed together.

The bus traveled down 64th Street, and I pointed and counted for the last time how many rocks lined the large ditch that sat in the middle of the road and ran parallel with it. As we moved farther away from my place of refuge, my heart ached, and my support system slowly slipped away. I don't know why, but the ditch reminded me of Tasha from my old school and how I sometimes managed to outrun her. The thought of going back and reliving those days with Tasha haunted me. I tightened my lips and pushed my shoulders back. I believed the school district had pity on me and paid for me to attend Devereux because of Tasha and my mother being ill all the time.

Karen turned around in her seat and tapped my leg. "Don't you graduate from junior high tomorrow?"

I pulled my hair away from my face and wished they had air conditioning on the bus so all the windows didn't have to be opened. "Yup, and it will be the last time I see Kenny, too."

Karen got yelled at by the bus driver for not sitting. When the bus came to a stop, she quickly moved to my seat. "Is he your boyfriend, Rose?"

"Kind of, I guess. I only see him at school, so I guess he is like a school boyfriend," I said, but I was only telling part of the story. I was amazed, shocked, that I had a boyfriend at all. It was amazing that a boy would like someone like me—a one-eyed freak.

I did tell Karen, "But you know, Karen, his life and his goals are very different from mine. So, maybe it's best that it's the end of the school year, and I won't see him anymore."

Karen rubbed her forehead. "I have a horrible headache." She leaned forward and rested her head against the back of the seat in front of us.

I thought about our conversation and how being fourteen had brought lots of adventures into my life. Like, the Saturday-night youth dances, a boyfriend, and having an incredible mentor, Ms. Humble.

I closed my eyes and pictured a new school with kids like Tasha that I would have to cope with. These changes were killing me. My palms started sweating, and my Holly Hobbie was difficult to hold on to. My voice bounced off the window. "No more private school, no more Kenny, and no more being a cookie jar."

After dinner that night, I pleaded with Mom to ask Grandmother if she would pay for me to attend Devereux in the fall. Maybe—just maybe—my dream of returning to my magical school for ninth grade would become reality.

7
WISH ON A STAR
July 1978
Believing in yourself is recognizing your inner beauty.

I strolled behind my brother Bobby when we entered the building for the Saturday-night dance and was shocked at my pale face in the full-length mirror in the foyer. Thank goodness, my new peach-colored wraparound skirt and flowered blouse were appropriate for this dance.

We entered the double doors to the gym, and a chill of fear held me hostage but thawed with the sunset lighting, knowing the dimness would disguise my deformed right eye.

Within seconds, I was a kernel shoved down in bowl of popcorn, surrounded by teenage bodies—girls in either a dress or a skirt to their knees and boys with open-collared, buttoned-up shirts tucked in. As I followed Bobby, the aroma of different perfumes attacked my senses at full force.

Music glided through the gym, and my heart wanted to dance to songs I loved. Bobby disappeared onto the dance floor, so I searched for a less-crowded area. I spied a spot near the stage. With courage, like the lion from *The Wizard of Oz,* I ventured away from the spot where my brother had left me. Weaving in and out of groups of people huddled together like they were teammates getting last-minute game plans, I tried to avoid bumping into them, but it wasn't easy. Once I got to the other side of the gym, I took a statue-like stance, leaning against the stage in a poorly lit area. I didn't want others to see I was a one-eyed freak, as Tasha had labeled me.

A tap on my right shoulder startled me, but when I turned, there stood a boy my age with dark, curly hair. His sweet smile was different from any guy's I had ever seen.

"Hi," he said.

I turned so I could see him better.

"Oh, hi."

He relaxed his hands on his hips. "Have you been to the dances before?"

I didn't look at him directly, and I hoped he couldn't see my right eye. "Yes, I have been coming for a while. Is this your first dance?"

He rubbed his chin. "No. Where are you from?"

"Uh . . . from here."

He smiled. "My name is Kahuna. Would you like to dance?"

I looked at the dance floor and then back at him. "Sure."

"The Hustle" song played, and the fast rhythm gave me a chance to dance with him without holding his hand or being too close. Once the song was over, he followed me to my spot near the stage.

He moved closer to me. "I am from a small town west of here."

"Do you like it there?"

"Yes, I do." he said.

I rubbed my hands to stop the trembling from the nervousness. I shuffled a few feet back and hoped he would go ask someone else to dance.

"Do you have any brothers or sisters here?"

I leaned against the stage. "Uh . . .I came with my brother, Bobby. How about you? Who did you come with?"

"I came with my cousins." He pointed. "They are over there."

"I see. Why aren't you with them?"

He tried to make eye contact, but I looked down.

"Because I wanted to talk with you and ask you for your phone number. Can I have it?"

He pulled a paper and pen out of his shirt pocket.

I clasped my hands. "I guess."

He handed the paper and pen to me. "Here you are."

"Thanks." I laid the paper on the stage and wrote my name and number.

The music made it hard to hear what Kahuna was saying, but I didn't dare look at his face to read his lips. I did get a look at his round face and dark curly hair so I would remember him.

I handed him the paper with the pen on top. "Here you go."

He smiled and put the paper in his pocket. "Do you mind if I call you tomorrow?"

I glanced at his platform shoes and then looked at him momentarily. "Sure, I guess that would be fine."

He snapped his fingers. "What time can I call you?"

"Well, church ends at five, so any time after that would be all right."

When I took a quick look at Kahuna's face, I noticed the intensity of his gaze, as though he were taking a final snapshot of me. "Okay, then. I'll call you after five tomorrow."

I waved goodbye, but not with much enthusiasm.

When he left, I watched him with disbelief. *Why did he want my phone number?* I danced with other guys with a hope it would take my mind off of Kahuna's smile, which was lingering in my mind.

After each dance, I found myself at the same spot against the stage. My brother checked on me, and he even danced with me, but each time he came, he'd quickly leave to mingle with his friends.

There were four years' difference in age between us, and he was tremendously popular. I couldn't believe he had time to dance with me.

The DJ announced the last dance. The song "Wishing on a Star" flowed through the gym.

Seconds after the song began, I jumped when someone touched my right arm. I turned to see who it was, and there was Kahuna, with a pleasant smile on his face. His brown eyes sent a message with a plea attached to it.

"Rose, can I have this dance?"

"Sure," I said. I could feel a wide smile spreading across my face.

I followed Kahuna to the center of the dance floor, and we faced each other. He held my hand with a gentleness and wrapped his arm around my waist, and I rested my left arm around his. We swayed back and forth to the music in small circles. I turned so he couldn't see my deformed right eye, but I looked at him through the corner of my left. His small eyes were set close together, and his smile reminded me of a Polynesian actor from Elvis Presley's Hawaiian movie. He had wavy dark hair, broad shoulders, and a skinny waist, and he wasn't much taller than me, about 5'6". Once I got a look at him, I focused on the ceiling.

"What high school will you be going to?"

I lowered my gaze. "I'm going to West high school; where are you going?"

He pulled me closer to him. "I attend East high school."

A comfortable silence rang between us. Warmth flowed from the firm touch of his hand, and my heartbeat raced. My stomach rose to my throat each time he looked at me with his attractive smile. I doubted if giving him my number was the right thing to do. Once the song ended, I made a break to find my brother. I couldn't remember if I said goodbye to Kahuna or not. I wanted to be far from him when the lights came on, so he couldn't see my eyes.

Kahuna kept his promise. He called me that first time as planned, and then, as the weeks passed, his calls became more frequent.

8
WET WHITE PANTS

September 1978

**Unforeseen stories are missed
even when your eyes are wide open.**

Bobby and I were sitting on a sofa in an unfamiliar home. Stretched across the wall was a banner proclaiming, "Happy Birthday." Friends of Taiana walked in, each calling out birthday greetings. I'd been invited to the party only because I was Bobby's little sister.

My eyes widened as Kahuna waltzed in. My head lowered with the hope that he wouldn't notice me. With each step closer, I couldn't avoid him. This witty boy, who liked me for some bizarre reason, gave Taiana's mom a hug.

His phone conversations were dreary but sometimes hilarious. Often, I placed the receiver down and walked away while he rambled on. I learned to be patient with the phone calls and letters, but to tolerate him at this party was not humanly possible. At the dances, I escaped to the restroom, like a squirrel into its burrow. I knew that, at this party, I had no options.

I eavesdropped on others, as they talked about school and who would drive to the ice-skating rink. Listening relieved the anxiety about Kahuna being there, but as he moved toward me, I bowed my head and prayed.

Perfect Rose Cracked Vase

Moments after I lifted my head, my brother motioned with his hand as he yelled, "Rosie, it's time to go ice skating."

My lifeless legs didn't want to move, and it wasn't that they were dead. It was an excuse so I wouldn't have to walk by Kahuna, who was leaning against the wall with his legs crossed. He looked hungry for attention. I told myself: *You can do it. You can do it. You can walk near Kahuna.*

Kahuna purred when I strolled by him. I tapped my brother. "I'm ready to go." I followed my brother across the dormant Bermuda grass to the parked cars, and Kahuna followed like he had an invisible dog leash connected to me. I climbed into the back seat and—boom—like a bomb, Kahuna was sitting next to me.

"Hi, Rose."

I scooted away from him.

"Oh. Hi, Kahuna. Have you been ice skating before?"

He raised his eyebrows. "Yes," but when I looked at his white pants, it gave me a clue that he'd never been ice skating.

Who in their right mind would wear white pants ice skating? The rest of the way to the rink, Kahuna's shoulder rubbed against mine. It spoke volumes.

I laced my skates and remembered when my father, brother, and I skated around the rink together. A tranquil peace descended, reminding me of how special those times had been. The first time my feet glided across the rink, I was two years old and had no vision because the doctor kept a cover over my good eye to try to get the blind eye to work. I had a surge of gratitude that, at the age of two and a half, the surgery to remove the cataract in my eye had been a success, even though I never gained vision in my right eye.

Dad instilled in me the beauty of the sport, and I developed a passion for it.

I glided on the ice and marveled at the 200' × 85' rink. My heartbeat synced with the music that blared through the speakers as I made my first left turn at the end of the rink. Within seconds after my turn, I noticed the small, slippery steps Kahuna made. It confirmed that I was more proficient at skating and could make him fall. When I passed him, I imagined how amusing it would be to see him fall in his white pants. So, on my next lap, I went in for the attack and "accidentally" bumped into him. Down he went, and he hit the ice and slid in his now-wet white pants. I skated backwards to watch him try to get off the ice.

Around I went again. This time, I stopped and tapped his arm.

"Are you all right?"

His hands were whiter than normal, and he was hanging on to the rink wall for dear life.

He turned and, within minutes, he lost his balance, and then he smiled. "Oh, yeah . . . Thanks for asking."

Under my breath, I said, "That's for all those countless phone calls."

"Glad to hear. Bye," I said and ventured off.

I snickered, and, the next lap around, I snuck behind him and said, "Boo."

His skates flew forward, he lost his balance, and his bottom hit the ice. I raised my fist, "Yes!" and skated off.

My brother bumped my arm. "Rose, you need to be pleasant and kind to him."

After my brother lectured me, I pictured Kahuna strapped to the top of the car in his saturated pants.

I was relieved they let him in the car, and, yes, he did sit next to me.

We arrived at Taiana's house; we walked to her grandmother's residence next door and into the back yard, where the smell of grilled hot dogs and hamburgers made my mouth water. The sparking pool seemed inviting, and, after standing in 110-degree heat with sweat dripping down my back, I had only two choices: sweat to death, or change into my swimsuit.

I entered the kitchen. I questioned myself, considering if it would be more dreadful to stay in my clothes and continue to sweat or ask Taiana's grandma for directions to the bathroom. I took the plunge and asked her. She pointed and said, "That way."

I thanked her and scurried. Closing the bathroom door, I was startled to see Kahuna in his wet white pants leaning against the hallway wall. Our eyes connected, and I shut the door.

I put on my one-piece red, white, and blue Speedo and stared at my rib cage and small breasts in the full-length mirror. I looked at my blue eyes and how my right eyeball was small and drifted underneath my eyelid. I gingerly opened the door and jumped.

"Oh, hi, Kahuna. How did you like skating?"

I held the towel around me to conceal my thin and shapeless body.

Kahuna responded, "Except for you tripping me, I liked it."

"Are you going swimming?"

He rubbed his hands. "Yes. I just need to get my trunks."

He pulled at his wet white pants and moved like he was inventing new dance moves.

"Well, I guess I will see you a little later, then."

He moved a step closer. "See you out at the pool. Bye." We paced together to the end of the hallway and parted. I glanced back and observed his stiff, uncomfortable steps.

9
WISHY-WASHY

November 1978

Dream without fear, and love without limits.

The school bell rang, and I rushed to my locker. I said, out loud, "Twenty-five, fourteen, and thirty-two." I didn't care if anyone heard my combination. My hand shook as I turned the dial. After three tries, the lock opened, and I sighed with relief.

Anxiety stirred within me, and I reminded myself not to crumple. I reached for my English book and wished that Ms. Humble was still my teacher. The large hallways, big crowds, and six different teachers to deal with made me feel like I would self-destruct.

One swift slam of my locker echoed off the walls. I clenched my books to my chest and gathered my thoughts to what class was next. Oh, yes: English. Guilt surrounded me as I took my seat and waited for my name to be called to hand in the assignment I didn't finish.

Joyanne waved from across the hall when I exited English, where she was kneeling in front of her locker. I'm sure she wanted to know who Bobby was dating. I can't tell you how many times I'd seen her in that position and wanted to put my shoe on her skirt. Would her skirt slip off?

That day, I wished I was home watching "Little House on the Prairie." I believed someday I would have a little girl named Melissa like the main actress on that show.

Classmates were rushing after the second bell rang, and I was right along with them. Lockers banged shut, and the noise drowned out the conversations taking place. I followed behind a football player who opened the heavy door leading out to the quad, and I hurried to another building.

Class began with Mr. Cott filling us in on the do's and don'ts for the test, but I was not able to focus on what Mr. Cott was saying. Instead I was thinking of what pretty outfit I could wear to the Saturday night dance. I pulled my hair behind my ear and rubbed my blind eye. *I bet Bobby would advise me as to which dress I should wear,* I thought.

The dance, the dance. I thought, *How am I going to handle Kahuna following me at the dance?* Kahuna's love letters had been pouring into the black mailbox glued to the front of my house. Letters came often, each one showered with his drawings, stickers, and messages inside meant only for me. His letters started off with, "Hi there, sexy," or "What's up, cutie?"

Would he ever get the hint I didn't want to be his girlfriend?

One envelope smelled like cologne, and, another time, I found a bloody thumbprint on a letter.

I hid each letter in a special cardboard box that I named my "Liberty Box," because it had a stamped Liberty Bell on the lid. Several times when my friend Robyn visited, we'd read the letters and laugh at how humorous they were.

We particularly giggled at the comments Kahuna wrote on the envelope. Robyn held an envelope and read, "I want to marry you. Marry me, you fool." I had forgotten about that letter and quickly grabbed it from her.

Robyn laughed so hard her face turned several shades of red. She grabbed her sides and tried to speak, but the laughter took over. Then, when she caught her breath, she spoke loudly: "Now I understand why you avoid him at the dances, Rose; he's crazy. He's crazier than Kenny. Read the letter in that envelope."

I held it far enough away that Robyn couldn't grab it from me.

Hello! Beautiful!

How's your little Kenny doing? Has he moved to the other side of the country and deserted you?

So, you want me to talk about LOVE.

Let's first start with me . . . That's enough of that. Now, let's talk about you:

You're cute—you're so cute that every time you smile at me, my ears wiggle. My heart curls and my toes start drumming in my head. My knees pop out, and my eyes turn to jelly. Sometimes I even start stomping with my foot, and my face turns red.

You're smart—you're so smart that when your brain needs recharging you short out the outlet. Your ears start to smoke.

You're shaped perfectly—your shape is so perfect that celebrities use your measurements for publicity.

You're straight—you are so straight that Billy Graham thought you were an angel from heaven and wanted to hire you for his shows.

You're modest—you are so modest that you go swimming with an inner tube sewed onto your bathing suit, which isn't so bad except it covers your body.

You're all this and more. That's why every boy in the world is in love with you. Now, with me, it's different. I can't stand it here. I want to be with you, because I can't help falling in love with you. But if you want me to "Drop Dead," I'll understand. I'll die in the gutter, but I'll understand.

Love you always and forever, Kahuna.

Perfect Rose Cracked Vase

Robyn grabbed another letter out of my Liberty Box. "Oh, my. Rose, look at this one with all the green-pen artwork on the outside and crazy drawings of faces on the back. Let's read it." Robyn held her head high and read as if she were reading the most important letter in the world.

> *Dear Sweet Rose,*
>
> *How are you feeling? I'm just fine, as usual. I'd just like to tell you how much I appreciate you. You know you're the best friend a guy like me could have. You're different from most girls. You're different from any girls. Let's face it, you've put up with me for this long, and I think you know me better than I do. I know a lot of girls, but none of them are as patient and ambitious as you are. I know you don't think you're perfect, but you have done a good job of taking care of the little clichés and things. Sometimes I think your family are too modest, but then there's no such thing as too modest. Sometimes I wonder if you are perfect. If there's anything I do or have ever done that bugs you, tell me because every time I think I may have offended you, in even the smallest way, my conscience starts working on me. And tells me how badly I blew it, and I start to hate myself. It seems as if I do something wrong every time I see you or talk to you. The only thing that makes me feel better is to talk to you. Then I feel rotten again. Now you know why I must call you all the time. But it's not just that. I call you because you're so nice and fun to talk to. Even when I find myself listening to you blab about things that don't really interest me, I never regret hearing them or even wasting time listening to you hum into the phone. What I'm saying is, you're special. Not just because you're cute.*

Not just because of anything. You've done things I can only hope to do. You seem to do everything right. I consider you the luckiest girl in the world. Having the best girl in the world for a friend is something I sometimes think I don't deserve.

Still loving, Kahuna

P.S. I hope you can read my handwriting. I miss you.

Robyn folded the letter and laughed. "Man, he is crazy about you." I said nothing but reached for another letter to share with Robyn.

Salutations, Rose,

Do you think you deserve to read my letter after the way you tore my envelope? I don't think you do. But who's stopping you?

How's witto Kenny? Does he still sit on your thumb . . . Does he still attract flies?

Hey, I'm not so bored anymore. Thanks for . . . wait! Why am I thanking you? I know! Thanks for being so nice to me and making me write this sloppy, messy letter.

I've got a terrible crush on this girl. She's cute and she has long blond hair. I have her phone number and her address. She isn't stuck up, but she should be. Yes, she has only two big brothers. Her house is the same color as mine, but I've only been there three times so far. I'm having a lot of trouble trying to get her to dance with me, and she dances well. When she comes to the dances, I can't keep her away from this guy named Billy, and she's always around two or three friends. That's who I like, Rose. Tell me who you like?

Love, Kahuna

I placed the letter and envelope back into my Liberty Box. "Robyn, haven't you noticed how he follows me around at the dances? I wish he would get the hint I don't like him."

Robyn reached for another letter. "He is a weird guy who likes you. Let's read one more before we leave for the dance."

I put the lid back on the box. "Nah. Let's get ready, so we will be on time to the dance. I think Bobby is taking us."

"Rose, are you kidding me? Bobby is taking us to the dance? I hope he will dance with me. You know how much I love your brother."

10
CRUSH OR NOT TO CRUSH
June 1979
Never let your first opinion dictate your actions.

School was out, and now the anticipation of youth conference had arrived. I was seated comfortably next to Robyn after putting my suitcase in the compartment below the large Greyhound bus. The bus climbed the mountains, and my mind pondered the events ahead. Twelve hours later, we arrived. Within seconds after I stepped off the bus, a cool breeze touched my face. It stirred a new liking for summer days with my friends Heidi, Tyli and Robyn. The cool weather made playing our favorite game of when we saw a good looking guy we would freeze like a statue and stare at him.

Each day was filled with speakers on interesting topics: *Parents Are People, Too*, giving tips about how to get along with the people you should love the most. *Frog or Prince/Princess?* was on self-esteem. *Perfection a Bite at a Time* was one of my favorite talks, I guess, because it was on improving ourselves, which I needed to work on.

One talk, *Are You Getting Older or Getting Better?* made me think about the choices I had made and whether they had altered my growth. One thing I had chosen long ago was to have a boyfriend. I craved a boyfriend like others crave chocolate. I wasn't driven to smoke, drink . . . but what I was hooked on was having a boyfriend, and it had been a year since Kenny.

I pulled at my ear and hoped it would help me concentrate on what the speaker was saying, but Kahuna entered my thoughts. How splendid it would be to have his warm fingers locked in mine. I rubbed my chin. *Rosie, what are you thinking?*

Then, right at that moment, I yearned to call Kahuna. My thoughts ventured into a world I never had with Kenny. My heart coached me to make a break and leave during the speaker's words of wisdom. I pinched myself. *Am I dreaming?*

The last night of the week long retreat ended with an outdoor dance near the center of campus. Disco music played, and I stood near a tree. I noticed a few guys I had exchanged phone numbers with earlier in the week. Brett, from Colorado, was one of the guys I gave my number to. He walked toward me in his dark-blue jeans and tan button-collared shirt. I loved his light blond hair, parted down the middle. I danced with him twice. When I looked at Brett, I didn't get butterflies in my stomach like I did when I thought of Kahuna. Something in me had changed, like a match had lit my heart. No words, no reason for why, but I had a sweltering desire to be with him. I finished my dreary dance with Brett, returned to my dorm room, packed my suitcase, and dreamed of Kahuna as I slept that night.

As the bus drove into the church parking lot, I was pleased to see Dad in our car. I didn't care how hot it was—I was glad to be home. I retrieved my suitcase and hurried to my dad. His eyes sparkled with delight with his arms opened wide.

Seated next to my dad in the front, I soaked in his smile as he handed me an envelope from Kahuna. I thanked my dad as I ripped open Kahuna's letter.

Hey Foxy!

Welcome home! Aren't you glad to be back home? Hey, where's my letter? You never sent me a letter from youth conference? You never even called! Don't try and write now because it won't get to me. You can't write here, either. I guess you don't like me anymore because you won't even write. But in case you change your mind, I'm still here. I mean I'll be back next week. I hope you're still getting your bike because I think I'll get one.

Rose, I miss you again. I don't suppose you'll be missing a muggy thing like me. Can you tell me why I haven't been chasing girls anymore? That doesn't mean I've forgotten about you, but I don't stare at good-looking girls anymore. I don't even get excited. I think I know the reason, but I'm not sure. I know you are waiting for me to say it, Rose. Just don't skip lines. Be patient while I waste paper. If you've read this far, you must want to know, so I'll tell you. It's probably because I'm stuck on you. You've probably guessed by now that you're my favorite tootsie roll. If you have, you're right. I guess you could say I like you more than anybody else. Not because you're my last resort, either. Maybe if we get some bikes, I might see you again, only more often. If you want, I could ride my bike to the dance. It's only eleven miles from home.

I've got a friend who's only sixteen, and she's already engaged. Her brother's eighteen, and he already has a kid! Hey, don't get the wrong idea. I'm not getting married until I'm 21. No exceptions. I'm running out of space, so I might as well quit. Sorry I didn't write earlier. I miss you.

Love Always, Kahuna

I slipped the letter back into the envelope, and the words, "I love you, Kahuna," flowed out of my mouth.

11
BIKE RIDE

July 1979

Nothing can stop genuine love.

At the age of fifteen, I was in love. With each turn of the phone dial, my emotions swirled—love, hope, and fear. My hands sweat as I anticipated the sound of his voice.

I waited; it seemed hours, but it was just a few seconds.

"Hello."

I spoke with hesitation. "Hello. Is this Kahuna?"

"Hi . . . Rose. This is Kahuna."

I held the phone cord tight. "Kahuna, I wanted to know if I could come see you."

"Hum—that would be cool. When did you want to come?"

I focused on our red pole lamp and then spoke. "I was thinking of riding bikes to your house tomorrow with my friend Robyn."

"That would be fine. Just let me give you some directions."

"OK. Hold on a minute." I released my grip on the cord, placed the phone down on the telephone chair, and looked for a pen and paper.

"Did I hurt your eardrum when I put the receiver down?"

Perfect Rose Cracked Vase

"Mm . . . hum . . . Just a little."

"I'm sorry. Didn't mean to."

My left shoulder balanced the receiver, while my chin held it in place so I could write.

"You will need to watch for a dirt road on the left side, right after you pass the intersection that has a traffic light. That dirt road will take you to my street."

I tried to picture what he was saying while I wrote down his directions. "OK. I think I have it."

When we finished our phone call, I called Robyn to make plans and to ask if I could use her brother's bike.

My alarm clock went off at eight, and I jumped out of bed. I did my chores and ate breakfast. I dressed in my favorite outfit and curled my hair. While I applied my strawberry lip gloss, I noticed Robyn in my mirror behind me.

"Hi, Robyn. Are you ready to go?"

"Rose, it's more than a hundred degrees outside. I think it's ridiculous you want to go see Kahuna."

I turned to face her. "Well, if you don't want to go, I'll go by myself."

Robyn gave her famous fake giggles before she spoke. "I can't let you go by yourself. What kind of a friend would I be?"

After we had ridden about four miles, I couldn't remember if I'd told Mom goodbye. I was pretty sure I had. We rode our bikes through several four-way intersections, and, several times, we had to maneuver our bikes to avoid trucks and cars that pulled out in front of us.

Robyn slowed down with each turn of the wheel.

She finally spoke. "How far have we come?"

"I think about eight miles."

Minutes later, I looked over at her. She was two bike lengths behind me. Her face was red as a beet, and she was struggling to yell at me.

"How much farther?"

I pictured the directions I'd written down and left on the telephone chair before I could answer.

"About five more miles, I believe."

She yelled. "You have got to be kidding!"

I didn't look back at her, but I slowed down so she could catch up. When she did, I glanced at her.

"I wish I were," I said.

With each thrust against the pedals, sweat dripped down my back, and my mouth craved water. Robyn drifted back again, so I slowed down and waited. When she was about a bike length behind, I turned my head so she could hear, but when I spoke, my mouth was empty of moisture.

"We need to keep a lookout for a dirt road on the left side of the street after we pass the traffic light; that's where we will turn left."

Still, within a few minutes of my attempt at encouragement, Robyn drifted farther behind. Large trucks zoomed past and caused us to move onto the dirt path near the fields.

"Rose, I can't see with this sweat burning my eyes."

While I listened to Robyn complain, I tried to envision the directions Kahuna had given me.

The narrow road was dangerous, as trucks hauling hay and other harvested crops zoomed past us.

"Rose, my back hurts, my head hurts, and I want water."

I tried to get her to think about something else. "Robyn, can you feel the cool breeze when we go past a field of crops?"

"Yes, I can, but it still doesn't stop the sun beating down on me. We have already passed the traffic light, and there is no dirt road; it looks like we are farther than we should be. I feel sick and need to stop."

I noticed the street sign Kahuna had told me about a while back and was baffled that we had missed the dirt road.

"Let's make a left turn here," I suggested.

I loved the fields of crops that blanketed the land around us. There wasn't a store or building near, only a ditch that flowed down the street, which I hoped would lead us to Kahuna's house—just like Dorothy in *The*

Wizard of Oz, who followed the yellow brick road. When I glanced back for the millionth time, I didn't see Robyn. I had to go back and retrace my path. I found Robyn near the irrigation ditch, and I thought maybe she could put her feet in it to cool off. I jumped off my bike and grabbed her arm.

"Robyn, let me help, and you can cool off in the ditch."

Robyn glared at me with sweat dripping down her face.

"Rose, I can't ride my bike any farther."

"Put your arm around my neck, and I will help you."

I doddered with her arm around my neck over to the ditch. I caught my breath before I spoke.

"Okay. I will get help and come back for you."

I bent forward and rested my hands on my knees; my energy had vanished. I tried not to collapse. I tried to encourage myself by thinking, *stay focused, stand, and move forward.*

Robyn used whatever reserves she had to pull off her socks and shoes and immerse her feet in the muddy water.

I pedaled off on Robyn's brother's bike and pictured Robyn's desperation.

I gained strength from my eagerness to see Kahuna. My staggering urge to share my deep feelings with him increased like the heat did. I traveled south, pushing my feet against the pedals to move the tires down the hot paved road. Nausea set in, and my head throbbed. My vision became blurry, and, within seconds, my body hit the ground near a white picket fence. My sweaty face impacted the dirt, and my mouth craved moisture. I closed my eyes and prayed that someone would rescue me and bring water to my lips. The idea that I could die flooded my thoughts.

My skin was scorched, and I felt a stillness around me; a truck stopped nearby. Then I heard the shuffle of footsteps creeping in my direction.

A man in brown boots bent to his knees. "Do you need help?"

I tried to speak: "Yes, please," but I couldn't. I lay there paralyzed and watched him lift the bike up into the bed of his blue truck. The touch of his cold hands on my arms sent a chill down my spine as he carried me to his truck. I smelled tobacco smoke on his shirt as my head rested against his chest. I contemplated that this had to be a dream, but it wasn't. I needed to have faith he wasn't going to hurt me but was going to save me from this heat. I envisioned him taking me to his home and strapping my arms and legs to a bed post and then hitting me with a large, spiky belt. I winced at the image that came to mind of me naked and of him taking my virtue.

He positioned me in his truck, and I thought the world was spinning. For a minute or two, I believed I was on a carousel. I couldn't see what he looked like or which direction he was driving, but the odor made me believe he was a smoker. My head pounded in pain, and I struggled to look at this man, who now seemed more like a captor than a rescuer. I managed to move my head and noticed his muscular, dry hand on the gear shift. His hands could have killed or raped another human and left them dead on the side of the road. Maybe he was someone my parents wanted me to watch out for. My mother told me never to hitchhike, and here I was, in a stranger's truck. I gasped for air.

It reminded me of a time when my father came into my room, and I was lying on my bed, screaming at him for always taking my brother Kevin's side. He hastily placed a pillow over my face, trying to stop me. Would this man put a pillow over my face and never let me have air? Even though I was afraid of him, I succumbed to his arms as he carried me into a building. A pat on my shoulder startled me out of a daze. My blurred vision focused on a fluorescent ceiling light while I sat on a cold metal chair. I couldn't tell where I was. A man dressed in a weird uniform huddled above me.

"What is your name, young lady?"

I tried to look at the person, but it was difficult, because of the black dots in my eye. He touched my arm, and I flinched.

"Would you like some water?"

My lips were glued together with some form of paste, and the inside of my mouth was dry. I strived to move my tongue around to moisten the inside of my mouth, and, after a few times, I attempted to answer him, but it wasn't possible. It was hard to concentrate.

He looked at me and asked, "Do you want a drink?"

I nodded yes and closed my eyes.

"Here you go."

Stars were floating around my head with each throb of pain.

The police officer asked me questions, and I couldn't remember, but I did remember Robyn. I talked slowly because the horrible headache intensified with each word I spoke.

"My friend, Robyn, is sitting in a ditch near a road."

The policeman looked at me with a concerned look.

"What did you say?"

I took a sip of water and released the street name. "My friend is soaking her feet in a ditch."

The policeman left without a word. The thought of how I could have been imprisoned by a stranger made me cringe. I closed my eyes and dreamed of how I would tell Kahuna I loved him.

A different policeman walked in.

"We located your friend, and they are bringing her here."

"Glad to hear you found her."

The policeman leaned against the doorframe. "Do you have friends or family who live nearby and who can come get you?"

I attempted to speak so he could hear me. "My friend, Kahuna Pali (Pa-lee), lives near here."

The policeman grabbed his pen. "Do you have a number for him?"

"No, I don't know his number, but I know he lives in town."

He pushed himself away from the doorframe. "I'll go look in the phone book."

Minutes later, Robyn walked in. "Man, Rose—what I do for you. I'm sick."

I sat and listened to Robyn complain about how horrible she was. Thank goodness, my Prince Charming came into the room with his curly, dark-black hair and deep-brown eyes, and gave me a smile.

"Hi, Rose. Where's Robyn?"

I pointed. "She is right behind you. You passed her when you came into the room."

He turned to see her.

"Hi, Kahuna."

"Hi, Robyn. Boy . . . your face is beet red."

"Thanks a lot, Kahuna."

A policeman came in and asked if we wanted more water.

Robyn made a flirtatious smile to the policeman. "Sure—I would love that."

The policeman stepped out of the room. Robyn looked at me. "Man . . . he's cute."

"You think so?"

Robyn patted her leg. "Heck, yes."

Kahuna gave me a smile. "I'll be back."

"Robyn, are you all right? You have got to be joking! I can't count the number of times you dragged me down to the fire station during lunch hour, just to talk with the firemen, and now you like policemen, too?"

Robyn rolled her eyes. "Where did Kahuna go?"

"I believe he is calling his mom."

Robyn strolled to the missing-children poster board. "Okay."

I looked at the pictures of the children. "Boy, I'm lucky that man brought me here and didn't butcher me and drop me off in an alley like the stabbed dead man we found months ago when we were hanging clothes on the clothesline in my backyard."

Robyn turned to face me. "That was a horror movie in real life when we found that dead man."

"Robyn, I still have nightmares about that man face down in my alley."

Once we arrived at Kahuna's house, he scooped his brother up in his arms and hugged him. I struggled to listen to Kahuna over his other two little brothers as they scampered around the house, screaming.

"This is my youngest brother, Tony, the baby of the family." Kahuna held Tony and pointed at his other two brothers.

"Dakota is my blond-haired brother, and the other one is Troy."

They went in circles around Kahuna while chasing each other, but Kahuna acted like it was nothing. Kahuna's friend Dax, whom I had never met before, spoke without any hesitation.

"Yes, Tony is my favorite."

With his dark curly hair, big brown eyes, and a smile identical to Kahuna's, I could see why.

Kahuna sat Tony on the floor near the TV and then moved the pile of folded clothes off the couch.

"Why don't you and Robyn have a seat over here?" I sat next to Kahuna, and, within seconds, his shoulder rubbed against mine.

He grabbed my hand. A warmth entered my heart—not the type of warmth of the blazing sun that had cursed me earlier. I wanted to spill out those three words I had trapped in me.

I whispered in his ear, "I love you."

"Rose, I love you, too."

Robyn stood near the phone. "Kahuna, can I call someone?"

Kahuna kept his hand locked in mine while he spoke.

"Sure, Robyn."

Robyn pranced into the family room. "Rose, your dad is on his way to get us. He said he would be here in about twenty minutes."

I scowled at Robyn, and she smiled. Dax sat on the brown chair and focused on Kahuna and me holding hands.

"Rose, is your dad going to be able to fit the bikes in the car?"

I turned toward Kahuna. "No."

Kahuna raised his chin. "Hey, Dax, do you mind going for a bike ride over to Rose's?"

Dax glared at me while he spoke. "No problem, Kahuna."

My brow furrowed. "Robyn, are you all right with us leaving the bikes here?"

Robyn sauntered near me.

"That's fine, as long as I can go home."

Robyn opened the family room door several times, and Kahuna glared.

"Rose, it's time to go."

From the front seat, I waved goodbye to Kahuna. The warm air hit my face with an uncomfortable speed, but it was more tolerable than Robyn complaining about how hot she was in the back seat. With each cottonfield we passed, I pictured my next moments with Kahuna. The silence broke after we were a couple of miles from home.

Robyn grabbed the back of the front bench seat. "Can you take me home?"

In a joyful tone, my dad said, "Sure, Robyn."

I collapsed on my bed and dreamed of my new boyfriend. Seconds later, my mother's voice echoed from the hallway. "Yes, Mother, Rose is fine; she has heat stroke, but she will be all right." I imagined Grandmother's words like this: "Rose shouldn't be around boys." Mom's voice faded as I fell asleep.

Mom broke my slumber with a tap and held the phone in front of me.

"It's Kahuna on the phone."

"Hey, how are you?"

I kept my head on my pillow. "Oh, I'm fine. Thanks."

"Well, I won't keep you on the phone. Thanks for visiting me."

I rolled over to look at the alarm clock on my nightstand. "I'm glad I rode out to see you. It was worth it. We can talk later, if that's okay."

"Sounds great, Rose."

12
DAD'S MAGIC POLISHER

August 1979

Look beyond the frame, and you will see the full picture.

Like other Saturday mornings, irregular *whooshes* of Dad's polisher awoke me from a deep sleep. I rested on my bed, listened, and envisioned his stubby, short fingers wrapped around the silver handle. For some reason, it made me feel a desire to help him clean. In a flash, I jumped out of bed, dressed, and dashed to the kitchen. I leaned against the wall to observe. His eyes were focused on the floor, and his body, in perfect form, was seated on his green typewriter stool with wheels. His pudgy hands directed the polisher. Minutes passed before he noticed me. Once he did, he moved the handle forward into the upright position to stop the machine.

I smiled. "Good morning."

"Good morning, Rose." An illuminated smile spread across his face, and dimples appeared. "I am just getting started on the floor. You know we have Bobby's farewell party tomorrow, before he leaves for the Philippines."

I waved. "I can see. Have you had breakfast?"

He pulled a white cloth out of his back pocket and wiped his forehead. "No. I thought I would wait for everyone else."

"Would you like me to make you some toast?"

Dad looked at the dining room floor and then at me. "That would be nice."

I put his toast on a small plate, covered it with a kitchen towel, and waved above my head to get his attention. I figured those two buttered slices of bread would be there for hours. He stopped the polisher, and silence filled the room.

"Would you like me to sweep the living room and hallway for you?"

He grinned. "Oh, that would be wonderful."

"I'll do it right now. Please don't forget about your toast."

Why did he love cold toast? With each movement of the broom down the hallway, I thought of the dance routine Dad had invented for the polisher. I knew his dance by heart, each step narrated, before it was executed.

Dad would squirt soapy water onto the floor before he used the three hard-bristled, brown brushes attached to the dark-green triangular metal base. The base had a strip of three-inch white rubber to prevent it from marring the furniture, walls, or cabinets. The bottom portion of the machine was versatile—one could exchange the three brushes for pads or buffers. Dad invented a contraption to replace the broken liquid container that came with the polisher, by using four squirt-bottles labeled with their respective solutions. Each squirt-bottle dangled by its handle levers on the welded metal crossbar that connected halfway down on the horseshoe-shaped handle.

The polisher slithered across the floor and created dark-water-squiggle pictures on the cream-colored linoleum tile. After the hard bristles scrubbed, he located the mop and bucket. Dad demolished the dirty-water designs that I sensed matched his mood. I tried to figure out what the circles, straight lines, and wavy lines meant.

It was comical the way he muscled the polisher on its side to change out the bristle brushes, replacing them with buffer pads. He squirted the wax concoction on the floor. Each movement he made with the buffer pads developed a view of a still pond of water resurfacing beneath the layer of embedded dirt. The polisher was an expensive purchase, but it gave Dad a wealth of gratification, and it helped unleash the stress he dealt with. It was more productive than picking at the sores on his scalp when he was upset.

The advantage of the polisher was that it drowned out the chime of the doorbell or ring of the telephone. It made the day peaceful, with no phone calls from Grandmother. Dad couldn't control the emotional trauma of Grandmother's negative words or Mother's constant battle with depression, but he could control the polisher. Each movement of the polisher gave Dad power, control, and accomplishment. The machine didn't talk back, scold him, or cause pain.

When Grandmother called, it was like a virus that came through the telephone wires. This invasion brought winds of contention that stormed the house for the rest of the day after Mom talked with Grandmother. Dad protected Mom with his machine and broke the cycle of abuse. I was impressed at how, after each change of the brushes, he would check on Mom, and it never failed that Dad would find her asleep in bed.

Dad had no backbone when it came to Grandmother, and he used his polisher as a crutch. I witnessed it, but no one else did. Dad wasn't ashamed of his physical shortcomings—just of his weakness against Grandmother. One humorous shortcoming Dad had developed was a trick he loved to perform for everyone. My smile expanded when Dad pushed his nose in and showed off how he could flatten it out, fold it over, and smile with pride. However, when Grandmother called, his spineless back folded and crumbled. Grandmother washed him out better than he could ever wash the dirty floors, so he drowned her in noise.

The thought of how important it was to keep the polisher alive made my energy level escalate when helping him. My skinny arms dragged the three red Indian throw rugs outside to shake. Each time I shook one, I wished instead I could shake out the sadness that dwelled in our home. Each swipe of the broom brought the dirt pile to rise and gave some type of story to what had been tracked in by those who lived here. Once I finished sweeping, I moved the furniture, so Dad could focus on the floor.

When the floor was complete, Dad played the piano I had bought for him with my baby sitting money at a yard sale to drown out the phone.

Perfect Rose Cracked Vase

I always sat near him and watched his hands dance across the keyboard, his stubby fingers soaring and stretching to reach all the notes. When he was on the piano bench, it was as if his body could release and fly. I sung along to the songs he played for his mother, the grandma I'd never met, but I believed her spirit was near when he played. "You Are My Sunshine" and "Tennessee Waltz" are songs that brought life not just to him but also to me and our home. My grandma must have been warmhearted, like my dad, because she taught my father traits that created a spark that never went dim. I wished for my mother's sake that *her* coldhearted mother, who lived among us, could see the value of love and compassion.

13
BEST FRIENDS

November 1979

**Friends may come and go,
but best friends never abandon you.**

Peace entered my room when I knelt in prayer at the side of my bed. Yet, when I looked in my closet, my heart raced. Each piece of clothing gave me confidence, and today I needed to choose an outfit that made me feel attractive but comfortable. My hands shook as they filed through each hanger. I picked the perfect outfit, laid it on my bed, and took a bath.

After I dressed, I returned to the bathroom to dry and curl my hair and brush my teeth. I had no desire to eat breakfast, with the feeling of butterflies in my stomach. I peered in the bathroom mirror and applied a few rolls of my strawberry lip gloss. With each stroke of the gloss, I craved a kiss from Kahuna.

The doorbell rang. I hurried to my parents' bedroom and knocked faintly on the door. I couldn't see them well, but I knew they were in bed.

They didn't respond, so I opened the door.

"Mom, Dad. I'm leaving with Kahuna and his family."

"Okay, Rosie. Have fun."

"Thanks, Mom. See you later."

I closed their door. My heartbeat skipped when I caught sight of Kahuna through the three rectangular windows in the front door. I opened the door, and his smile greeted me. I wished he'd kiss me, but it wasn't the right time, with his large family gawking through the windows of their oversized van.

Kahuna's eyebrows rose. "Ready?"

"Let me lock the door first."

When I finished, I turned. "Where are we going?"

"I believe we're going to the park for a picnic and then to the zoo."

He grabbed my hand, and I responded with three squeezes, which meant "I love you."

The van seemed larger with each step I took toward it. I glanced in the window while Kahuna opened the side door. Familiar voices, matching the ones I'd heard during our telephone conversations, were audible. It was as if Kahuna had unlocked the door to a noisy room. I smiled at the young children moving freely on the two rows of bench seats. I waved to Kahuna's little brother, who looked like him.

"Rose, we're sitting in back with Dax."

I scooted to the back seat; it was like an obstacle course. Once I was seated, all I could see was the tops of small heads.

I tapped Dax on the leg. "Hi, Dax. How are you this morning?"

Dax smirked. "I'm awesome—and you?"

I clapped my hands. "I'm happy."

Dax raised his eyelids. "So am I."

Kahuna closed the door and slipped his fingers in mine.

I was amused with the small arms waving in the air. One of Kahuna's little brothers kept turning around and staring at me.

Kahuna reached for his brother's arm. "Turn around and sit down."

Troy plopped down, but a split second later, he was on his knees, staring at us. It became a game for more than thirty-five minutes.

Kahuna's mother drove into the parking lot and parked. "Kahuna, can you get the ice chest?"

Kahuna released our clasp. He spoke over the voices of his siblings. "Just a second, Mom."

The weather was cooler than usual for this time of the year, and it was sweater weather, but I didn't want to cover my blouse with my long, thick white sweater. So, I left it in the van. I stood next to Kahuna and hoped his mother heard me as I spoke to her.

"Can I help carry anything?"

Kahuna's mom grabbed a brown cardboard box and handed it to me. "Here—take this."

She gave me the box, and I answered her with enthusiasm. "Sure."

I placed the box on the picnic table and rubbed my arms to serve as a barrier from the wind. *Should I have put my sweater on?* I looked around the park. It had been established years before I was born, with large pine trees and outdated playground equipment. Kahuna's three little brothers rushed over to play on the twenty-plus-year-old, dark-black, life-sized train.

Kahuna grabbed my hand. "Mom, do you mind if Dax, Rose, and I go for a walk?"

"Sure, that's fine."

"What time is lunch?"

She glanced at Kahuna. "We'll eat in about an hour."

Kahuna set the alarm on the watch he wore on his right wrist.

Then Kahuna patted his mother's shoulder. "You'll be fine here with the kids, won't you?"

She smiled at him with confidence. "Of course, I'll be fine; just get back here in an hour."

Dax appeared happy but quiet as he sat at the picnic bench.

Kahuna tapped Dax on the back. "Let's go."

Kahuna and Dax argued about correct French pronunciations as we walked near the basketball court. We sat on the dead grass under a large pine tree. Dax and Kahuna talked about band and French club.

Kahuna wrapped his arm around my shoulder, which sheltered me from the wind. Then, he looked at his watch, his arm still around me, and pulled me closer.

"We'd better head back. My mom is probably wondering where we are."

Dax stood. "Let's walk on the other side of the park."

At the picnic tables, the little kids were eating.

Kahuna opened the ice chest. "Dax and Rose, do you want a sandwich and pop?"

When we pulled into Kahuna's uncle's and aunt's driveway, everyone got out fast. Dax and I hesitated about going into the house, so we sat outside on the porch and waited for Kahuna.

"Rose, don't you feel weird out here while everyone else is inside?"

I rubbed my shoes over the dirt, making circles. "I do, but I think I would feel awkward being inside. How about you?"

Dax scooted closer before he spoke. "Yes, I agree with you."

Twenty minutes later, Kahuna strolled out. Dax sprang to his feet and stood on the porch. "Hey, Kahuna, let's go to the school playground."

Kahuna stepped back. "I'll go ask Mom."

Dax sat on the edge of the porch, and I sat next to him.

"Dax, do you think Kahuna's mom will say 'Yes'?"

Dax took a snuffle. "Aw . . . I sure hope she does."

We both turned our heads when we heard the front door open.

"Mom says we can go."

We raced to the school, and Dax won every time . . . and I always came in last. Then we played on a metal slide, like the one I had at my grade school. Kahuna forgot to set the alarm on his watch, but, from the field, we could see his uncle's house. When Kahuna's siblings were piling into the van, we sprinted. Dax and I climbed in and sat in our same spots, and Kahuna hugged his aunt and uncle.

When we arrived at the zoo, we helped unload the strollers. I stood next to Kahuna's mother and gathered enough courage to speak. "Mrs. Pali, can I please push Dakota around the zoo?"

Mrs. Pali buckled Dakota into the stroller. "Yeah, sure. That would be helpful."

She pushed the other stroller toward Kahuna. "You need to take Troy."

Kahuna grabbed the stroller handle. "Okay, Mom."

"Kahuna." She pulled his arm to get his attention. "You can go anywhere—just meet back in an hour at the picnic area. Watch the kids."

"Sounds great."

Kahuna and I pushed the strollers while Dax walked beside me. At the entrance to the zoo, a lady with bell-bottom pants and a bright striped shirt faced us. She pointed at the strollers and spoke loudly. "You are a flower child."

I stepped back and kept hold of the stroller. She continued to yell the same sentence. Dax grabbed the handle of my stroller and helped me. Kahuna backed up also, and none of us said a word to her. We looked at each other and walked away while the lady continued to bellow at us. Once we were far enough away from her, I teased Kahuna. "Are you a flower child?" Dax and I laughed, but Kahuna just smiled.

When we climbed the slope, I changed the subject. "How would you guys like to meet Ruby the Elephant? She paints and draws pictures. I remember her from grade school on field trips."

"Sure. Which way is it?"

I pointed. "We will have to make a right on the path over there."

Dax glanced at me. "You're familiar with this zoo, aren't you?"

"Yes, I've been here several times. There is one visit I wish I could erase from my memory. It still haunts me."

Kahuna spoke. "What happened?"

I paced between them. "I was nine, maybe ten, when my brother and a group of his friends brought me and my friend Lindsey to the zoo. Lindsey and I were excited but not for long. My brother guided me to the trashcans near the zoo entrance and asked if he could have my purse. I handed it to him, and he took out the money Mother had given me. He gave me enough money for the entrance fee and then shoved the rest into his back pocket. He threw my purse into the trash, but I didn't dare protest. I can still envision it. I loved that cream-colored purse and didn't like the idea of losing it. He and his friends circled around Lindsey and me. His eyes widened, and I feared what would happen next. I focused on his lips as he spoke. 'Rose, you and Lindsey stay here, and we'll be back later for you.'

"Lindsey and I stood near the trashcans. Kevin and his friends piled into the car. I wanted to run and get in, but I knew he wouldn't let me. Tears formed and I sobbed. A worker approached me, but I couldn't answer her. Lindsey was a stronger soul and told her our names and gave her my phone number. I believed my brother would come back for us. But he never did."

By the time I finished my story, we had arrived at the elephant exhibit. We sat on the benches facing the huge exhibit. Kahuna gave me a slight smile while he bent down to check on Troy. "How horrible," he said.

"Well, it was a long time ago, and I still love my brother. It hurts to remember, but I need to forgive. Oh, look: There's Ruby, and she's painting; look how she holds the paintbrush with her trunk."

Kahuna put Troy on his shoulders. I grabbed Dakota and held him next to the fence so he could see.

Dax pointed at Ruby. "Do you think she's painting a picture of how to escape from here?"

People commented on how amazed they were with Ruby. Troy got fussy, so Kahuna seated him back in the stroller.

"Let's go."

I put Dakota in his stroller and tucked a blanket around him. We headed toward the turtles and farm animals and listened to bird calls in the bushes and trees. Dakota and Troy giggled as they interacted with the sheep, goats, cows, and horses, and we lost track of the time.

Kahuna tapped his watch. "We need to leave for the picnic area right now."

When we arrived at the picnic tables, we were glad we'd gotten there before his mother did. I sat and observed how loving Dax was with Kahuna's siblings. Dax reminded me of a swan, because of his slim build and long neck. He was attractive, and lots of girls liked him, but I understood Dax like no other girl did. I knew Dax's heart; I knew the tender soul that lived in him. We both loved Kahuna, and we both understood the need to have him for a friend. I rested my cheek against my hand and listened to Kahuna and Dax talk about the future.

"Kahuna, are you still thinking of attending the Academy?"

"Yes, Dax. I am. I just need to get some health issues under control."

I chimed in, "Where will we be in four years?"

Would Kahuna continue to be Dax's friend after high school? Kahuna was often annoyed with Dax. The question Dax asked me several times on the phone, "Why doesn't Kahuna call me or talk to me at school?" lingered in my mind. It was like a tape recorder repeating the same sentences. I constantly reminded him, "He likes you, and he's just busy with his paper route and family."

Kahuna tapped my hand. It startled me. "Rose, where do you think you'll be in four years? Dax and I will be at the same college."

"What? Uh, I . . . think that's great for both of you."

A large water fountain near the picnic area produced a soothing water sound. As each drop descended, so did my plan for the future—because I had none, besides marrying Kahuna. Friendly, colorful peacocks walked around us as if they didn't have a care in the world, and I thought to myself, *Why have a plan? I'm slow, handicapped, and unable to afford college. Rose, you're just a one-eyed freak.*

I changed the subject. "Kahuna, where is your mother?"

Kahuna stood and then looked at me. "I think I see them coming."

I turned, and there was Kahuna's mom. She motioned for us. "Time to go."

Kahuna yelled. "We're coming."

When I pushed Kahuna's little brother in the stroller, I also tried to push away the uncomfortable conversation we'd had at the picnic table.

14

CHRISTMAS EVE

December 1979

**Pluck your negative thoughts out of the
deep soil before they grow roots.**

Christmas Eve morning seemed as dull as Mom's blue-and-red-flowered, loose-hanging muumuu, which had seen years of wear and many visits to the clothesline. I stretched in bed and relaxed while I reminisced about Dax's baptism that was the day after Kahuna's sixteenth birthday. I pictured Kahuna and Dax dressed in white, standing in the font side by side with water to their waist. Their hands connected, ready for Kahuna to submerge Dax under the water. Kahuna looked uncomfortable with Dax's hand in his. I nestled my hands under my head, stared at the ceiling, and thought about the conversation I'd had with Dax after he was baptized. I remember smiling when he came out of the dressing room. He looked handsome in his dry white dress shirt, slacks, and tie. I yearned to hug and congratulate him but waited my turn behind others. When I stood in front of him, I hesitated, before making eye contact. "Nice baptism, Dax."

He rested his hand on my shoulder. "Yeah, it was pretty awesome. Thanks for coming."

I moved an inch closer. "I wouldn't have missed this for anything."

I recalled the next part especially, when I balanced on my tiptoes to reach around Dax's neck to give him a hug while I whispered in his ear, "Thanks for inviting me. It was marvelous."

I didn't want to release him, but he was eager to let me go.

Dax glanced at Kahuna and then smiled at me. "I'm glad you came."

My sweet memory was shattered when Mom yelled from across the hallway. She was loud enough to wake the neighbors.

"I wish Rose wouldn't have put water on the top of the TV. She knows we haven't any money to replace it."

"Sweetie, when I get the money, we'll buy another one."

I rolled out of bed and dropped to my knees. I folded my arms against the bed, like I had been taught as a little girl in church.

"Dear Heavenly Father, with a faithful heart I ask that thou forgive me." I paused before continuing.

"Heavenly Father, I never meant to leave a cup of water on the TV and never thought it would spill."

I switched my weight from one knee to the other to relieve the pain from kneeing on the hard linoleum floor.

"I hope you hear me, Heavenly Father. I hope you can hear how miserable I feel for breaking the TV. Mom and Dad don't have the money to replace it, and it's my fault, Heavenly Father."

I closed my eyes tight and wished that my heart would stop aching, while listening to Mom hollered at Dad.

My arms were wet from tears cascading down them. I took one more pause before I ended my prayer. I wanted to ask for help with Kahuna and my relationship, but I knew this wasn't the time, because I wanted God to focus on helping Mother.

Who could I turn to for help? I wished I still had my bike I'd saved money for, but my mother made me give it to my brother, Kevin, and I never got it back.

I dashed out the front door, and, with each pound of the pavement, pain traveled up my legs. I wanted to hurt physically to relieve the emotional stress settling into my soul. With each quick movement my legs made, I thought of my brother, Bobby, who I longed to talk to but who was millions of miles away on a church mission in the Philippines. Our family had dilemmas, and I wished my legs could have taken me far away from them. How to spend money was not a subject in our home, and we were scraping for pennies. My legs moved faster, and the bottom of my feet stung. To avoid the thought of the pain, I focused on how devastated Mom was about the TV.

Once I got to the park, I sat under a small tree and leaned my back against the narrow trunk with my legs folded. I wanted to scream. This had to be the worst day of my life, with Bobby gone, Mom upset, and Dad unable to come to my rescue. My anxiety only intensified because, later that evening, I had to go visit my grandmother.

"Christmas Eve at Grandmother's and then home to a quiet house." I spoke out loud, though I knew no one heard me. I observed the diverse groups of people playing football and Frisbee. Ants were crawling on my legs, so I quickly forced my feet to push me up—a trick I learned in ballet class years ago. I jogged toward the sidewalk near the edge of the park. And I cried.

Each time my foot touched the pavement, I tried to pound out frustration. I wanted to make Mom happy, but it wasn't possible. The air seemed motionless, without a breeze, and the sun pierced me with heat. The weather was as stagnant as the tension that lingered in my house. I ran home with an uncertainty about what would happen once I got there.

I opened the front door and heard Mom yell.

"Rose, is that you?"

"Yes." I closed the door and headed down the hallway.

Mom looked at me with despair. "Where have you been?"

I stood at my parents' bedroom doorway and leaned against the frame. "I went for a run."

"You know we are going over to Grandmother's?"

I wiped the sweat from my forehead. "Yes, I remembered."

"We will leave at four-thirty."

"Okay, that sounds fine." I glanced over at Dad, who was standing near his dresser. His fingers were digging at sores on his head, a dead giveaway he wasn't happy about going over to Grandmother's.

"Dad, how are you?" He removed his hand from his head, slipped it into his pocket, and jiggled his keys. "Good, as usual, honey."

Mom sat on the edge of her bed and stared at her closet.

I stepped into the hallway. "I guess I'll go take my shower."

Mom wore her red blouse and dark slacks that covered her black hairy legs she'd stopped shaving decades ago. She wore lipstick, something she hadn't done in years. This was her invisible shield of protection from Grandmother's intolerable comments.

Dad knocked on my door and then talked loud with his deep voice so I could hear him. "Rose, it's time to go."

I pulled the phone away from my ear so I didn't shout in Kahuna's ear. "I'll be out there in a minute, Dad."

I spoke. "Kahuna, it's time for me to go over to my grandmother's house. We can talk again later."

"How about I call you at nine tonight?"

I walked with the phone to my bedroom door. "I *think* I'll be home by then."

"Talk with you later."

I placed the receiver back on the tan rotary phone and carried it to the end of the hallway. I made sure to roll up the twenty-foot cord on the chair so no one tripped over it.

I walked to the end of the hallway and shook my head at the pitiful, artificial Christmas tree centered in front of the living room window. Mom always took a five-gallon bucket, turned it upside down and balanced the tree on it. She dressed the tree stand with a Christmas Raggedy Ann cloth. After six years, the tree's limbs were dilapidated. No wonder why our neighbors down the street donated it to us. For some reason, my mother loved the tree and believed it was an heirloom to leave me; I, on the other hand, didn't agree. The worn-out tree had similarities with my mother. Both appeared weak and worn-out, and both needed extra care.

Mom and Dad argued as we drove to Grandmother's house. Money was usually the source of all their problems, but, this time, it was Grandmother. Our cream-colored 1963 Buick LeSabre was as worn out as our Christmas tree. Its air conditioning came through the rolled-down windows and not through the vents inside the car. For the first time ever, after twenty minutes of listening to Mom and Dad arguing, I was happy to arrive at Grandmother's. Before we got out of the car, Mom pulled her comb out of her purse and pulled it through her brown, curly hair. The wind had moved the natural curls in every direction. It never failed. After she combed her hair, she rubbed the tooth part of the comb over the palm of her hand. I could never figure out why she did that. I wasn't sure if her hand itched or if she was nervous. Years later, I asked her, and she said, "It's my hand itching for money."

Seven knocks on Grandmother's door was always a must for Dad, a rhythm like music. *Dum, da-da dum dum, dum dum.*

The door opened.

"Well, come in."

Dad held the door for Mom, and I followed. The living room's blue couches, blue carpet, and blue-framed pictures blended together, and I liked them more than the red living-room furnishings Grandmother had years before with a previous husband. I glanced at the ridge of the back of the sofa. It looked bare without her doll collection—dolls she would tell me not to touch because they weren't meant for me but for my cousins. I always wished, as I looked at their beautiful clothing and striking hair, that I could have one of them. Only twice had she given me a doll, but they were never as adorable as the ones she gave to my cousins. Right before I sat down, Grandmother reminded me not to stiffen her seats. After years of hearing this, I finally figured out that it meant "Do not pass gas on my furniture."

Mom sat next to Dad and rubbed her hands together with anxiousness. My step-Grandpa sat in the blue rocker with his eyes only half open. His large tummy stuck out, making it look like there was a beach-ball underneath his button up collared shirt. He reminded me of a skunk, with a gray stripe in his hair that went from his forehead to his neck. I don't think he said one word while my grandmother babbled on about the family gossip. Mom just turned her head toward Grandmother, like always, and said, "Yes, Mother," or, "I know, Mother." Dad's fingers were half buried in the sores on his scalp—a sure sign he was frustrated.

Often, I cut in to their conversation, hoping to distract Grandmother and give Mother a break from her rants. I sat at the edge of the couch and turned toward Grandmother.

"Grandmother, where is your Christmas tree?"

"Oh, Rosie, Christmas doesn't mean much to me anymore. No one comes to visit during the holidays, so I said, 'Heck with it.' She swiveled her blue rocker to get step-grandfather's attention.

"Isn't that right, Grandpa?" Grandpa slowly moved his head, as if he agreed.

I tried hard to be sincere and made eye contact with her.

"I hoped to see a tree, Grandmother."

"I *did* get you a gift, if that is what you really wanted to ask me."

I sat back in the couch. "No, Grandmother. I just wanted to see your Christmas tree, because you always decorate it so pretty."

Grandmother pointed. "On the end table near the love seat is a small box with a gift for you. Why don't you get it and open it?"

I scooted forward and pushed my hands against the couch. I stood there near the couch and hesitated for a few seconds, unsure if I should take the gift, because then it would impose guilt, and she would expect a favor in return.

Grandmother scowled at me. "Go get it, Rosie."

I walked the three steps toward it and three steps back. Before I sat down, I smoothed out the towel on the couch. I opened the small box and saw a silver watch with a blue oval face.

"Oh, Grandmother—you didn't have to get this for me."

"Well, Rosie, I got it to help you realize how much time you spend on the phone with that boy, Kahuna."

Mom gave me a half smile and then continued to rub her hands. I think she wanted to pull her comb out and use it to scratch her palms. I walked over to Grandmother and bent to give her a hug.

"Thank you, Grandmother. I love it."

"Thank your Grandpa."

I think he was her fourth or fifth husband. I believed she'd killed her previous husband by giving him the wrong dosage of insulin on my birthday. Mom and Dad talked often of how they believed it because she was a registered nurse and purposely gave him the wrong amount of insulin, which threw him into a diabetic coma. She'd married this new Grandpa when I was 13, and I hadn't known him that long, but I gave him a hug and thanked him. He didn't respond other than a small movement of his head. I sat and stared at the watch and thought about the time. *Kahuna calling me at nine.*

Dad dozed off and slept with his head down and hands now rested on his lap. Mom pushed her hand against his leg several times to wake him. "I think it's time to go, Honey."

Dad scooted forward. "Whatever you say, Sweetie."

I gave Grandmother another hug and thanked her.

"Rosie, I hope your granddaughter comes and sees you when you are old like me." Guilt became my middle name because I had destroyed our TV, and now Grandmother was reminding me that I hadn't visited her enough.

"I will try to come over and see you, Grandmother, but, remember, I don't drive or have a car."

Dad stood by the door and watched Mom hug Grandmother. He didn't like hugging Grandmother, and I don't think she liked him hugging her, either. Once we got in the car, Mom told Dad all the filth Grandmother had said to her.

On the drive home, I sat silent in the back seat. I thought about the events I had to look forward to next weekend with my two best friends. I looked out the window, and all I could see was my reflection. It was too dark to see beyond the outline of my face—a face I never favored or cared much for. As I exhaled, my breath fogged over the outline of my reflection. I'm glad my Mom had used an invisible shield of protection from the pain Grandmother would shoot at her.

When we walked in the front door, Mom headed for the kitchen to take her medication, and I walked straight to my room. I think Dad followed Mom.

15
FRENCH TOAST

January 1980

Service brings a new perspective
on the value of loving others.

The morning sunlight traveled through my sheer Priscilla curtains and brightened my light-green walls as I nestled between my sheets and the strawberry quilt Grandmother helped me tie. It was one of those rare moments; I didn't want to make the effort to leave the covers that protected me. The heater hummed through the vents, and I pondered on the stories Mom shared with me of the trials I'd had as a toddler.

A world of no sunlight, unable to see the beauty of radiance it gave. I scooted in my bed and rested against my headboard. The faint sounds of dishes clanking made me curious about who was in the kitchen early on a Saturday morning. Dad must have been making Mom's breakfast.

I lazed in bed, not motivated at all to get up. After sitting there for a moment, I smoothed the covers and adjusted my pillow. Just then, someone knocked on my bedroom door.

"Who is it?"

"It's me, Kahuna."

"Just a second, Kahuna."

I readjusted my pillow for back support. Then I checked my nightgown to make sure it covered me. I smoothed my hair and then pulled the covers to my armpits.

"You can come in now."

He walked in.

"Good morning," he greeted me.

"Oh, Kahuna!" I rubbed my eyes in disbelief.

He placed my plate of food on my nightstand and handed me a cup filled with milk.

"I told you I wanted to do this, and here it is—French toast."

"Thanks for making breakfast. That was nice of you." I wanted to throw my arms around him and touch his lips with mine.

He glided my desk chair near me and sat down. "You're welcome."

I took a sip of the cold milk. "Are you hungry?"

Kahuna stood. "I have mine in the kitchen. I'll be right back."

When he left, I made sure my bra wasn't in sight.

He returned with his plate and cup in hand, put his cup on my desk, and then took a forkful of food. He swallowed and then spoke with the smile I adored. "Why haven't you tasted your French toast?"

I placed my cup on my nightstand and grabbed the plate. "I wanted to wait for you. How did you get in my house this morning?"

"I spoke to your mom last week, and she said it would be fine. I arranged with your dad to be here by seven. He let me in this morning. Your dad is still in the kitchen cooking eggs for your mom."

I sniffed the food and could smell the cinnamon. "Smells yummy."

I took a bite of the soggy French toast—and the moment it entered my mouth, I wanted to spit it out. After I swallowed, I cleared my throat and swallowed one more time.

I tried to hide any facial expression that would show how awful I thought it tasted. I smiled and said, "Well, this is a surprise. I never thought you would make me breakfast."

Kahuna walked with his plate over to my door to see if he could hear or see anyone coming down the hallway. Once he thought it was clear, he put his plate on my desk and sat on the edge of my bed. He moved my chin and leaned closer to me. When our lips connected, a tingling started at my heart and traveled to my toes. I peered into his dark brown eyes and hoped my fondness for Kahuna would never fade. Our kiss was gratifying, and I loved the sound our lips made while we shared a moment of tenderness. When he tore his lips from mine, my hunger for his affection grew. Sweat covered my palms, and a sensuous flame burned in my heart. Did he notice my face turning different shades of red? I licked my lips and wished he would never leave my bedside. When he did, I wanted to pull him toward me, but I didn't dare. I bit my lip and told myself there would be many more moments when the sound of his voice, the sparkle in his eyes, and his smile would fill the empty hole in my heart. I swallowed and squeezed my lips tight, so it wasn't obvious that I craved him like my mother craved the chocolate pinwheels that she hid all over the house.

He began to eat after he sat down. Each time I took another bite, I had to force myself to swallow. There had to be an ingredient that had been left out. Neither of us spoke while we ate, but we did exchange frequent smiles, and he winked at me.

I took my last bite and glanced out the bedroom door as my dad carried a plate to my mother. I guess she wasn't feeling well enough to get out of bed.

"You ate fast, Rose, so you must have liked it. I'll take our plates into the kitchen and clean while you get dressed."

When he walked toward the door, I wanted to ask him what he put in the batter, but I bit my tongue instead.

I jumped out of bed and rushed to close my door just as my dad left his room. "Good morning, Dad."

He smiled and placed a hat on his head. "Good morning to you."

My dad stepped away from his door, and then I closed mine. I put on my white shirt with different-shaped hearts and orange painter pants. I hadn't done my laundry since last Saturday, so I didn't have a lot to choose from. I brushed my hair and walked out the door.

In the kitchen, Kahuna was at the sink, washing dishes.

"Kahuna, where did my dad go?"

"He went outside to the storage room."

At that moment, the lawnmower roared. I couldn't resist any longer, so I asked, "Kahuna, how did you make the French toast?"

"Oh—I'm allergic to eggs, so I left that ingredient out."

"Really? I didn't know you were allergic to eggs. Then what ingredients did you use to make the batter?"

Kahuna rubbed the soapy washcloth over the last plate and put it in the dish drainer. "I soaked it in milk, and then I put butter and cinnamon on, and then put it in the toaster."

Water ran through the pipes—a dead giveaway that Mom was in the shower.

"Oh..." He washed the silverware. Once he was done, he turned toward me, wrapped his arms around my waist, and pulled me close. We hugged, and our lips found each other. I gazed into his eyes, which I didn't often do because of my deformed eye. "I appreciate you coming over to make me breakfast. That was really nice of you."

He kept hold of me. "Rose, it was nice of your dad to let me in this morning. Can you believe that, next week, you'll be sixteen?"

I grabbed his arm and led him into the living room. "No, I can't, and I'm excited about us being able to date."

We both sat down on the couch at the same time as though our bodies were connected at the hip.

Kahuna grabbed my hand. "Would you go with me on a church snow outing next weekend?"

I squeezed his hand. "I would love to." His lips touched mine, but he cut it short, saying, "I need to get home. I have chores to do."

I moved to get a full view of his face. "I wish you didn't have to leave."

Kahuna got off the couch. "Me, neither."

And I followed behind Kahuna. We embraced, and the comfort of his arms made me wish he would never let me go. When Kahuna opened the door, I observed Dad struggling to mow the lawn.

We walked hand in hand to his brown bike. He jumped on, and his arm muscles flexed when he grabbed the handlebars. I stood in that same spot and concentrated on Kahuna until he was out of view. Dad tapped my shoulder. "Are you all right, Rose?"

I gave Dad a firm smile. "Yes, I'm fine." I pointed at the lawnmower and asked if he would like me to finish mowing. I pushed the lawnmower and thought about how Kahuna gave off a certain radiance—something I'd never experienced. I used my leg muscles to push the lawnmower as I made a pattern of diagonal lines in the grass. When I finished, I viewed the lawn, and my thoughts of Kahuna were even stronger than the desire to be home when I lived in foster care.

16
DATE

January 1980

A date is like a bowl of popcorn. It can fill the tummy, leave kernels in our teeth, and make you want more.

The secret is—don't bite the uncooked kernels.

My friends and I huddled together outside the school cafeteria, waiting for the bell to ring. My anticipation of being with Kahuna made it difficult to listen to my friends. Gail hit my shoulder. "Who do you like? Answer me, Rose."

I smirked when I answered her. "Oh, no one right now." I thought to myself why is Gail asking me this question when we have double dated with our boyfriends Floy and Kahuna? Maybe she wanted to spill the beans with our friends that I had a boyfriend.

Kahuna didn't attend the same school, so, I might get away with the cover-up.

Gail rolled her eyes while she spoke. "I like Floy's blue eyes, and he is so nice. I love having him for a boyfriend."

Gail turned to Barb and asked, "Who do you like?"

Perfect Rose Cracked Vase

Barb shaded her eyes with her hand and spoke. "I like Greg—he's so friendly."

How boring that discussion was. Neither of them had ever had a boyfriend like Kahuna, who wrote special letters.

I glared at Gail. "Enough of the guy talk."

Gail continued to ramble on about Floy even after the bell rang. And I wondered while walking to my next class why Gail felt a need to write me notes asking me to never take Floy away from her. I knew that would never happen because no guy was better than Kahuna.

Dad drove me to Kahuna's house after school. His home was a perfect picture, with his mom holding Dakota and his sisters sitting on the couch.

"Rose, would you like to rock Dakota to sleep?"

"Sure. I would like that."

I held my arms out to take him.

"Here you go." Kahuna's mom placed Dakota in my lap.

I held his back against my arm, slowly moving the rocking chair.

Kahuna's mom sat on the couch, sharing stories, while Susie and Mollie put down blankets for me to sleep on. Kahuna's mother made it clear several times while she spoke that, when she left the living room, Kahuna needed to leave, too, and sleep in his own bed. I glimpsed at Dakota's eyes to see if he were asleep.

Each story Kahuna's mom told I filed away in my mind to store them so that, when Kahuna and I had kids, I could share the stories with them. After two hours of storytelling, Kahuna's mom yawned, and it was obviously time to end the night. Kahuna stood and looked down at me with one side of his mouth drawn up and a wink of his eye. An invisible wave of love flowed between us. I smiled and wished I could run into his arms for a goodnight hug.

Kahuna's little brothers' yelling woke me. *Was there an incident like this in Kahuna's house every Saturday morning?* I wondered. Mollie was peacefully asleep on the couch and Susie on the floor.

I stared out the window and spoke. "I'm finally going on a date with Kahuna."

The long drive made it seem hopeless that we'd ever see snow, until we reached the top of the mountain. Wow! The white blanket of snow came into full view. It looked brighter than I had ever imagined. It looked as if an artist had painted the branches and ground.

I jumped out of the van in my new boots that Kevin had bought me and my new gloves and coat that Mom and Dad had bought me, though they really didn't have the money. Kahuna reached for my hand, and we climbed the hill. To touch and hold the snow against my bare skin was amazing—it was my first experience with snow. The tips of my fingers were numb, and it made me think of how Grandmother was like snow: Beautiful on the outside, but once you are a part of her life, you feel a cold sting before your body goes numb.

Experiencing such treatment had disrupted Mom's circulation, preventing her from becoming the mother I knew she was capable of being.

I'd had enough of the lightweight cold stuff, and I let it slip out of my hands, rubbing them over my coat before putting my gloves on. I wished Mother could let Grandmother's horrible stings slip out of her heart as fast as the snow slipped out of my hands.

Kahuna's Polynesian skin stood out against the backdrop of white snow. We chased each other, and he threw a snowball at me. I ran behind a pine tree and fought the cold breeze. I was confident he wouldn't get me—until a snowball hit me unexpectedly.

"Kahuna, you got me. There's snow in my boot, so I need to go to the van and take my boot off."

By the time I took off my boot, my sock was soaked, and my foot was white and numb.

"Rose, we should stay in the van and let your foot thaw."

I rubbed it, hoping to get some feeling in it, while watching others from our group around the campfire.

I grabbed my sock. "Bag this. Let's go by the fire and have hot cocoa."

"Are you sure you want to?"

"Yes—it'll be fun."

I slipped the cold, wet sock on and hoped the boot would keep my foot warm. When I jumped out of the van, Kahuna pulled me close. Our eyes met, and then he kissed me. The kiss didn't last long, and it wasn't an earth-shattering, death-defying kiss. But it was a long-awaited one, as far as I was concerned.

That night, as I rested on my bed and stared at my alarm clock, I asked myself, "Why do I desire to be close to Kahuna? Why do I love him?"

17
SECOND GO-AROUND

February 1980

Don't let another person's actions dictate your attitude toward life.

When I awoke, I didn't hear Dad's polisher and thought how unusual it was to hear pigeons outside. Dad had to wait to use his polisher until we returned from my regional singing competition.

I reached twice in the closet for the same dress, but I knew it wasn't pretty enough to wear in front of judges who would listen to me sing. I put it on anyway, because it was the prettiest dress I had that matched my cute white sandals. Mom yelled for Dad to make sure Pepe, our white poodle, was in the house. I walked past Dad while he was calling outside our front door for Pepe.

When I turned into the carport, I caught sight of sweet Pepe lying on the cement beneath the passenger side of the car. Blood surrounded his gashed ear. I knew right away that our neighbor, named Tree, was the culprit. Tree had warned my parents that, if he caught Pepe in his yard one more time, he would shoot him dead. Well, Pepe must have gotten caught.

My confidence for singing shattered, and the sheet music slipped from my fingers. I reached for Pepe, and my tears fell on him. Within seconds, memories of my dog Gigi lying helpless in the bathtub came back—a memory I'd hoped never to relive.

Footsteps echoed toward me. The tap of the shoes on the cement vanished when Dad spoke. "He must have crawled home, Rose."

I cried with no intention of stopping. "Why Pepe?"

Dad pulled my arm. "I don't know how to answer you. . . . I do know we need to get down to the high school for your competition."

I hugged Dad. He hugged me. I was glad he was with me. He provided a comfort that was priceless. My soul melted in his arms. I wished I'd had his comfort when Gigi lay still in the bathtub.

"What should we do with Pepe?"

Dad squeezed me tight. "We need to roll him in a blanket and, when we get back from your vocal performance, bury him next to Gigi. Let me go get a blanket, and then we need to leave."

Dad rolled Pepe in the blanket and gently placed him against the wall of the house. We left, arriving ten minutes late. I was unable to concentrate on the words, because I couldn't block out the sight of Pepe's lifeless body. I focused on the wall behind the judges, and, when I finished, I told myself, "Never again will I audition, never again will I have another dog die at the hands of a human, and never again will I have another dog as special as Gigi or Pepe."

Our ride home was unbalanced, with emotions swirling around in the car like a tornado. Dad wasn't mad at me, and I wasn't mad at him. We were both overcome with grief. Father's face lost the smile that lived with him as a nearly constant, daily presence. Frustration showed when he gripped the steering wheel as though he had to hold on for dear life. I think he was worried about how my mother would take this tragic information he would have to share with her. Would it throw her into an emotional turmoil, making it even harder to keep some form of happiness within our family? I wanted to hug my dad right at that moment and tell him everything would be all right.

Dad walked in front of me as we entered the house. His head dropped after he closed the front door and heard mom's voice. "Honey, is that you and Rose? Where is Pepe?"

Dad inhaled through his mouth and exhaled before he clamped his mouth shut. He immediately picked at his scalp, his face filled with despair as he struggled to give a smile. With his hand still planted on his head, he marched back to see Mom. I followed behind him partway and then turned into my room to change my dress. Their room mumbled in pain, and, within seconds, Mom howled out as though Dad had driven a knife through her heart.

Dad and I carried Pepe to the back of our bare dirt yard to lay him to rest next to Gigi. The yard was our desert graveyard, with not a lick of grass, that rolled right into the alley without a change of scenery. My legs quivered as I watched Dad shovel out the dirt. I anticipated that I would be able to see the blanket Gigi was rolled in. A small piece of Gigi's blanket came into view. Dad pulled out a hefty rock. Sadness entered me—a shock as though lightning had seized my heart. I looked at Pepe and then back down at the small but deep hole. My backyard didn't ever serve to hold a swing set or pool; it served to hold my dogs' bodies.

When Dad and I entered the arcadia (sliding glass) door, we heard Mom bawling. We looked at each other, and then Dad made an abrupt dash to Mom.

"Sweetie, are you in the bathroom?" No response through the kitchen vent.

I sat at the table, and Dad stumbled into kitchen. "Rose, Mom took a lot of medication. She is not responding as I would like."

Dad called Terros, an organization that helped people like Mom. Once before, Terros had pumped her stomach and had her stay overnight with a counselor available. Now here again, Mom would be staying the night at this special house, where others could look after her. Tomorrow would be a brand-new day, with no mistakes in it. At least that was what I hoped.

18
REJECTION

March 1980

As my paternal grandma always said, "Opinions are like bellybuttons—everyone has one."

Kahuna stood in my kitchen, and I was delighted, but it was unusual for him to stop by without calling first. He reached into his back pocket and pulled out an envelope. He held it in front of me. It looked like a card.

"Rose, I know what I am doing looks as if I don't love you."

I folded my arms. "Kahuna?" I moved closer to him.

He shook the envelope. "It's not because I want to break up with you."

I took the card. "I'll agree to this, Kahuna, but I know it won't work. We love each other, don't we?"

His smile disappeared, and his eyes squinted. "Yes."

Kahuna moved his hands behind his back, standing like a soldier ready to give a command, and then he took a step closer to me.

I moved back but kept focused on his hair. I knew if I looked in his eyes, I would crumble.

He caressed my shoulder.

I shrugged his hand off my shoulder.

I couldn't explain to him how many times I had felt rejected when I had to leave my home and live in foster care. I don't care how you see it—rejection is painful in every aspect. I pointed the card at Kahuna. "Can I ask you one question? Do you want to date other girls?"

Kahuna moved closer. "No, Rose."

Kahuna wrapped his arms around my waist and pulled me close. His tender lips were a warm welcome. With my eyes closed and his lips connected to mine, I thought of my deformed eye. *That must be it. Kahuna wants to find a girlfriend with two perfectly good eyes.*

Our luscious kiss ended, and Kahuna moved away from me.

"When should I read the letter?"

He squeezed my hand. "Wait until I leave."

"Okay—I'll read it later."

Silence came between us before he spoke. "I need to go; I have to run errands for my mom."

He wrapped his arms around me and squeezed with a sincerity that gave me a glimpse of hope that we would always be together. After he left, I shuffled to my room, knowing there wasn't any medication that could mend *my* broken heart.

I closed my bedroom door and glanced at the artwork he had drawn. I grabbed my plastic letter opener and slit the envelope.

> *Dear Very Important Rose,*
>
> *I decided to write you instead because you're so special, and I know you're the most important cause at this time.*
>
> *I've spent a lot of time talking to my mom, and I'm becoming even surer of you and myself. I feel this is the most correct decision I've made in a while, and I'm doing it for both of us. I feel that we've become too dependent on each other, more than we should. Our love of concern and dependence is blinding us from the companionship of love. If we continue depending so much on each other,*

we won't be able to love each other fully. In so many words, I'm leaving both of us on our own to deal with our own problems in order to develop self-dependence and confidence for both of us. This is something we can't have others do for us. We ourselves are the only ones who can develop self-dependence (which means Bobby can't do it for you).

I know that after we can develop this, I will indeed know whether we love each other. I said before, "I want to eliminate all the impurities from our relationship." I believe you love me with a love of dependence only. Your life depends mostly on me, and my life depends mostly on yours. That is the WHOLE ORIGIN of our uneasiness and my indecision. If I'm going to "fall in love" with you, I don't want to do it because I depend on you. It may take years, Rose, but when you're ready, I want to be the first guy in your path, ready to meet you. I think it's worth waiting for. I think you are worth waiting for.

As for myself, I'm going to try hard to do as I've been taught and warned, and I'm going to keep myself worthy and clean so I'll be ready for you. I'm not trying to make you wait for me, Rose. I'm asking you to rid yourself of the terrible dependence you have on me. Then we'll see just how in love we really are, and the spirit tells me it'll make us both happy. I also am very confident that we will love each other very much, and I'm very anxious for it to happen. I know that after we are independent, you'll be very happy with yourself and your life.

I placed the letter on my desk and stared at my wall, which Kahuna and I had painted light green a year ago. Me? Not happy? I was happy . . . with him. I loved my life with him. I didn't think I had become dependent on him. If anything, I thought you were supposed to help the person you love and feel a strong connection.

I continued to read.

> *Maybe you don't understand how dependent love can affect you. It stops your development. Man and wife were meant to progress together—not exist on, or live on, the presence of their companion. Dependent love is like two people in wheelchairs waiting for each other to push them.*
>
> *I know I'm loading a giant hunk on you at one time, and it's my fault because I allowed it to get so big, but I think it was good to wait so we could understand it better.*
>
> *Rose, now I feel in my heart that I really do have some love inside for you, but it's all covered up by dependence. That's why we question whether we really love each other.*

I read the last sentence again, maybe questioning whether he loved me. Then I read on.

> *I think that independence will help you control your emotions. I know it will. I also know that this is probably the biggest problem you'll ever have to face.*
>
> *Remember, I'll stick with you and support you, but only you can do the job. Pray often. The Lord will stick with you, too. He's got the answers to your problems, and I know independence is the first problem.*
>
> *I'm not trying to dump you off, Rose! It would kill me to do that. I believe you're the bag of gold the Lord has promised me if I live right.*
>
> *I'm NOT asking you to be PERFECT or SOLVE ALL your PROBLEMS. I know you can do it. You're wonderful, Rose. I'll always believe that. It's very hard for me to imagine loving anyone else but you.*

Don't worry about Mom. She feels the same way I feel, and Dad does, too. I've done the right thing! I'm almost proud of myself. But the battle isn't over yet. There's so much hard work ahead.

Persistently Loving, Kahuna

P. S. You'll always be special.

Prove it to yourself how special you are. I know you're always doing your best, and I'll stand behind you. 11:50 PM

I slipped the letter into the envelope and noticed what he had written on the back.

Love me for myself, not because you depend on me, not because your life is run by my welfare.

Does he understand the mountains I had to climb alone without a soul to count on? How could he be proud of himself after pulling the carpet out from underneath my feet? I'm independent and forced to be. I was never able to rely on my parents like he had.

I was tapping the envelope, hoping his words would explain why his mother had to manage our relationship. I placed the letter in the Liberty Box and shoved it underneath my bed. With the box out of sight, maybe the words he wrote would vanish.

All I wanted was a friend to like me and care about me. Why did Kahuna feel a need to tell me I couldn't depend on my brother when he depended on his mother? Humm!

19
LIBERTY BOX

April 1980

Friends come against the tide, the wind, and your raw emotions.

My smile awoke from its slumber when I tilted my head back, speaking words I wasn't sure I'd ever hear myself say: "I can survive."

Kahuna wrote after three agonizing weeks of torture. I traced my name written in his handwriting and clutched the letter close to my heart. I sniffed the envelope. "Thank you, Heavenly Father, for hearing my prayers." My legs turned to jelly as I darted for my room. I dropped to the cool linoleum floor and rested my back against my bed. I held the pages and blocked out sounds beyond the walls of my room. With each word I read, I ached for Kahuna.

> Hi Rose,
>
> Thank you for all the sunshine you bring me every day. If there was only one person on the whole Earth I could share my thoughts with, you would be the one. You've never given me reason to be disappointed. You always

press forward when others die out. Keep going, and you'll reach your goals.

What would I do without you, Rose? I could've ruined both our lives, and you stuck with me. Now I'm afraid to keep trying because I'm afraid I'll make another mistake. I think it was a mistake for me to end our relationship. I hope I never do that again to you. I have missed you!

I know I'll always love you, Rose, but what can I do to prove myself? Is it possible for me to get your faith back? Every time you were feeling down, it was because of me. Will I ever grow up?

I still want to take you to the ROTC dinner-dance Saturday if you want to go. I'll call Wednesday to get your answer. Don't worry; I don't want to embarrass you any more. And I won't act like I'm going steady with you unless that's what I'm doing.

Rose, I feel so small and ashamed; I'll always love you!

Love, forever, Kahuna

P.S. You're the best friend I've ever had. You're the nicest and prettiest girl I've ever known. Don't think I like you just for your looks.

I folded the cream-colored paper and kept the creases intact so it would fit into the envelope. I understood his insecurities in our relationship, and the physical attraction for one another was like a magnetic pull. These last three weeks of rejection were killing me. Rejection from Grandmother, Mom, and then Kahuna.

He still loved me and didn't want to discard me. It was time to let the tears fall, with relief that he realized we needed each other.

I waited by the phone Wednesday night.

"Rose, did you get my letter?"

"Yes, Kahuna. I did."

"Would you go with me to the ROTC dinner-dance?"

"Yes."

"Well, let me get with my mom on what time I can come get you, and then we can plan from there."

"Do you think your mom will mind me going with you?"

"I don't think so."

"I sure hope not, Kahuna; I really don't think your mom likes me."

"She does, Rose; she is just worried about us getting too close."

"Kahuna, do you realize that we are already closer than most teenagers our age?"

"Yes, I do, and I am concerned about how to keep things on the right path for both of us. I think we need to keep the faith."

"I do, too, but, to be honest, Kahuna, I have feelings for you I never thought possible."

"I know. I do for you, too. We need to pray and figure out the best path to take. I'll call you tomorrow, Rose, with the details of what time we will pick you up."

20
ROTC BALL

May 1980

Love walks, talks, and intensifies when nurtured with tender affection.

In the midst of silence, the image in the mirror screamed: *Why would Kahuna ever want you to be his date to the ROTC Ball?*

To curl my hair on my blind side was a slow process.

"Please work with me." I held tight to my pink brush and begged my hair to obey. My shoulder-length hair listened to my plea as it took shape and curled.

The roar of Mom's TV went silent. "Rose . . . the doorbell."

"Thanks." I peeked through the door window, smoothed out my dress, and, when I answered the door, butterflies danced in my stomach. I was face to face with my handsome young friend, Kahuna, dressed in his ROTC uniform and shiny shoes. I moved away from the door and welcomed him in. My heart raced when Kahuna's mom walked in behind him. He brushed against me, and, at that moment, I wished my plain dress was a lacy blue formal instead. He winked, and I gave him a smile.

Kahuna held out a gold box. "Here, Rose. This is for you."

When I took the box, our fingers touched. "Thanks, Kahuna."

My parents came into the living room, and we gathered in a semi-circle. I removed a small envelope taped on the front of the box and read the note, which had these words on the outside:

Stop! Do not open it unless you are the most beautiful girl in the world.

I wanted to open the envelope, but I didn't feel it was an accurate description of me.

Kahuna gave a half smile. "Open it, Rose—please."

I handed the box to Kahuna, opened the envelope, and read the pink card with roses on the front cover. It read, "*Love to Rose, the most special and loving girl in my life. I love you.*" Kahuna pinned the corsage on my left shoulder, where I could see it. I captured a mental picture of his handsome face and locked it deep inside. "Thanks, Kahuna—I love it."

The corsage had a light-pink carnation intermingled with pink, sparkly ribbon and sliver pipe cleaner. I raised my eyebrows and mouthed, "I love it."

Kahuna tapped my back. "We'd better get going."

"Bye, Mom and Dad."

Mom smiled. "You look beautiful."

I hugged her. "Thanks."

Dad rested his hand on my shoulder. "Yes, Rose. Mom is right. You look pretty."

With my arms wrapped around Dad's, I kissed his stubbly cheek. "Thanks."

Mom pulled on my dress to get my attention. "We'll see you later. Have an enjoyable time."

After hugging Mom, Kahuna wove his fingers in mine as we walked to the van.

When we arrived at the school, other ROTC students were near the school bus to board for our journey to the Air Force Base. Dax sat across the aisle and a row in front of us, and Kahuna's mom sat in the driver's seat. I squeezed Kahuna's hand and believed she had an internal clock to know when to look in the rearview mirror at us. Kahuna squeezed my hand three times, our signal for "I love you." I gazed out the window and wished his mother liked me. She hated me, like my grandmother and Tasha, who beat me in grade school.

My mood shifted from anxious to peaceful when we strolled through the double doors into the ROTC ballroom. The lights dimmed, and we saw a forest of helium balloons anchored to the tables. Kahuna greeted a friend, and I took in the grand magnitude of the decorations—like Cinderella, so eager to partake of all the night's activities. Familiar songs came from the corner of the room, making me want to dance.

Tables, dressed in navy-blue cloths, stood in organized lines.

Kahuna pointed toward the center of the line of tables. "Let's sit over there, Rose."

I gazed at him with pure delight. "Okay."

When we walked over to the table, Dax came from behind Kahuna and reached for his shoulder. "Can I sit with you guys?"

Kahuna shrugged his shoulder and wouldn't answer, so I spoke on his behalf. "Sure, you can sit with us."

Members of the drill team, including Dax, carried in the Arizona and United States flags so we could recite "The Pledge of Allegiance." Passion within me intensified with each word that flowed out of my mouth, and my heart acknowledged that we are blessed with splendid freedoms.

We were served *baron of beef au jus*; Virginia baked ham, ranch-style baked beans, Mexican corn, tossed garden salad, old-fashioned potato salad, cottage cheese, molded fruit Jell-O, and rolls.

Kahuna always sat to the left of me, and tonight was no different. It made it easier for me to see him, especially when he tapped me on my shoulder. "Rose, when you are done eating, let's go for a walk outside."

I swallowed before I responded. "Why outside, Kahuna?"

He took his arm off my shoulder. "I just want to show you something."

Before we walked out the door, I peeked at Dax, sitting by himself. I had a sneaking suspicion that it bothered him that we left. Kahuna scooped my hand in his and guided me to the courtyard. He held my hands and spoke, "Rose, I know we broke up a month ago, but I wanted to know if you would officially be my girlfriend again."

He squeezed my hands while I spoke. "Sure, Kahuna, but aren't you worried about our physical weaknesses?"

Kahuna rubbed his forehead. "I can't stand not having you in my life, and I promise I will treat you better, particularly in regard to your body."

I pulled him close. "I guess now we are boyfriend and girlfriend."

He spoke in my ear. "I like that, Rose."

After we hugged, he stepped back. "I have a gift for you."

He pulled a thin, gold-chain necklace with my birthstone out of a small white box. "How beautiful! I love it!"

He held it in front of me. "Would you like to wear it?"

I moved my hair away from my neck. "Of course." After Kahuna attached the necklace, I promised myself I would wear it to my grave.

21
SUMMERTIME

June 1980

**Some might think my life is tasteless,
but to me, it's a yummy jar of dill pickles.**

Mom's words traveled from the kitchen before I closed my bedroom door. "Is the swamp cooler on high?"

I collapsed on my bed and thought about how much I loved my summer breaks from school, even though our swamp cooler was useless when the humidity soared. My stomach rumbled while I was dressing, so I rushed to the kitchen.

Mom sat at the table with a heap of butter on her toast. "Are you glad to be out of school?"

"Yeah, I love sleeping in." I smiled at Mom, thinking of all the other reasons why I was happy school was out. In the summertime, I didn't have to worry about gas money for our old, dilapidated vehicle that lived in the single driveway. I didn't have to make embarrassing phone calls to friends to bum a ride to school or walk the three and a half miles.

My mouth watered for a bowl of crumbled saltine crackers mixed with milk. Bobby and I had invented this cereal recipe years ago. I searched the half-empty cupboards and found all that was left was stale boxes of cereal. "Mom, there isn't anything good to eat."

My mother motioned with her chin. "Have some toast."

"No, I'll eat later. I think I'll go strip my bed and wash my sheets." I strolled out of the kitchen with a neglected stomach that growled.

Each taxing pull on my strawberry-printed sheet made me wish I could pull the strawberries off and eat them. Still, living our poverty-stricken lifestyle wasn't all that bad. At least I had my own bed and wasn't sleeping at someone else's house.

I turned on the washer and put in a small amount of laundry soap. I loved the sound the water made when the agitator moved. Bubbles formed, and, when I dropped the sheets in, they disappeared as quickly as the saltine crackers from our cupboards. I focused on the water and thought about how glad I was that Kahuna was my boyfriend and hadn't disappeared.

I put the washer lid down and headed inside to the shower. On my way to the bathroom, I walked through the kitchen and imagined there was a large ham on the table, ready to be eaten. Frustration came with each brush stroke over my knotted hair. Oh, how I wished we could afford hair conditioner. I stared at the face looking back at me in the mirror and tried to focus on my unruly hair, but I couldn't help but notice the blank, hollow stare back at me from my blind eye. I spoke out loud to the familiar teenager in the mirror, with a hope she would understand me.

"Kahuna and I are sixteen and able to get jobs, but I'm scared. I do love babysitting on weekends, but five dollars isn't enough to pay for gas, food, deodorant, hairspray, and panty hose."

I brushed my hair away from my face and smiled at the girl who couldn't take her eye off me.

"We are both so excited about getting our driver's license, but I'm afraid the Motor Vehicle Department will reject me." I covered my blind eye and spoke as though my friend in the mirror would console me. "With vision only in one eye, my confidence is brittle. I know they will kick me out the door when they see me."

I uncovered my eye and smiled at the one consistently friendly face I had in my life. She was the only person who could give me encouragement. Deep inside, I craved for the support that I desperately needed. Then, I remembered a bit of positive news and shared that with the girl in the mirror. "I'm so excited I was at least accepted to be volunteer counselor at the Easter Seals Camp. Yippee. I will get out of the heat and be useful helping special-needs children—and I can certainly relate. Definitely, this is a blessing."

The thoughts about Easter Seal Camp reminded me that Kahuna was away. He had gone to Washington on a trip to visit family. I was nervous that he wouldn't get back before I left for camp in two weeks.

Mom yelled from the kitchen, "Rose, the mail. Can you get it?"

I hurried out of the bathroom. "Sure, Mom."

Kahuna and I promised each other to write while on our separate trips. It had been five days since he'd left, and I was hoping my first letter from him had just been dropped in the black mailbox that was glued to our house.

When I found one, I squealed and hurried inside. I sat in the blue recliner that my grandmother gave us and read his letter.

> *Dear Sunshine,*
>
> *How's my favorite person? Mom told me you got a job. Are you rich yet? I might be staying in Oregon with Valinda's family to work for the summer, but I don't know if I can because of school. I sure would like to hear from you. I wish you could be at my house when I talk to Mom long distance. A letter or anything would make my day. I'm beginning to miss you pretty badly now, but I try not to think about it.*
>
> *I've really enjoyed my stay here at Dothan's. My Mom can explain who they are. They treat us so nicely. I ran 6 miles today.*
>
> *I thought I'd take the time to add in this little letter full of sweet nothings that being away makes me see a lot of*

the nice things about you more clearly. Where before I dearly loved you for fifty reasons, now I love you more for a hundred different reasons. I guess I forgot how hardworking and charitable you are. I feel like I took our relationship for granted in a way. Although I didn't downgrade it, I forgot some of the neat things we share. I admit I did sort of downgrade it sometimes, but I didn't realize what I was doing, and I let my emotions take me away. I still feel bad about that, and I'll need your help to correct them. Rose, you know I can be very, very bullheaded and stubborn, but I know that there is not a being in existence who can persuade me to change my mind like you can. If there is one person in the world who could influence my thoughts, it's you. You have much more control over my actions than you think. Just because I love you. I trust you with my life, and I have faith in your feelings. I constantly depend upon you to keep me in line and making the right choices.

I know now and always that I can leave my welfare in your hands whenever I need to. Other girls may be nice, pretty, and have some good qualities, but there is not a girl alive who has what you have.

You have more faith and love than any person I've ever seen. I've known this for a long time, but sometimes I forget it because of my emotions. As you can see, I still love you very, very much.

Love forever, Kahuna.

A poem for you . . .

You are the rose, white, untouchable by man or beast, blooming brightly with a thousand soft, glistening petals of moist, snow-white velvet.

You are the moonbeam, shining through my window, brightening and changing a gloom right into a softly glowing dream.

You are the teardrop in the face of an infant, pure and heartfelt and knowing no sin or unclean thing.

You are a picture in a museum, bright, happy, and spreading sunshine, never changing.

You are the girl I prayed for and waited for and searched for and prepared myself for because I knew you were here, but I didn't know where. I loved you before I met you because I knew you before. You are the girl of my dreams. I love you.

His words were golden, but not in a material way. I rubbed my fingers over my name he'd written. I thought about how handsome he was—yes, very exotic. Kahuna was my pot at the end of the rainbow, and his words were more valuable to me than even God's words. He was my source of happiness.

Our large living-room window captured the mulberry tree that stood tall and strong—and I wanted to be that way for Kahuna.

I didn't have the emotional strength to get a job or a driver's license, but I had the force of will to hold on to Kahuna's words and trust in his judgment. With his letter in my hand, I thought of my Liberty Box and how it held deep secrets that only the two of us knew.

The days passed, and I waited for more letters from Kahuna, but, two weeks later, I hadn't heard from him. Easter Seals Camp was in three days, so I forced myself to pack.

My hope of seeing Kahuna before I left for camp waned, and I begged Heavenly Father to let me see him.

Days later, my prayers were answered when Kahuna arrived at my front door. My heart skipped when he gave me a warmhearted smile and hug. Oh, how handsome he was, even with his whiskers. I rubbed my cheek against his and told myself: *This isn't a dream. He is here, and he is real.* I grabbed his hand and led him into the kitchen to see Dad.

"Hi," Kahuna said.

Dad turned with a smile. "Oh, hi, Kahuna; how are you?"

"Good, I just got back from Washington last night."

"Well, I'm glad you got home safely, and I know Rose missed you." Dad turned his attention back to the egg he was cooking, and Kahuna fixed his eyes on me with a tentative expression.

"I missed Rose, too," he said with a grin.

Kahuna and I sat at the table.

"Rose, my cousin Justin thought he had to have a picture of his girlfriend taped to the sun visor the whole time he was driving us there. He looked at her when he should have been paying attention to the road. We could have been in a car accident if I hadn't yelled, 'Watch that car!' or 'Stop!' I was relieved when he let me drive. I didn't need a picture of you taped to the sun visor because I had you pictured in my mind."

I reached over and rubbed his hand. "I'm just glad you got home so I could see you before I left for camp."

I don't know what Dad thought of our conversation, but he snickered.

Dad set my egg in front of me and left the room.

Kahuna grabbed my hand the minute Dad left. "When will you be back from Easter Seals Camp?"

"I come home next week for one night and then leave the next morning for girls camp."

Kahuna moved closer. "Can I get the address to the Easter Seals Camp?" he asked.

"Sure, it's sitting on my dresser. Just remind me to get it after I brush my teeth."

We talked about the letters he had sent me.

Kahuna squeezed my hand three times, and I squeezed his three times back. It sent a chill and comfort that he was my light, my star, and my best friend.

"I will be leaving for Boys State tomorrow. Then, while you are at girls camp, I will leave for Band Camp. I will write you."

I pulled my hand away from his. "Sounds good."

Kahuna's eyes got larger, and he raised his eyebrows. "Don't you want me to write you?"

"Of course, I do." I couldn't tell Kahuna I was jealous of the girls in his band. He'd written in a letter about how the girls in his band are nice, pretty, and have some good qualities.

After I carried my dishes to the sink. I said, "I need to brush my teeth and finish packing my suitcase."

Kahuna followed me to the bathroom. I didn't want to hurt his feelings, so, even though embarrassed about it, I let him watch me brush my teeth. I tried not to let toothpaste drool out of my mouth. I usually looked at myself in the mirror while I brushed my teeth, but this time, as Kahuna watched, I couldn't. Then, I grabbed my hairbrush and put my hair into a ponytail. With each twist of the rubber band around my hair, I thought of the invisible rubber band that was mentally around Kahuna and me. Kahuna stood with his head leaning against the doorframe with his full lips and curly, thick chestnut hair.

"I'm going to miss you," he said.

I walked closer to him. "I'll miss you, too."

I headed for my bedroom, and Kahuna followed.

I placed my toothbrush and hairbrush in my suitcase. "There. I think I have everything."

When I put the suitcase lid down, the buckles couldn't connect.

"I have too much in my suitcase."

"Here, let me show you the proper way to close it."

Kahuna used his broad shoulders and muscular arms to lift my opened suitcase and placed it on my bed. He sat on top of my suitcase, and his arms flexed to close it.

"Put the latch down below my right hand, Rose."

I put my hand underneath his arm and closed the latch.

"Good; now get the other one."

Once it was locked, we both sighed.

Kahuna's years of being a discus thrower made carrying my suitcase into the hallway effortless for him. I glanced at my room to make sure everything was the way I wanted it and closed my door.

Mom and Dad were at the table, with mail scattered all over.

"Dad, I'm ready to go."

"Do you have a jacket?"

"Thanks for reminding me, Mom."

I turned toward Kahuna. "Let me get my jacket."

When I re-entered the kitchen, I could see frustration in Dad's face, and I interrupted their conversation.

"I'm ready to go."

"Did you leave me the address so I can write you?"

"Yes, Mom. It's on my dresser."

I bent down to hug Mom. She flinched, and I sensed her loneliness.

Dad spoke, "Time to go, Rose."

"Honey, you hurry back, and drive carefully going over the train tracks. Make sure Rose is signed in before you leave."

"I will, Sweetie, and when I get back, we can go over the bills."

Mom glanced at Kahuna. "It was nice of you to come and see Rose before she left."

"Oh, I'm glad I did."

I gave Kahuna a hug. "Thanks for coming over. I'll send you a letter this week."

"Sounds good, Rose. I'll wait for your letter, and then I'll write you."

Dad opened the front door to instant heat. "Let's go."

Dad reached for my suitcase at the same time Kahuna did. Dad opened the trunk, and Kahuna put my suitcase in.

I stared at Kahuna. "See ya."

He winked. "Bye."

22
COWBOY DALLAS

June 1980

Value your imperfections, because
they are what make you a masterpiece.

I slammed the car door and rolled down my window. Dad drove, and the warm air circulated through the car.

"Rose, do you have a nametag for your suitcase?"

"No. Should I have one?"

"Yes, so we'll stop at the store."

Because the radio was broken, Dad usually would sing songs that he'd written. This time, he stayed silent.

"How about this store, Rose?"

"Looks good."

Dad grabbed suitcase tags, looked at the price, and gave a sigh. "Let's go pay," he said.

While waiting in line, Dad jingled coins in his pocket and then searched in his wallet for a dollar.

Dad asked me, "Do you have a pen to write your name on the tag?"

"I do, in my suitcase."

Perfect Rose Cracked Vase

He pulled one of his many pens from his shirt pocket protector. "Well, here."

Dad drove in front of the building where I needed to catch the Easter Seals bus. Teenagers were standing there, dressed in shorts and sleeveless shirts, and I had on my T-shirt and ditto pants.

"Let me get your suitcase and sleeping bag."

"Oh, Dad—you remembered my sleeping bag?"

"Yes, I put it in the trunk last night."

"Thanks for thinking of me."

"Anything for my little girl."

I smiled and jumped out of the car.

"Here, Rose. Take the sleeping bag, and I'll take your suitcase."

Dad's stubby fingers wrapped around the handle, and he took a deep breath before lifting my suitcase out of the trunk. After he dropped it onto the pavement, he stretched his arms and pulled his shoulders back. "What do you have in here, Rose? It's heavy."

"It's just my clothes and toiletry items."

Dad grabbed my suitcase and motioned with his head for me to close the trunk. We walked past handicapped children, in wheelchairs, and some with walkers.

"Rose, go inside and sign in."

I pointed. "Do you think I should go through those doors?"

"Yes. Leave your sleeping bag with me."

I wove between clusters of teenagers.

A lady wearing a cowboy hat and blue jeans was standing next to the desk.

"Hi, my name is Rose, and I need to sign in."

The lady pointed to a paper on the desk. "Sign in is right there."

Exiting the door, I caught sight of Dad, who looked exhausted.

"Dad, I'm signed in. You can leave."

"Before I do, find out where to take your suitcase and sleeping bag."

I approached a group of teenagers. "Sorry to interrupt, but where do we take our suitcases and sleeping bags?"

A tall, husky boy my age, pointed. "Over there behind that building is a trailer."

After we'd put my suitcase and sleeping bag in the trailer, Dad hugged me. "You have fun, Rose, and I'll see you next week."

"Thanks, Dad, for the ride and suitcase tag."

I squeezed my father's shoulder. "I love and appreciate you."

"I love you, too, Rose."

There are no words to describe Dad's short, stocky legs that carried him away. How blessed I was to have a loving, devoted father.

The campers got on the bus before the volunteers. "All you volunteers," Terri bellowed out as she stood near the bus, "please sit in the back!"

I sat in the third seat from the back and opened my window. The husky boy I'd spoken with earlier sat behind me.

We got on the road, the teenagers around me talked, and I looked out the window, at places I had been to with Kahuna.

A tap on my shoulder startled me. I turned so I could see who it was.

"Hi. I'm Conner Kramer."

"Oh, hi. I'm Rose."

Conner rested his arms on the back of my seat. "Where do you go to high school?"

I cleared my throat. "I go to Maryvale High, but before that, I went to West High. How about you?"

"I attend Brophy College Preparatory, a boys' school."

"Really? Well, my mother attended Xavier."

I leaned against the window so I could see him better.

"What's your favorite subject, Rose?"

"My favorite class is concert choir."

Conner rubbed his chin. "You like to sing, huh?" He moved his head closer.

"Well then, we will have to do a skit together. They have a skit night, where all of us volunteers entertain the campers."

"Sounds fun. I would love to do that."

"What kind of music do you like to sing?"

"The songs my father wrote or *Sound of Music*."

"What is your favorite song from *Sound of Music*?"

I rubbed my forehead and thought for a minute.

"I am not sure of the title, but the song starts out, 'I am sixteen going on seventeen.' Have you heard it before?"

Conner beamed. "Yes—let's practice it and do a duet for the campers."

I looked around the bus before I spoke. "Do you know 'Sippin' Cider'?" Conner smiled. "Yes, I do. Let sing it right now."

"Okay; maybe others will join in."

We had sung only a bar or two before we had the back section of the bus singing, and it reminded me of riding the bus to Camp LoMia. We finished that song and started in on another, and another, with several of the campers singing along.

After two hours on the school bus, the camp leader, with beautiful blond hair and piercing blue eyes, stood near the bus driver. "Campers and volunteers, my name is Asa. We will be arriving at the campsite in about forty minutes. When we're there, the volunteers will get off the bus first. A worker will retrieve your camper for you. Then, you will take your camper to the large building, which is the dining hall, for lunch. Between here and the camp, some cowboys will try to get on the bus. Please be aware that we will need to obey their orders."

Conner tapped my shoulder. "What do you think she means by '... some cowboys'?"

"I have no clue. Are they workers?"

Conner moistened his lip. "I think it's for the campers."

I studied Conner's large eyebrows and pimpled face.

"You're right."

Three cowboys, in full gear, galloped in on horses and stopped in front of the bus. They pulled their plastic guns out of their holsters. The campers screamed and yelled, "Cowboys!"

The bus stopped, and the smallest cowboy rode his horse to the door and banged. "Hey, ya—open up."

The driver stood. "Should I open the door?"

One of the volunteers yelled, "Open the door."

The bus driver opened the door.

A cowboy entered and pointed his plastic gun at the driver, saying, "I'm taking your driver hostage, and y'all have to stay here forever." An albino cowboy with white hair came aboard. He smiled at me, and my face flushed with warmth when he clutched his straw hat to his heart. "Please, please, water. Take me to camp, and I will free your bus driver. Will you save me?"

Campers shouted, "Yes" and pounded against the windows and seats.

This incredible creature that I couldn't take my eyes off turned to the other cowboy. "Let the driver go."

The cowboy who was holding the gun on the bus driver gave in and left the bus. The one who threw me a smile sat next to me. The bus moved, making a breeze to cool my flushed face.

He spoke. "Hi, my name is Dallas. Is this your first time at camp?"

I rubbed my cheek. "Yes."

He put his hat on and stretched his leg into the aisle. "Well, I think you'll love it. The campfires are fun—not just for the campers but for us workers and volunteers, too."

I moved my hair away from my eyes. "Campfires."

Silence followed, and I thought of Kahuna. Guilt pierced right through me.

I sensed peace when we arrived, with the clean, wide sidewalks that stretched from cabin to cabin to give the campers mobility and independence. There were pine trees and wildflowers.

Terri, the director, climbed on. "Dallas, come here, and everyone else stay seated until I call your name."

My eyes followed him through the window, as I waited for my name to be called.

I inspected the campers when I exited the bus.

Judy guided this young girl with two forearm crutches, whose left leg dragged. "Rose, this is your camper, Katrin. She is twelve years old and loves to camp. Katrin, this is Rose, your counselor for the week, and she will be with you during your stay at Easter Seals Camp."

After the introduction, Judy vanished to retrieve another camper.

"Hi, Katrin. So, you're twelve?"

Katrin took a few deep breaths. "I'm almost thirteen."

"Are you hungry?"

She shook her head "Yes." I guided her. "It's this way, Katrin. Would you like me to carry your purse?"

"No, I can handle it." She stopped walking and pulled her purple purse up on her shoulder. My heart swelled with how much energy it took for her to walk. "We're almost there, and I think they are serving sandwiches."

"I . . . I like sandwiches."

"I do, too, but I can't handle tuna fish. Do you like tuna?"

Before she answered, we entered and stood at the end of the food line. "Yes, I like tuna fish with cheese."

The dining hall was spacious, with tall silver beams on the ceiling. A pool table occupied the far-right corner, and the tables had benches connected to them. Windows covered the walls that let the sun shine in to give the appearance of being outside. Voices bounced off the walls with laughter.

She leaned against her forearm canes and observed the other campers.

"Katrin, here's a tray for you. Let me know how I can help."

She smiled and leaned against the railing that held the trays. I was hungry, but my first responsibility was to Katrin. "There are lots of different sandwiches to pick from."

Katrin looked at the rows of sandwiches. We each picked the sandwich we wanted, and then I nodded toward a table in the middle of the dining hall. "I see a place over there where we can sit. Let's get you seated, and then I'll get my tray and our drinks."

I put her tray on the table and caught her forearm canes when she sat down. "What would you like to drink? I think they have milk, orange juice, apple juice, and water."

"I would like apple juice, please."

I placed her forearm canes underneath the bench and retrieved my tray and our drinks. Returning to the table, I sat to the right of her.

"You must have been hungry. You finished half of your sandwich."

"My mom didn't have time to make me breakfast."

I didn't respond and dropped the subject, because it brought back memories of my youth. The nurse approached us and handed Katrin a small, white paper cup with pills.

"Rose, while Katrin is down for a rest and relaxation, could you come to the nurse's station? I need to go over some items with you."

"Where is the nurse's station?"

"It's on the other side of the dining hall in the small, white building that looks like a house."

The nurse took a seat to the left of Katrin and talked quietly to her.

"Katrin, do you have a catheter in your purse?"

She wiped her mouth with the back of her hand. "Yes. I have two."

"Good, but if you need more, Rose can get them from me."

"I have six of them in my suitcase."

"Well, if you run out, let me know. Okay, Sweetie?"

She took a bite of her sandwich.

The nurse gave me a friendly look, and I smiled. "Make sure to come by the nurse's station."

I'm sure the tone in my voice made me sound uneasy. "I will."

"Katrin, are you ready to go find the girls' cabin and pick a bed?"

"Yes, I'm ready."

"Here are your crutches."

Katrin used her crutches to pull herself up from the bench. I wanted to protect her from falling and instinctively extended my arms out. She gave me a puzzled look; I drew my arms to my side and forced myself to let her manage on her own. My senses trickled through me with the realization that the tables had been turned. Instead of feeling sorry for myself, it made me better appreciate my physical abilities that she didn't have. I could run, walk, and have a boyfriend who loved me. At camp, I needed to be a positive influence on Katrin. It made me feel worthwhile.

Sweat was seeping down my back as I trailed behind Katrin, and I observed that her left leg dragged behind her. We stopped several times before we made it to the cabin. I opened the cabin door, and she struggled to lift her leg over the threshold. Once inside, she found the nearest bed and plopped on it.

"Would you like to use the restroom, Katrin?"

She looked at me, her eyes wide open. "Yes, I would."

"Let me get a look at the restroom, and then I will help you."

The restroom had three toilet stalls, and the first stall would be the easiest for her because it was larger.

When I entered the room, Katrin was resting, and other campers were settling in with their counselors' help.

"Okay, Katrin. It's time to use the restroom. Do you need help?"

She glared at me. "I . . . I can do it."

I held my hands behind my back and reminded myself to be patient. She strolled like a turtle, and I shuffled behind her. My stomach coiled because I knew my deformities and hardships were minor compared to hers. With that, my stomach twisted and lurched to a sickening stillness. In a way, Katrin was better off than I was. At least people could immediately see her challenges.

She entered the first stall and pulled her pants down with the door open. Did she care to have privacy? All girls do, including me.

"Can you bring me my purse?"

"Sure."

I handed the purse to her. She unzipped it and pulled out a long, thin, flexible tube and inserted it into her body.

At first, I was nervous standing next to the door watching her, but, for Katrin, it was a necessity. When she was finished, she gawked at me. "Did you put on plastic gloves?"

"No. Where do I get them?"

"They're in the front area of my suitcase."

"I'll go look—just a second."

I riffled through her suitcase and pulled out the plastic gloves.

"Okay, I have the gloves on."

She held the catheter in her hand. "Wash this out, and then dry it with a paper towel. Here, take this."

I grabbed the catheter. "Do I run it under hot or cold?"

"Hot water."

My fingers stung from the hot water, and Katrin grumbled from the stall. In the mirror, I could see Katrin behind me.

"Can you dry that off and put it in the plastic bag in my purse, please? I left the purse on the floor by the toilet."

Katrin slept, and I attended volunteer meetings to learn of my responsibilities at camp. I was glad that they'd assigned a worker to stay in each cabin, because if something went wrong or a camper needed help, they could assist them.

They gave information on Katrin's physical and emotional needs. The best part was that Dallas sat across from me.

The evening air was nippy, but the flickering campfire made the temperature comfortable. I moved closer to Katrin and observed campers' faces, glowing—from not only the flames of the fire but from the spirit of the songs we sang. Harmony flowed, and campers waved their hands above their heads. Energy doubled when Kate knelt to ask a camper their favorite song. A girl my age, with shoulder-length hair, cried. I rubbed her shoulder and grinned as I sang along. She responded; others needed to be coaxed, but, gradually, like snails, the campers emerged from their fragile shells.

When it was Katrin's turn to tell Kate what song she liked, she didn't answer. Instead, she looked at the worker with a haunting stare—a type of gaze I know I held inside me when I didn't feel valuable. For a second, I connected with her. Thoughts of home life as a young girl surfaced.

One day, we took the campers to the local swimming pool. Another day we slept under the stars on the side of a dirt road. Katrin beamed with energy as we gazed at the sky, overflowing with stars.

The morning after the campout, we counselors pushed wheelchair campers through the dirt back to the bus. I lifted and carried, until my scrawny arms cried in pain, but the minute we arrived back at camp, a worker placed letters in my hand. I was flushed with temptation to open the letters, but I slipped them in my coat pocket and kept focused on Katrin.

I helped Katrin shower, dress in clean clothes, and lie down for a nap before I left.

I relaxed on a bench near the campfire pit, looking at the light-blue envelope with a drawing of Ziggy on the front and my name in bold letters. I didn't want to destroy Kahuna's drawings on the envelope or the sticker on the back that said, "A job well done is time well spent," "I miss you," "Good work," and "Hi!" Not wanting to wait, I ripped the end of the envelope.

Hi, Fruit Pie,

> This seminar is continuing to be a unique experience. I learned that I really don't smile enough like I used to do. I'm also a little shy around strange people. I've got a lot more free time than they said I would have.
>
> There is one small thing wrong here. I'll tell you the problem, and you can help me figure it out: Here at Boys State, we play a lot of games and have a lot of activities. My problem is that when everyone around me gets rowdy and excited, I just smile and participate.
>
> While everyone is out talking about trivial matters on free time, I'm in the dorm practicing my trumpet and reading my scriptures. I think I've impressed everyone as being the quiet, intellectual type. I do think I don't talk to people as much as I should, but I also think that maybe I'm just doing what I should. The main thing that worries me is that I'm so busy being a goody-goody that I don't have time to do good with my neighbors, but I don't know if that's correct. I really doubt it. Well, I know I seem and am very different to a lot of people, but I'll hold my ground, and I'll try to pull them up instead of going down to them.
>
> I still love and miss you very much.
>
> HAVE FUN AT CAMP!

I know you're doing great things; say your prayers. The world loves you.

Love forever, Kahuna

The wind danced through the trees, and I believed we all feel awkward. The bench where I sat turned into a place of refuge from the sorrow of knowing that these campers would never live a life such as mine. I tapped my feet against the dirt and spoke. "I'm blessed."

A kind of tranquility descended on me, and I realized how fortunate I'd been that the German measles hadn't damaged my life like other disabilities had affected the other campers' lives. Some of them had to wear diapers. *Did the campers have the same kind of feelings, wants, and desires to belong to someone, like I did?* I placed my letter in the envelope. *Kahuna, thank you for loving me.* Dallas waved and walked toward me. He sat next to me. "Hi. Are you enjoying camp?"

I put the letter in my coat pocket. "Yes, I love camp and my camper." Dallas looked around and seemed uneasy. "Hey, I see you got your letters."

When Dallas saw his boss within eyeshot of where we were, he said, "I'd better go. See you tonight at the dance."

Before the dance, Conner and I practiced for our song "You are Sixteen going on Seventeen' and rehearsed the scene from *Sound of Music* for our skit. We dressed in our costumes from props we found in a box from years past.

The dining hall had been transformed into a Disco Dance Hall, complete with a disco ball. The campers shined like stars with the enthusiasm of a dance. Even Dallas danced with the campers and stirred a certain kind of special, jovial emotion—exactly like the Saturday night dances were for me. A girl camper, my age, named Roxanne, had developed a crush on a counselor named Martin, a guy I had met in 9th grade. Roxanne followed him to get his attention, and she told everyone she loved his blond hair and dimple. He heard about her crush, and, days before the dance, she got enough courage to ask Martin to go with her. He accepted this opportunity to make her feel important. He went to her cabin and escorted her to the dance. Her crippled body needed the same type of forearm crutches Katrin used. All the counselors pitched in by curling her hair and applying makeup. She was the light of the ball.

The evening ended around the campfire with songs. Katrin clapped to the beats, and her face glowed. The pop and hiss of the fire was the background soundtrack when the director gave her final goodbye to the campers. After I had tucked Katrin in, I met my friends at the firepit. Dallas was there, slouched in a picnic chair with his legs crossed. Words of the week's events were exchanged and brought many laughs—how much we enjoyed our campers! Dallas moved his chair closer to me. Conner told a joke, and Dallas laughed along with us but said nothing. He smiled and then winked at me. The flames in the fire sizzled out, and so did my friends, as they left one by one. Before I knew it, Dallas and I were alone. He reached into his coat pocket and pulled out a paper. "Here, this is for you. Can I walk you to your cabin?"

"Sure." We strolled on the paved path.

"Nice night, isn't it?"

We bumped into each other. "You know, Dallas, we would never have cool summer nights like this in the city."

He stopped. "Well, I hope you like my note. I'd better let you walk the rest of the way alone."

His white hair shone in the moonlight, and he moved closer to me. I backed off. "Thanks."

He touched my hand. "I sure enjoyed the skit you and Conner did before the dance. You have a beautiful voice. I hope to walk with you more often."

I shrugged my shoulders. "Okay."

On the bus, I waved back at Dallas through the window. Then I studied Katrin, resting her head against the bus window. She looked empty, as if she were in a glass bubble, unable to be touched or be heard. I was glad she had been my camper—I learned from watching her struggles. Her physical limitations helped me to see there is always someone worse off. I observed the other campers and imagined what their lives back home were like. How many came from broken homes, homes with emotional problems, homes with low income? How many lived in foster homes? How many of them had friends they could call or receive a letter in the mail from, like I had from Kahuna?

23

TRUTH OR LIE

Summer 1980

The truth can impair, but a lie can leave anguish.

I entered my bedroom and saw a letter on my dresser. On the front of the envelope, a small koala bear sat at the top of a tree, holding on for dear life, and the words, "Thinking of you." I pulled the card out of the envelope and read the front. It said, "This is the next best thing to being there." A letter fell out and landed on the floor. I picked it up and dove onto my bed.

> *Dearest,*
>
> *Well, Rose, this day, July 9th, is the day we fell in love. It was the first day you held my hand.*
>
> *Now, as I think about all the wonderful things we have, I want you to know how much I appreciate all the things you've given me. You mean the world to me. You are the most beautiful girl in the world and always will be.*
>
> *I know now how special and sacred our relationship is. Thank you so much for your continued effort.*

Perfect Rose Cracked Vase

> *Continue to keep fighting the battle, and keep the promises you gave me. You will be making more in our future.*
>
> *I love you very much,*
>
> *Love, now and forever, Kahuna*

I read the sticker on the envelope: "Happy days bring a smile to my face when I'm around you." I rolled over onto my side, facing my ceramic-doll lamp. I wanted stay in my bed, but I knew I needed to take a shower.

I dumped my dirty clothes out of my suitcase, and Dallas's letter followed. A letter I hadn't read . . . a letter from a man who was going to be a doctor. A real doctor.

> *Hi, there, Rose,*
>
> *It was wonderful meeting you at camp. When I return home from summer camp, I want to take you on a date.*
>
> *Maybe we can go to the movies or take a walk through the park.*
>
> *Take care, and I can't wait to see you again at camp.*
>
> *Love, Dallas*

I folded the letter and hoped my feelings for him would fold, too. I couldn't put his letter in my Liberty Box, so I placed it in my dresser drawer.

I carried my dirty clothes to the back porch to put in the washer. We could never afford a clothesbasket, so it was always a trick to open the arcadia door with a load of laundry in my arms.

The phone rang just as I entered the house.

"Hi, Rose—this is Dax; you're home?"

I plopped down on the telephone chair. "Yes, I am home, and Easter Seals Camp was cool. I supervised a camper."

"Have you heard from Kahuna?"

"If you count the letters from Easter Seals Camp."

"You know, Rose, I wish he would respond to me like he does to you. I think he is home, and he won't answer my phone calls."

"Well, I haven't heard from him, but if I do, I will let you know." I leaned my head against the wall and slouched over in the telephone chair. "I don't know what to tell you, Dax."

"Did you get my letters?"

"Yes, I did, and I appreciate you expressing how much you think Kahuna loves me. I love you for seeing the good in Kahuna."

"I'm glad I could write you, Rose."

I swung the long telephone cord in a circular motion. "How is your job at the mall going? Are you making lots of juice drinks?"

"It's good, and the bike ride there and home isn't too bad."

"What are the rest of your plans for the summer?"

"Well, I will be going to band camp with Kahuna."

I stopped swinging the cord because I couldn't hear Dax very well. "Are you rooming with Kahuna at band camp?"

"No, he didn't request to room with me."

"That stinks. I'm sure that hurt." I paused and thought for a moment. I bit my tongue to hold back from saying anything that would hurt Dax.

"You know, Dax, he will realize what an awesome friend you are. Just give him some time."

"I don't think he cares about me anymore."

I scratched my head. "Be patient, Dax."

"I hope you're right."

"I know I am right. I would love to talk more, but I need to take a shower. So, I'd better let you go."

"Thanks for talking. If you do hear from Kahuna, let me know."

I stood. "Sure, I will."

After my shower, Mom yelled. "Rose, can you come here?"

I mumbled, "What does she need?" Then, I hollered from behind my closed door. "Okay, let me get dressed."

Mom was getting off her bed. "Rose, I was going to get a snack. Do you want one?"

"Sure, I would love that. How was your week, Mom?"

"Besides Grandmother irritating me, it went well."

When we entered the kitchen, it smelled of floor cleaner. "Mom, you need to hang up on her. I wish I would have been home to answer the phone for you."

Mom opened the refrigerator and continued to talk. "I wish you would have been here, too."

My mother's hunched back showed her hopelessness.

"I made new friends at Easter Seals camp, and it was a neat experience. Those campers had handicaps worse than what I have. They couldn't do things I take for granted. Oh, I met this cute guy named Dallas, who's going to be a doctor."

Her hand flew to her mouth. "Oh, a cute guy, huh? When do you go back?"

"I have girls camp next week, and, then, three days after I return home, I leave for Easter Seals Camp."

I propped my hand against my cheek while seated at the table. "But, I can't wait for girls camp, Mom. It's the greatest place in the world. I wish you could come with me—we would have so much fun together."

My mother spoke with a strong yearning, "I wish I could, too."

"Can you believe this is my fifth year? And I'm going to be a junior counselor. I'm not sure what all that means, but I'm excited."

Mom rubbed her hands. "I'm glad we had the twenty-five dollars to pay for camp."

"I appreciate all you and Dad do for me."

I waited for a minute, got up from the kitchen chair, and headed toward the arcadia door. I called over my shoulder, "I'd better check my load in the washer. I have lots of clothes to wash."

I carried each individual piece of clothing out to the clothesline and wished we had a clothes basket.

The next day, my mother called me to the phone.

"Hi, Kahuna. Thanks for the letters."

"You're welcome. What did you do at camp?"

All I wanted to do was listen to him, so I briefly told him about camp.

Then I soaked in every word as he told me about Boys State and events he'd forgotten to tell me about visiting his cousin Valinda. As he shared stories, I wished they were of us together and not with her.

My throat tightened, and I pictured Kahuna and myself on our porch swing, when he said, "I can't wait until we get married and can move to Washington. You will love it, and so will I."

I wanted to move there right then; skip girls camp, skip the rest of my teenage years and run away with him. But I knew it wasn't time for that yet. My church leaders had taught me dozens of lessons about morality and about being careful not to get too close to someone of the opposite sex. Even so, I didn't feel one ounce of guilt for the relationship I had with Kahuna. My desire to love him overpowered any thought of guilt.

After our phone conversation, I washed the lunch dishes. No sooner did I have my hands in the dishwater that I remembered that I had forgotten to remind Kahuna of the Easter Seals Dance Marathon. "Okay," I told myself, "tomorrow I will ask him."

24
GIRLS CAMP

Summer 1980

My house is my home, but camp is my heaven.

I waved at Dad through the Greyhound bus window, and his charming smile sent a warm hug as he waved back. The bus circled the building that sat on a street island we called the Pink Palace, because of its cherry-pink paint, small circular windows, and white pillars.

I eased into my seat and went over a mental checklist of what I'd put in the brown suitcase. I gripped the paper sack that contained my lunch and listened to the driver's deep voice, as he announced over the intercom the rules of the bus.

A girl I hadn't met before sat next to me, named Rose, but everyone called her Wil. She attended a high school near Kahuna. When we hit the Beeline Highway, we sang camp songs.

Each landmark we passed took us farther away from the desert heat. I watched out the window as we passed the large man-made fountain that, every hour, spews water to a height of 562 feet (171m).

Then, through one section, saguaro cactus lined both sides of the road, standing boldly across the landscape and marching to the base of the rock mountain. The cacti, each in a different shape and size, reminded me that my friends and I were different. Some of the cacti had large holes; some looked like they had been hacked. I imagined myself as a peculiar, hollow-shaped cactus, standing alone, without spines or the beautiful blooming white and yellow flowers. Where others fit in naturally, I never had the ability to be noticed or look normal.

We drove through a small town called Pine, made a right turn off the Beeline Highway, and bounced along the dirt washboard road before arriving at camp.

The bus stopped near the lodge, and we were still singing camp songs. When I stepped off the bus, I soaked in the beauty of the pine trees that reached to heaven. I retrieved my worn brown suitcase and sleeping bag from the luggage bay and placed them by the side of the dirt road; then I walked to the lodge. After four previous years at girls camp, the routine was automatic.

The lodge was the heart of camp, with all the skits and activities. I chose the same bench to sit on because, from there, even without vision in one eye, I could have a complete view of the stage.

I ate my lunch and listened to the camp director tell us what cabin or "Addie" (Adirondack) we were in for the week. Then I dragged my suitcase and bulky sleeping bag up the mountain.

Brenda, with her red, wavy hair, was walking in front of me. Several times when my mother was either in the state hospital for mental issues or another hospital for health issues, I lived with Brenda's family. I loved Brenda's smile. She wasn't much for words, but she was such a pleasant person, and I admired her gentle soul. Kim was behind me, complaining that she couldn't carry her suitcase. Other girls around her seemed to follow suit, and it turned into a major pity party. Several times, I stopped, sat on my suitcase, and held my sleeping bag on my lap. Girls passed me, and others joined me.

I reached my Addie, a structure with three complete walls and a window centered on each of the walls. The fourth wall had an open front, covered with a tarp that we rolled up during the day. The beds were made of wood and anchored to the walls. I chose the top bunk on the right corner.

Each evening, we gathered around the flagpole and held hands. We sang a song that genuinely touched me, "No Girl Is an Island." We swayed, side to side, while this song rose in the air. I never had a sister, and my mother was always sick, so those words meant a lot.

> *"No girl is an island*
> *No girl stands alone*
> *Each girl's joy is joy to me*
> *Each girl's dream is my own*
> *We need one another*
> *So, I will defend*
> *Each girl as my sister*
> *Each girl as my friend."*

After we sang, we prayed together and went off to bed.

25
HAUNTED OR NOT
Summer 1980
Be a hero, and let your honesty be shared.

"Here you go, Rose—the *Happy Snappy News* of Camp LoMia."
Friends squealed in anticipation of a haunted house, and I looked at the sky and then at the *Happy Snappy News* and read:
The following poem is dedicated for your enjoyment of tonight's camp fireside and Thursday's haunted house:
The Hag
The Hag is astride as night for to ride,
The devil and she together;
Through thick and through thin, now out and then in,
Ne'er so foul be the weather.
After reading, I told myself I could endure this tribulation.
I sat on the log and gazed at my friends as they danced.
Then, I remembered Kahuna's letter of support. I needed to speak to my Addie Mom. But how?
I approached my Addie Mom at breakfast. "Ms. Roberts, I don't think we should have the haunted house."

Her body stiffened, like a block of ice. "Okay, Rose. I'll talk to the camp director."

I shrugged and scuttled to the restroom. Two of my friends asked me if I was all right. I put on a fake smile. "No, there is nothing wrong . . . I just miss Kahuna."

Brook chatted. "Well, Karen and I are going to the bridge. Do you want to come?"

"Sure, Brook. Just let me use the restroom."

Brook screamed, "Yuck."

I yelled from another stall. "What's wrong?"

"Someone smeared peanut butter on the door handle, and it's all over my fingers."

"When I'm done, you can use mine."

We rushed down the hill and sat on the white bridge under the pine trees. I tapped Brook. "Hey, Brook. How far can you throw a rock?"

Brook pointed. "Oh, to that big rock near the pine tree over there."

"Let me see you do it."

Brook threw the rock, and I wanted to tell her congratulations on hitting the big rock, but Ms. Roberts interrupted. "Rose, let's go talk to the camp director."

"Okay." And I whispered, "How did I get into this mess?"

Brook gave me a stern look. "See you later, Rose."

I gave her a tight smile. My legs trembled, following Ms. Roberts. I prayed. *Oh, please help me, Heavenly Father.*

The lodge came into view, with its different-shaped rocks on the lower half and logs layered on top. Crushed leaves beneath our feet interrupted the silence. *I never should have told Ms. Roberts. Maybe, I should have gone to the camp director myself.* We stepped in, around the picnic tables and benches, and then down the wide, dim hallway.

This isn't fun, I thought. When we came to the end of the hallway, we passed the nurses' station, and I wished I had poison ivy again.

Ms. Lee was seated on the edge of her bed, and her smile went right through me. "Rose, what is bothering you?"

I focused on her hairdo. "Ms. Lee, I don't feel good about the haunted house. I'm terrified of haunted houses, and I'm sure other girls are, too. Besides, I think it would bring an awful spirit."

I wanted to observe Ms. Roberts' reaction, but instead I looked at my legs' trembling.

Ms. Lee grabbed my hand. "Well, Rose, the older girls have worked many hours on this, and everyone is looking forward to it. I appreciate your concern, though."

Okay, she does not understand.

Ms. Lee continued, "Rose, you don't have go to the haunted house."

I stared at her white hair. "I know I don't have to go to the haunted house. I'm just worried about others."

Ms. Lee moved forward. "Thanks for sharing your thoughts, and, Ms. Roberts, could you stay?"

When I arrived at my Addie, Brook was singing a silly song. *How can she be reserved one minute and then loud seconds later?* I tiptoed in, and she stopped and came to my bunk.

"What was that all about, Rose?"

"I had a question I needed to ask the camp director."

"Can I ask you what the question was?"

I climbed up on my bunk and looked at the wood beam and then at Brook. "Oh, something is bothering me at camp."

"Sounds like you don't want to tell me, but if you want to, I'm here."

I grinned. "I appreciate your friendship."

"Well, how about going to the Sacred Grove?"

I jumped down from my bunk. "Okay, let's go."

I stopped under the "Sacred Grove" entrance sign that hung from a horizontal log and marveled at the peacefulness. The pine logs were anchored horizontally on top of small rocks, like pews in a church building. The best seats rested against tall pine trees, with shade. The front area of the Sacred Grove had an enormous, rectangular rock, which served as a pulpit, and a stream trickled parallel to the Grove.

Brook pointed. "Let's sit against those pine trees."

"Okay."

I sat on the edge of the log. "Gosh, I am having a tough time with our cabin Mom."

Brook sat next to me. "I'm having a difficulty with her, too. She's not friendly with anyone who's not a friend of her daughter, and she never smiles."

The clouds moved above us blocking the sun.

Brook bumped me. "Tell me about your letter from Kahuna."

I drew circles in the dirt with my foot. "I think, someday, I will marry Kahuna."

Brook moved her head. "Wow!"

I wrote Kahuna's name in the dirt with a stick. "So, tell me about Peter. I know you like him."

Brook rolled her eyes and smiled. "Rose, he is so darn good-looking. Oh, how I love his dark-black hair and miniature nose. Don't you think he is cute?"

I shook my head. "No. I have known him since I was seven, and he's not my type."

Brook turned toward me. "At the Saturday night dance, Peter asked me to dance the last dance with him. My hands got sweaty when we were dancing, and I hoped I didn't have bad breath. When I gazed into his eyes, a tingle went down my back."

The pine branches moved above us and produced a scent I could never get tired of. "Sounds like love. Have you ever thought of writing him a letter?"

I repositioned my bottom on the tree log, and a cool breeze danced around us.

Brook rubbed her arms. "It's cold. Let's go get our coats."

"I was thinking the same thing."

When we left the Sacred Grove, Brook asked the question.

"Are you excited about the haunted house?"

I focused on the dirt path. "Umm hmm . . . I hmm . . . don't like haunted houses."

"I don't like them, either . . . and I don't want to go Thursday."

I stopped her and made eye contact. "Brook, you don't have to go."

Brook smiled. "Really? Seriously—I don't have to?"

"Nope, you don't."

Brook looked past me, over my shoulder. I turned and saw our friends running toward us and yelling. Karen rushed ahead of Robyn and reached us.

"Did you hear? Did you hear what happened?"

Brook clapped her hands. "No, what happened?"

Karen jumped and held on to Brook's shoulders to keep balance. "Someone hoisted Kim's bra up the flagpole."

Brook laughed. "That's awesome. Is it still there?"

Brook grabbed Karen. "Who did it? Who put the bra up the flagpole?"

Karen smiled. "I'm not saying a word."

Brook pulled on my sleeve. "Let's go see it."

We sprinted to the flagpole.

Brook pointed at the bra, and her thunderous laugh echoed to the boys on the other side of the mountain at Camp Geronimo. Other girls joined in and gawked at the bra.

Karen grabbed her stomach. "Let's go. We need to get our flashlights."

On our way to the Addie, other girls were running in the opposite direction.

We entered the Addie. I climbed on my bunk and studied the grain in the plywood walls connected to joints of 4x4 beams and read, "Kelly loves Jim," and "Lisa kissed Dan." I grabbed Kahuna's picture, which was resting on one of the beams.

Brook sat on my bunk. "Aawww. Poor Rose misses Kahuna."

I replaced the picture. "Yes, I do, but I don't miss his mustache or the little bronze #1 in the corner of his left glass lens."

Karen came over to join us. "Brook, do you like someone?"

Brook combed her hair with her fingers. "Yeah, but I don't think he knows I exist."

Karen and I looked at each other before she spoke. "Are you guys excited about the haunted house?"

I hunched forward. "Honestly, Karen, I don't like haunted houses, and I don't feel good about it."

"Are you joking, Rose?"

The dinner bell ring. We grabbed our flashlights and headed down to the lodge.

Karen shook her flashlight. "Do you think Kim's bra is still on the flagpole?"

Brook grinned. "I hope it is—and do you think Ms. Lee knows?"

Karen moved close to me. "That is a good question, Rose."

"Yeah, and, umm . . . I'm curious if Ms. Roberts knows who did it. Aren't you, Karen?"

Karen turned on her flashlight and put it under her chin. "I just hope they never know it was me."

Brook nudged Karen. "We'll keep it a secret, won't we, Rose?"

"I'm not saying a word."

Karen rested her arms over our shoulders as she skipped between us. "You are both the best, and I hope Robyn doesn't tell."

26
CAMP LETTERS
Summer 1980

Words written on paper are captured in the heart.

At breakfast, a leader waved an envelope and yelled out, "Rose, you have a letter."

I approached her. "You have my letter?"

She held it in front of me and said, "You have one good artist for a friend."

I seized the envelope. "Thanks."

Karen, Robyn, and Brook tried to take the envelope out of my back pocket. Frustrated, I tried to speak civilly. "Please stop."

I finished with breakfast, excused myself, sat at a secluded picnic table underneath a gigantic pine tree, and opened Kahuna's letter.

> *Dear Camper,*
>
> *Here is letter #1. I'm so happy you love me. You don't say that much, so it means a lot to me when you do. I have always had feelings for you.*

I know I need to be more understanding at times. It's hard after what I go through all day. It makes it so much easier when you're nice to me. I miss you so much.

I hope you didn't get mad that I didn't approve of the dance marathon. I just don't want to defile my body by being with you night and day. That kind of exposure is too special and sacred for unmarried couples like us. Please don't defile your holy temple by attending such a function. FOR EVEN ONE HOUR! I strongly disapprove. If you really want to go, then don't let me stop you. You're a free person, and you deserve the right to choose.

Keep saying your prayers. I miss you already. Just don't worry about me. Worry about your responsibilities at camp, and the Lord will protect me.

Please write!!!!!!

Love Eternally, Kahuna

P.S. Do not open the letter in here—wait for me to open it. It's to see what you can endure. You'll be shocked if you open it. Wait for me, and you'll never regret it.

The second letter was sealed, and, across the front, Kahuna had written in big, red letters: "Stop. If you wait for me to open this, you'll be very, very happy."

I was tempted to open it right then, but I resisted and put it back in my pocket.

My friends strolled out of the lodge and headed right for me.

Brook stood in front of me. "So, what did the letter say?"

Robyn smirked. "He probably wrote how much he loved her."

Brook placed her hand on her hip. "Well, Rose, you are the first to get a letter at camp. How does that make you feel?"

I raised my eyebrows. "Uh . . . I don't know if it makes me feel anything, Brook, besides lucky."

Robyn rolled her eyes. "I know one thing; the letters are probably mushier than the ones he wrote two years ago."

Brook kicked the dirt. "Have you been his girlfriend for two years?"

I rubbed my forehead. "Um, I think I got my first letter when I was 13, and that was three years ago."

Robyn shook her shoulders. "At least we get to kiss more than one guy."

The memory of Gail's letter of how I should never steal Floy away from her caused me to open my mouth and speak. "Oh, my, you guys . . . Kahuna and I went on a double date with Gail and her boyfriend Floy, and they made out the whole night. I had to write in my journal how gross Kahuna and I thought they were. So, you see, we're not a crazy couple like Floy and Gail."

Robyn moved closer to me. "Isn't Floy Tyli's brother?"

Brook answered, "Yes, he is Tyli's brother. I've seen him come and pick Gail up at school."

Robyn applied chapstick to her lips. "Well, all I can say is making out isn't gross when you are the one involved in the action."

Brook's voice startled me out of my daydream. "Rose, it's time to go."

"Yeah, yeah, just a second. I need to pray."

Mail call came, and Ms. Lee placed letters in my hand.

At the breakfast table, the girls discussed who liked Donnie, a guy I'd known since I was three. Their eyes were all on me when I spoke. "I did have a so-called crush on him when I was about twelve, but that crush dwindled when he spit wads through a straw at me."

I placed my three envelopes on the table in front of me.

Brook peeked over my shoulder. "Wow, Rose—three letters. Who did you get them from? I see the first one is from Kahuna."

Perfect Rose Cracked Vase

I looked at the upside-down fifteen-cent stamp on Kahuna's envelope. "Oh, I got one from Dax and one from my mother."

"Now you have Dax writing you? How do you get them to write?"

"Brook, they are my friends."

Joyce looked over at me. "What? Uh, you got a letter from Dax?"

"Yes, I did . . . is there anything wrong with that?"

Joyce stuck her nose in the air.

Ms. Lee yelled, "If you are going on the three-day hike, you need to bring your sleeping bag and backpack to the large tree in front of the lodge within twenty-five minutes. Make sure you have your canteen filled."

The Tonto forest thickened with each switchback we completed, and my motivation soared with the thought I could read Dax's and Kahuna's letters when we arrived at our campsite. I struggled to keep my multi-colored green-and-blue safety glasses on when they wanted to slide down my nose from the sweat. Flat, green land appeared on our last switchback and gave us an inviting invitation to pitch our tents and build a firepit. We squawked at the idea of digging a hole for an outdoor toilet.

I marveled at the beauty of the forest as we sat around the firepit to eat our sandwiches for dinner. The sunset reminded me I needed to read my letters before dark. I excused myself, went into my tent, and read Kahuna's letter.

Dear Marshmallow,

Here's letter #2. I hope you don't get bored or confused after all my letters. My day today was different. I had a flat tire this morning and had to change it so my sisters, Dax, and I could go shopping downtown. Shopping wasn't complicated because Mollie and Susie did it.

I worked at the church for just a couple of hours and came home to eat lunch. Grandma's eating with us. Boy, she's tough. Her problem is that she judges people too quickly. She hollers at me for things I don't even care about. Well, now I know why mom went nuts. It just makes me want to work harder to satisfy her. I can handle it.

I went back to the church to practice my trumpet on the new stage. It was neat to hear what I really sound like instead of playing between my knees.

Now I'll talk about us. I know that I need to be more patient and understanding. Sometimes I think I do things without letting you say how you feel. Rose, there must be a million things you have to tell me, but you're afraid of what I will do or say. It makes me feel bad when I act hysterical; I hope my actions don't destroy our bond.

I hope you aren't still upset over me disapproving of the 36-hour dance. Rose, your body is a sacred temple—don't ruin it by letting any guy, even me, hold you for even one hour. I love you too much to allow you to do this with me.

Sleep well, and be an example. Don't forget to write me back.

Love forever, Kahuna

P.S. I'm bushed, and it's only 9:30 p.m.

I pulled Dax's letter out of my coat pocket and thought I would read it later.

When I returned to the firepit, we talked about how hard it would be to live without the conveniences of life . . . no running water or bathroom. Ms. Jen's warmhearted spirit rekindled a spark of energy with her positive values of what matters. She shared stories of the pioneers and read Joshua 1:9: *"Be strong and of good courage; be not afraid, neither be thou dismayed: for the Lord thy God is with thee whithersoever thou goest."* Wow, I wanted to be like her, a strong woman with courage.

Perfect Rose Cracked Vase

Lightning danced outside the tent, and raindrops made a peaceful sound as they rolled down the side of the tent. I was mesmerized by the raindrops *(How is it they don't leak inside the tent?)*. With a gentle touch, I moved my finger across the tent ceiling. Within minutes, the rain trickled down upon me. I moved from underneath the rainwater I had invited in, and I yelled out, "Oh, no."

Tyli shined her flashlight at me. "Rose, what happened?"

I was embarrassed, but I had to be honest. "I touched the top of the tent like this."

I brought my finger near where the water was coming in. Tyli hollered, "*No*, Rose."

I squeezed my eyes tight and prayed. "Sorry, Tyli. I didn't know that water would seep in."

Joyce pointed her flashlight at the water trickling into our tent. Then she shined her flashlight on me. "You're definitely a blonde."

Tyli moved her sleeping bag over and asked me to sleep next to her. I placed my shirt on the puddle of water and then moved to sleep near Tyli. "I will never again touch the tent when it's raining."

The campfire was popping and crackling in the early morning when Mrs. Jen tapped the tent with a wakeup call. I rushed to the outside toilet, and when I returned to open the tent, I overheard the girls inside. "Man, I can't believe Rose touched the tent last night when it was raining. Doesn't she know better?" My hand shook when I unzipped the tent door; silence entered with me. I crawled to my sleeping bag and secured it on my backpack and made my way out of the tent. Seconds after I left, the mumbling resumed. I told myself, "Ten years down the road, it won't matter what they thought." That same feeling of inadequacy and doubt went right through me, just like when Grandmother called me a "no-good-for-nothing-brat."

When we arrived at the main camp, the sixth-year girls had distributed the *Happy Snappy News*. They reported on us. It read . . . "*Girls* back, triumphant. Small groups straggled in all afternoon. Some laughing, some singing and some staring blindly into space, but they all had one thought in mind: We love you, showers. Apparently, the pack-in was a great success, though. Everyone stated it was fun, even though they missed 'civilization.' We congratulate all girls and leaders who survived the great LoMia Pack-in 1980."

At dinner, Ms. Lee grabbed my arm and handed me my letters. "Rose, you got three letters."

One of the envelopes was thick, with Kahuna's handwriting on it. The others were from Dax and Mom. I opened Kahuna's letter in front of friends and didn't care if they looked over my shoulder; I was too tired to move.

> *Good morning, Sunshine,*
>> *Our family woke up early and ate breakfast on time this morning. We were afraid Grandma would come over and feed us beans and hot dogs for breakfast, so we ate early. Sometimes, I feel like yelling back at her, but I know she is old, and it would only hurt her. She gets a lot of pressure. Besides, she only does it because she loves and cares for us.*
>>
>> *I was tired last night, but I feel good today. I think this raising a family stuff will be fun. It was hard for my parents to do it because there are so many of us. Nine kids are a lot.*
>>
>> *I miss you still. Do a good job at camp. I know you will. I'll always respect you and love you!*
>
> *Love forever, Kahuna*

I reopened the envelope and wished Kahuna could jump out. His unshakable devotion toward me brought a peace and assurance that I was lovable. I wanted him more than life. I folded his letter, and I reached for a second letter in the same envelope.

Perfect Rose Cracked Vase

Dear Honey Comb,

I'm tired. I guess my sleep is finally catching up with me. Today went okay. I took charge and assigned jobs for my brothers and sisters. It was a real challenge, but I did it. The hard part was getting the kids to not watch TV or waste time and get their work done. Not one of them finished their jobs. There were four kids and fourteen small assignments between them. When Grandma threatened to spend the night, things got done. They all did their jobs (sooner or later).

I talked to your Mom today. She told me how disappointed you were when I didn't want to go to the marathon dance. I do realize that both of us want to spend a whole night talking, and a whole 36 hours would, in fact, truly be three times as good, BUT, the Lord doesn't appreciate me embracing you for 36 hours. I know that nothing big will happen, but I haven't married you yet.

I know it would be a special experience, but I want to save it for after I take my marriage vows. I love you so much, Rose. You're pure and holy, and I want you to stay untouched and not abused. I don't want marriage to become boring because we do the same things, married or not.

I feel uncomfortable. I know there are a lot of things I say that you don't agree with. You go along with it or don't say anything because you're afraid I will get mad or put you down. Rose, we're in love, so whatever we say to each other must be okay with the other one. We both need to be more understanding.

I have a goal that we will be able to freely share all our thoughts with each other someday. We almost have a perfect love.

Love forever, Kahuna

Written at the bottom in a special ink were the words:

I miss you! Come Home Soon!

Why did Mom tell him what I thought about the marathon dance? I felt isolated, even though I was surrounded by girls. But when I thought of Kahuna, I wasn't alone. *It's tough to be sixteen and in love,* I thought.

Joyce yelled. "Have you gotten a letter every day?"

I patted my left pocket holding my letters. "Yes, Joyce."

"Wow, Kahuna must really love you."

"Do we have Kangaroo Court tonight?"

Karen unfolded her legs from underneath her bottom. "I think so, and I hope they didn't take our stuff while we were on the campout."

Tyli's face lit up. "I'm glad I didn't bring my violin, because they would've made me play."

Shelly was eavesdropping. "Well, tonight the judge comes, and tonight we have a haunted house."

Brook lowered her eyebrows. "Shelly needs to stop butting into our conversation." Brook motioned toward the door that led to the stage. We left.

We sat on the benches and faced the stage. The leaders leaned forward on the windowframes above us and smiled. The sixth-year girls sat on the edge of the stage and led us in camp songs. We sang, "Oh, I wish I were a little bar of soap," or "Sippin' Cider." It was magical.

Singing and swaying back and forth evaporated the thoughts of the haunted house.

A sixth-year girl announced, "All rise; court is now in session." We stood, and girls marched between the rows of benches toward the stage and chanted, "Here comes the judge."

They marched in rhythm. The judge followed with a red, fake-velvet robe and a cardboard crown painted gold with colored jewels and carrying a velvet bag slung over her shoulder.

The sixth-year girls and the judge huddled together on the stage and made "Aw...mmm" sounds. One girl named Mallory pulled a flute case out and held it up. Everyone in the lodge yelled out, "Rebecca, Rebecca." Within minutes, a little chestnut-haired girl stood and covered her ears. Girls guided her into the aisle. The poor girl's bright red face matched the velvet bag.

The girls asked the judge, "What would she need to do to get her flute back?"

The judge yelled, "Rebecca must play a song on her flute." Rebecca's hands trembled. Once she finished, her smiled grew as everyone stood and applauded her.

Five other girls were called, and each performed a different task; the bag looked empty. The girls huddled, tossed the bag in the air twice, and pulled out a brown picture frame.

Karen grabbed my leg. "Rose, it's your Kahuna!"

I looked at Karen.

Everyone yelled, "Rose, Rose." I knew there was no way out of this. Brook pushed on my back. "Rose—go reclaim your picture."

"I will. Give me a minute."

Brook pushed with force. "Get up."

The girls yelled, "Rose!" several times. I scampered onto the stage and looked at the sixth-year girl named Shani holding my frame for everyone to see. The judge motioned with her hand for all the girls to huddle around her. It was as if they had to get their last play worked out before they scored another touchdown.

The judge looked at me. "You must sing, 'Raindrops on Roses,' from *Sound of Music*."

I faced the audience, thought of my Dad as if he were there at the piano to accompany me, and sang my favorite song. I curtsied, and the audience clapped, whistled, and stood.

I turned to the judge. "May I have my picture now?" She took the frame from Shani and handed it to me.

Ms. Lee called from the corner of the stage. "Rose, how much does this letter mean to you?"

I scurried to Ms. Lee. "It means a lot. May I have it, please?"

She held it high. "What do you think Rose should do to get this letter?"

The girls yelled, "Sing, sing, sing . . . sing, sing, sing" This time they let me choose the song. I sang, "I'm Just a Girl Who Can't Say No," from the movie *Oklahoma*. My last note was followed by a loud applause. I skipped to Ms. Lee and begged for something that was rightfully mine.

Ms. Lee dropped Kahuna's letter in my hand, and I could smell Kahuna cologne on the envelope. "You have an amazing voice, Rose."

I thanked her and remembered that Dad liked my voice, too.

My memorable night ended when Ms. Lee said that we weren't supposed to bring flashlights into the haunted house.

I sat in the dining hall and waited for my friends to come back from the haunted house; even Brook went. I read Kahuna's letter and then wrote letters to Mom and Kahuna.

> *Hi, best friend, Kahuna,*
>
> > *Why am I afraid of a haunted house that the sixth-year girls are putting on tonight? Every time I think of the haunted house, Kahuna, I think of when I was at Robyn's house for a sleepover. I remember her wanting me to watch a movie called "Omen." I didn't realize at first it was R-rated, but after I watched someone have their head cut off with a machete and then witnessed the lifeless corpse fall to the ground with blood everywhere, I was frightened. I told her it was a horrible movie and I wanted to go home.*
> >
> > *Robyn repeated, "Watch this next part, it's neat." I told her I don't like movies that show little kids being killed*

and them killing someone. I told her the movie controls peoples' emotions. I couldn't take it anymore. I walked into her kitchen to use the phone without asking permission and called my dad. I asked him to come and get me. I was blessed my dad didn't ask questions. Dad knew that I had good judgment when something was wrong. Now this haunted house stirred the same fear and disgust I'd experienced at Robyn's. I'm glad that tomorrow I will be able to escape from this haunted house nightmare and go home to my safe bedroom. Even though I would have to deal with the hot weather, and there wouldn't be much food to eat, at least I could feel at peace. Plus, I would be able to talk to you. I miss you so much, Kahuna. You make me feel like I do matter and what I feel is important.

Kahuna, I believe I'm from a mold that no other girl was made from. I'm glad you like me for who I am. You bring sunshine into my life even on stormy, dark days. I understand why you don't want to go to the dance marathon, and your reason is correct. I hope never to lose you, Kahuna.

Love you forever, Rose

P.S. can't wait to hug and kiss you.

My friends entered the kitchen for hot cocoa and a bag of popcorn mixed with M&Ms while sharing their experiences from the haunted house. I could tell they wanted to know why I didn't go, but they didn't ask me. Had Mother's negative behaviors become part of me?

The sun burst through the Addie window, and those negative thoughts from the night before resurfaced. Was I a wimp? Tyli tapped on my shoulder, and I swung, not knowing it was Tyli I was hitting. She jumped.

"Rose, Rose. I went to see the nurse, and, as I left, Ms. Lee handed me this letter for you. I guess there isn't time for mail call at breakfast."

"Thanks, Tyli. I appreciate your delivery service, and I didn't mean to hit you. You know I can't see out of my right eye."

"I always forget . . . no problem, Rose."

After breakfast, I took pictures with friends, boarded the bus, and opened my letter from Kahuna.

> *Dearest Rugged Girlfriend,*
>
> *Today was worse than yesterday. I stayed home from work this morning to study water safety. I got really badly sunburned at lifeguard class today. I'm so red you wouldn't know me. At least I now have a red, but perfect complexion. My eyes were bloodshot from the chlorine, too.*
>
> *The house is still clean, and the kids have finally started to clean their rooms. They were even in bed by 9:30 p.m. I'm glad Grandma comes over to "motivate" them. I was so busy trying to be understanding with them that I missed how lazy they were. Dax didn't come again today. Besides, if he had been here while I was miserable today, I wouldn't have been able to keep his hands off me. He tries to massage my back, and sometimes he almost tries to tuck me in. He's constantly babying me. It drives me crazy! I'm a "big boy" and capable of taking care of my own affairs.*
>
> *Rose, you know that every night I pray for Heavenly Father to teach me while I sleep, and my prayers are answered. Every morning I wake up wiser than I was the night before.*
>
> *I wish Dax hadn't come with us to church. All he does is follow me around like my shadow. He's always telling me what to do as if I were his baby, and he looms over me like my guardian. I can't get rid of him. I like him and having him around, but sometimes it gets tough. I'm old*

enough and responsible; I know what I'm doing! Well, I'll be patient and hope for the best. Do you know what really bugs me? Sometimes he gets me so confused that it's embarrassing. He treats me like I need to "wake up." He makes me forget things and tells me I can't think about two things at once. I don't know how he does it! I can't stand it! There are a lot of other problems he has, but I won't talk about them now. I only hope you kept your promise when you said you would never, ever tell him anything.

Oh, well—I trust you. I know you keep your promises. Just remember that if you do break a promise, I'll try to understand. I love you very much, and I don't ever want anyone to put you down.

I have been hot and miserable and have wanted to sleep. I finally forced myself up at 4:30 p.m. and drove your letter to the post office. I then came home to clean house. I just barely got the house cleaned fast enough before Grandma came over for dinner. Grandma's a real sweet person when things go right, but she throws a fit at the slightest mishap. She just doesn't know the principle of free agency and forgiveness and how the Lord makes us suffer. She does, but she understands it differently.

Most of all, I just want to move out of this hot state. I'd like to take you and go up to Montana someday. I dream about just you and me going up north to live. I want the best for you. I still miss you a whole bunch! I hope you're enjoying camp.

I leaned against the headrest, closed my eyes, and pictured us together on a wooden swing that we would have on our front porch. I also wanted to leave this state. I hoped I would be as lucky as Cinderella, who also lived in unfortunate circumstances, but had a handsome prince take her away. Kahuna's—my prince—and my castle would be small compared to Cinderella's but would be filled with love. The bus engine rumbled and brought me out of my pleasant thoughts. I needed to finish my letter and continued to read.

> *Rose, remember always that I love you. So, when you're not feeling well, remember how attached I am to you. We're attached now, and no one can ever part us. I love you, Rose; you mean a lot to me. You're so special. You're a precious gem that I love to hold and look at. You have a lot of love in your heart for all those around you.*
>
> *Your mom called and checked up on us. She's nice, Rose. She really cares for you.*
>
> *Oh, my parents come back from their trip tomorrow.*
>
> Love Forever Eternity, Kahuna
>
> P.S. Don't tell Dax what I said about him.
>
> P.S. I like your smile the most.

On the stationery, there were cute printed drawings of a girl and boy holding hands with words above them: *Remember—you are never alone when you have a friend (me) to call your own.*

I put the letter in the envelope and read the words he'd written on the outside: *I think of you on a sunny, snowy, foggy, humid, cloudy, misty, balmy, icy, windy, hot, stormy, calm, breezy, blizzard, and a clear day.* I glanced out my window while the bus driver spoke, capturing a picture in my heart of camp. Anxiety set in as I pictured life at home. I closed that thought and sang with the girls.

27
BLINDFOLD

September 1980

Devoted friends never blow you down; instead, they help you stand strong against the storms that knock you over.

A firm knock on the front door interrupted the conversation I was having with Dax at the kitchen table. I put my finger to my mouth. "Ssshhh—that could be Kahuna." Dax motioned that he was going to stand behind the door. I peeked through the door window, and there was Kahuna. I opened the door and wrapped my arms around him.

Dax popped out from behind me while Kahuna squeezed me back.

"Hi," Dax called.

Kahuna's embrace loosened, and he glowered down at me. I hoped Dax hadn't caught the look.

Dax moved closer to Kahuna. "We have a surprise for you, but we'll need to blindfold you until we get there."

Kahuna rubbed his forehead.

Dax smirked after I gave him a smile. "Dax, tie the kitchen towel around Kahuna's head."

The stagnant air and sweltering summer sun were brutal as I guided Kahuna on the sidewalk. We passed rundown houses, and the thought came to me that my love for Kahuna would never deteriorate. I hoped our relationship would never falter, like my neighborhood had, with drive-by shootings and the gangs that had stolen our 1965 Mustang and driven it down to the river bottom. It all made me want to work harder to steady my relationship so it wouldn't crumble, like my neighborhood.

The squeeze and tug of Kahuna's hand made it difficult for me to stay steady whenever he struggled to keep his balance.

Kahuna was perfect. *How could he always look so gorgeous?* The heat rising from the black asphalt melted away any thought of being perfect. Sweat flowed freely in my armpits.

Dax touched Kahuna's shoulder. "Are you all right?"

"Yeah, Dax, if I hold Rose's hand."

"Are we walking too fast?"

Kahuna turned in the direction of Dax's voice. "No," he said, with an icy chill to it.

Dax took his hand off Kahuna. "Twenty houses to go, and we will be at the bus stop."

My hair flew in different directions from the cars as they passed. The heat from the blistering sun generated sweat on my skull; it gave me a sensation of bugs crawling. I wanted to scratch my head, but to let go of Kahuna's hand was out of the question.

Dax got on the bus first, and Kahuna followed, with me guiding him up the stairs. I dropped money in the coin box for both Kahuna and me and guided him down the narrow walkway, and people stared.

I directed Kahuna to his seat and then sat next to him. Dax sat in front of us.

Dax turned around, lifted his eyebrows, and pointed at Kahuna's face. I caught Kahuna with his head tilted back.

I grabbed his hand. "Kahuna, you're peeking."

"I am not. Just curious about where we're going."

Dax observed our hands interlocked.

After two more transfers, Dax tapped his watch and then pointed at Kahuna. I knew Dax wanted to know when I thought we should remove the blindfold. With a bend of my head to the right, I cup-mouthed, "I don't know."

Dax reached back and touched Kahuna on the shoulder, and he flinched.

"Are you ready to have your blindfold taken off?"

"I was ready from the moment you put it on, Dax."

"Turn your head to the left so I can take it off," I said.

Kahuna shook his head. "I'm glad that's off. What gave you guys the idea to come to the mall?"

"Rose and I thought it would be fun. Plus, you needed a break from the chaos at home."

Kahuna guided me off the bus.

Dax followed. "What store do you want to go to?"

"It doesn't matter to me, Dax, as long as you and Rose don't have any more surprises for me."

We entered through the electronic double doors, and I glanced in a full-length mirror to check my Medusa hair.

Dax tapped Kahuna on the shoulder again, making him flinch. Again, Dax didn't seem to notice. Instead, he called out: "Hey, you guys, let's go get a pickle from that store over there."

Kahuna didn't want one, but Dax and I bought gigantic pickles, and the three of us sat on a bench in the middle of the mall. Kahuna watched us race to see who could finish their pickle first. Dax beat me. He always won, even when we had a contest to see who could eat a bouillon cube the fastest on nights when we helped Kahuna with his paper route.

Kahuna stood, but when Dax got close to him, he acted uneasy. What could I do to make Kahuna happy with being with Dax? I was happy with my two best friends, and they had become my world, my life, and my existence—they made me want to live. They were the oxygen that kept me alive.

28
THANKSGIVING THANKS
November 1980

Love is priceless when shared with family members.

Grandpa was sitting in a cream-colored chair in the corner of my Aunt Carol Carlson's living room. His mysterious smile stretched from ear to ear and hid deep secrets. Dad's fingers danced across the spinet piano, producing familiar songs. Grandpa's smile never faltered as he sang along with the notes and my step-grandma sat across the room singing, too.

Sitting on the floor in front of the fireplace, I inhaled the aroma of the turkey, and my mouth watered.

I was mesmerized by the flames from the fireplace. Each pop and hiss stirred emotions I had experienced at girls camp, around the campfire. Emotions of events and how much Kahuna's letters meant to me. *Oh, no! I forgot that I told Kahuna that I would call him an hour ago!* I thought.

Aunt Carol sang while she checked each place setting on the two long tables that overflowed into the living room near the piano.

When Dad finished "Jingle Bells," Mom pointed at the table and asked, "Carol, where would you like my husband and me to sit?"

It warmed my heart to see my mother conversing with my aunt. Dad played another song, and Aunt Carol pointed at the table as her lips moved.

My mom acted like a lost black sheep that didn't know her place. Grandmother did a skillful job of convincing Mom she was incompetent with remarks like, "You could never measure up to your sister Carol."

I was absorbed watching Aunt Carol, with her beautiful red hair, directing everyone to their responsibilities.

When we first arrived, Aunt Carol let me know I was on the cleanup committee.

Aunt Carol raised her arms as if she were the drum majorette of a marching band. "Everyone to the table. I want a child seated between two adults."

I sat between Uncle Karl and my step-grandma. I was glad I got to sit near my favorite cousin, Jakob. Bottles of wine were on the table, which I never had, because wine, coffee, and beer were forbidden in our home. The adults held their wine goblets and, individually, expressed some sentiment such as, *"Here's to a good end of the year and new beginning of another."* Neither of my parents participated; they just held their empty wine glass after the toasts were offered.

The adults made their toasts, and I gazed at the vase full of sunflowers, carnations, and roses in the middle of the table. My three older cousins—Katrina, Greta, and Johanna—sat with their shoulders back; they all had beautiful eyes. They had style and exquisiteness that I could only dream of.

Aunt Carol often reminded me to stand straight. It was difficult, since I had kyphosis, a curving of the spine that causes a bowing of the back. I wasn't sure if I got the kyphosis from the Congenital Rubella Syndrome or if it was inherited.

Conversations filled the air. Uncle Karl eavesdropped on my dad's conversation with Grandpa. "I can get you a job where I work."

Uncle Karl's smooth, sleek voice was like warm honey each time he spoke. My dad pushed his plate forward, so he could rest his arms on the table, and faced Uncle Karl. "You can get me a job there?"

Uncle Karl leaned against the back of his chair. "I'll get you an application and mail it to you."

Dad's face gleamed. "Thanks, Karl. That would be a blessing."

Uncle Karl's influential demeanor made Dad seem like a disoriented boy begging for help. I wanted to chase away the pity I had for my father, but it wasn't possible. *Did my parents know I didn't care if we lived in a fancy home like my aunt and uncle, because I knew we had something superior? We had each other, but, more than that, we had Jesus Christ in our lives. Did Mom know I loved her and didn't care if she was like Aunt Carol, who was vice president of a bank?* Mom's leg moved from side to side, a clue that she was distraught.

Dinner was over, and I walked each china plate into the kitchen separately. After I got the last plate into the kitchen, my aunt wrapped her arm around me.

"Rosie, now you can wash them."

"Oh, no, Aunt Carol. I might break one."

Aunt Carol smiled. "You can do it, kiddo."

Johanna and Greta dried, and Katrina put them away. This was not the first time I had done chores in the kitchen with my cousins. We had often worked side by side on my summer visits, and I loved it that day, as I had before, even with washing the china.

Aunt Carol asked Dad to play the piano again to spark some more holiday spirit, and the music traveled into the kitchen, and we sang, "Up on the House Top." Aunt Carol inspected our work, peeking into the kitchen every five minutes to see our progress. She made sure everything was put away; then she gave her "Okay" with a smile, and we were free. We sat around the fireplace and sang songs. Jakob helped his Dad put the chairs and tables away. As I watched him, I thought of the fun we'd had as kids. The nights I slept in his room on a small cot and how we were forced to take naps; we would lie on our individual beds and pretended to be asleep when Aunt Carol checked on us. Then, when we believed it was safe, we would climb out the bedroom window. Jakob had climbed out his window a hundred times before and was always sure to tell me how kind his parents were for giving him the room that had a washing machine right below his bedroom window. Over the years, we had spent hours playing in the side yard, where no one could see us. Jakob showed me how to kick a ball and throw a baseball. I was never good at either. We had a unique bond, and when I looked at him across the room, I knew our relationship would last forever. There were many stories that we kept as secrets between us, like when we sneaked into the kitchen to grab cookies that Katrina baked and carried them back to his room to eat. We both thought it was funny that they believed we were asleep when really, we were in his room eating cookies. We laughed and said we wished we could have figured out a way to bring cups of milk.

Jakob was four months younger than me, and it touched my heart that he loved me, even though I was a girl and had a deformed eye. Now that we were teenagers, I missed the magic shows we would perform for Grandpa. Yet, even though our lives were filled with relationships with a girlfriend or a boyfriend, the warmth of each other's love never seemed lost or forgotten.

Grandpa divorced and remarried my grandmother twice before I was born. I don't think I had ever seen him near my grandmother. My step-grandma married him a year before my birth, and she was a compassionate lady who loved Grandpa. When Grandpa came to town from California, he seldom came to our house. If we wanted to see him, we would have to drive to Aunt Carol's house. I sat in the same spot I'd been in before we ate and glanced over at Grandpa, who was sitting in his same chair, too. His gentle slender frame and gray hair made him look easy to talk with, and he even had a substantial vocabulary, which was amazing, considering he'd never finished high school.

"Rosie."

I turned my head to look at him. "Yes, Grandpa."

He waggled his forefinger. "Could you come over here, please?"

"Sure."

I noticed a small gold box on his lap. He stretched his arm and held the box in front of me. "Rosie, I want you to have this."

"Do you want me to open it right now?" I was surprised how reserved I was acting, as if I were a mummy unable to talk or move. I wanted to rip the binding off that was holding me back from hugging him. He rubbed his gray hair. "Sure. I would love to know what you think of it."

I stood in front of Grandpa and moved my weight from one foot to the other. I pulled the blue ribbon off and opened it. I'm sure my smile grew bigger than ever, as I pulled out a piece of jewelry. "Oh, Grandpa, it's a beautiful gold necklace—I love it!"

I bent over, hugged him, and whispered in his ear. "Thanks, Grandpa. I will always cherish it."

When I stood, I took a picture of his face in my mind. I wanted to remember that moment forever.

I returned to my same spot on the floor and opened the box to marvel at my new necklace. Then the familiar doubts rolled into my mind, thoughts of my Congenital Rubella Syndrome and all my imperfections. Am I worthless, and did he do this to cover the guilt of never letting me come to see him in San Luis Obispo?

If I was attractive like my cousins—Katrina, Greta, and Johanna—I would have been allowed to visit Grandpa. I pictured myself on his front porch swing, with binoculars, looking out over the ocean and listening to the sound of the spectacular waves as they hit the shore. My grandfather's stories of how phenomenal the sunset looked over the ocean made me wonder if I would ever see it. His camera was always strapped around his neck, as if it were a part of his body. I would never see the pictures captured in his camera. A barrier stood between us, and it frustrated me, because I couldn't figure out what had caused it. Maybe it was the words that my grandmother had spoken when she described what a brat I was. Then I knew it couldn't have been that, because he wouldn't speak to her. Maybe he thought we were trash compared to my aunt's family. Mom often questioned if Grandpa was really her father. Grandmother always told my mother that he wasn't. I guess it's one of many reasons I never asked my grandpa or mother if I could visit him. She didn't feel like she mattered to him, so why would I?

I knew he was her father, because I could see some of Grandpa's traits in my mom, who also loved to write short stories and poems. Negative words Grandmother had spoken to Mom over the years continued to linger because of how awkward Mom acted around Grandpa. My grandmother painted an invisible canvas overflowing with rejection toward my mom.

Dad beckoned. "Rose, it's time to go."

I was sad to say goodbye to my relatives but anxious to get home and call Kahuna.

"Okay, Dad."

"Grandpa, I need to go. Can I give you one more hug?" Grandpa pushed himself out of the cream-colored chair.

I wrapped my arms around Grandpa's neck and felt the bones in his shoulders. His camera pushed against me and stopped the full embrace. My mouth was near his ear. I wanted to ask him a few questions, but I couldn't. He pushed me away and smiled, giving a clear view of his coffee-stained teeth. He raised his eyebrows and then looked into my eyes. Did he get a good look at my deformed eye? "Rosie, you be a good girl."

"Thanks for the necklace. I love it and will always remember you gave it to me, and I will be a good girl."

I focused out the car window on the Christmas lights as Dad turned into what our family called "Christmas Lane," with lights strung on every part of each house and yard. It never failed to thrill me with lasting delight. It was then I realized why Dad hung the Christmas lights before Thanksgiving each year.

Dad listened, rarely interjecting as Mom poured out her pain the whole way home, even when my mom's voice trailed off. It made me love my dad even more.

We arrived home at 9:30 p.m., too late to call Kahuna. Dad drove into our single driveway, and I stared at the Christmas lights Dad had hung over the two arches along our front porch. I loved the long strand of large bulbs on the edge of our roof. It made it shout that a happy family lived here.

Mom, Dad, and I entered, and bleakness followed. The lamp gave enough light to show Mom's expression that she was relieved to be back in her haven. Dad plugged in the tree lights. Mom walked straight to her bed, seeking comfort from her blankets. I sat on the couch, dreaming of happier holidays and wishing my brother Bobby were home. Had the years of Mom's visits with a psychiatrist and endless counseling sessions for our family serve any purpose?

Christmas morning was disappointing for Mom when she found out Grandpa was still in town and had been at Aunt Carol's since Thanksgiving. Dad tried to help Mom cope by serving her breakfast. I showered and waited for the phone to ring. It finally did.

"Merry Christmas, Kahuna."

"Did you open your present from me yet?"

"No, we are waiting for my brother Kevin to get here."

I sat down in the telephone chair and stared at the Christmas tree. "Have you opened the present I got you?"

Kahuna took a sigh before speaking. "No, I wanted to do it while on the phone with you."

I jumped out of the chair. "Just a second."

"Kahuna, are you there?"

"Yes, I just went to get my gift. You open your gift first."

"No, Kahuna—you first."

"Okay. Here I go. Wow! You got me a purple teddy bear."

"Do you like it? I bought it with babysitting money."

"It's cute. Now you need to open the gift I got you, Rose."

"Whatever this is, Kahuna, it sure is heavy." I ripped off the wrapping paper and uncovered two ceramic plaques. "Wow, Raggedy Ann and Andy. Where did you get them?"

Kahuna cleared his throat before he spoke. "I brought them at a specialty store and painted them. They reminded me of the costumes we wore for Halloween and won first place. Remember?"

"I thought our red mopped wigs looked funny, but the funniest part was the striped socks we wore."

"I need to go. We're going to my aunt's house for a family Christmas party. Do remember, Rose, you are special to me, and I value our friendship."

"I will Kahuna. Love you."

Knowing that, someday, we would be together for Christmas was a warm comfort.

29
GUILLAIN BARRE

February 1981

It's not important how others see me;
it's how I see myself that means everything.

Frustration boiled as I tried to squeeze my hand into a fist. I had been overtaken by a syndrome the doctors called Guillain Barre, an acute type of nerve inflammation, stemming from an infectious illness, the flu.

The flu subsided, and I developed a horrible migraine that never diminished. Mom took me to see Doctor Throw, who told me to stay in a dark room. Days of darkness didn't help; instead, my legs turned to rubber, and I was unable to walk. The weakness spread to my arms and hands, and it became impossible to lift a spoon or dress myself. I had unbearable pain, like knives jabbing me.

To block out the pain, I thought of happier times, including my 17th birthday party, a month before, with Kahuna's sister, who turned 14 on the same day. The problem was that Mom had been admitted to the hospital for an asthma attack. It became a ritual for her to enter the hospital on my birthday.

Speaking of bummers, though, this Guillain Barre couldn't have come at a worse time. I got a role as Minnie Faye in the play *Hello, Dolly*. I had made the pom-line—a girls' dance group that performed like the high school cheerline for next school year. It had been such a stretch for me to even try out. Not only that, but my time on running a mile improved after months of intense practice.

Now, stuck in my bed, I contemplated these activities. I rolled to see my digital alarm clock and fantasized about living normally. To see out of two eyes, to walk, and have a mentally and physically healthy mother were all out of the realm of possibility for me.

The bang of a hammer echoed through my window and clattered from sunrise till sunset. I tried to get the strength to pull the pillow out from underneath my head and place it over my ears, but it wasn't possible, so I rolled onto my side and covered the ear that was exposed to the racket with my hand. What my neighbor was building was a total mystery to me. I imagined a huge second-story wall with double doors and tons of red wood. Someday, I knew—if I got the strength—I could see what the mean man had built. I had always called him "the mean man" after he killed my dog, Pepe (others nicknamed him "Tree" because he was six feet nine).

I'd fought and won the war with mother's German measles. I wasn't a vegetable, as the doctors had predicted, and I'd learned to deal with the blindness and other challenges. Now I had a new battle to face—an unbearable—but winnable—battle.

Mom knocked on my door. It broke the repetitiveness of the hammering. She smiled, which I didn't often see, and handed me an envelope. "Rose, here is a letter from Kahuna."

I tried to grab it, but pain stole my strength.

Mom sat on the edge of my bed, so typical of our times together. "Can I open the letter for you?" she asked.

"Sure." Mother tore one end of the long business envelope and handed the letter to me.

"Thanks, Mom. I am glad you are well enough to help me."

Mom rubbed my leg to ease the ache. "I'm glad I'm over my asthma and able to help you, too. I'll let you read your letter, and I'll be back with a bowl of soup for you."

Dearest, Most lovable Bestest Friend,

Rose, I'm so sorry I hung up on you. It hurt me to listen to you in such an awful spirit. Shouldn't have done it, but I'll get stronger in time. I'll always remember I am given weaknesses for my own good.

Rose, I'm also very sorry I had to let you go after talking to you for only ten minutes. It hurt me a little, and I know it hurt you, but there was nothing I could do. Dad wasn't in the mood for explanations, and it would've made things worse. I'll be sure to talk to him about it later. It will make things much easier if they know basically what's going on before they get mad. If they only knew the way we talk on the phone and did things. I guess I must expect trouble, though.

I know it hurts you about our problems. Till I believe we can change that, oh, we'll always have problems, but we can learn how to cope with them so they don't bother us one bit. We'll learn to appreciate them just because we gain from them. The Lord appreciates problems.

I have hoped in the past and prayed that you will someday be so spiritual that your physical pain and illness will never depress you. That the pain and bad sickness you have will not get ahold of you, but that you can keep joy in your life. To do all these things, you need to do what you know is right.

Right now, I'm imagining what would happen to me if you died. I see myself staying up day and night with you in the hospital and banging my head on all the walls, and I see myself going into a pit of darkness and almost in shock, and I see myself marrying you by proxy and adopting kids to raise on my own.

I love you ever so much, and you know how it hurts to see you like this.

Rose, I feel bad about what I made you do months ago, but it won't bother me if it never happens again. I don't think I was quite normal. I'm tired, so I think I will go to bed. For the 100,000,000,000,000th (one trillionth time), I love you!

Love forever, Kahuna

I wanted to open my window and yell at the mean man, but all I could do was lie there and ponder on Kahuna's letter. My room had become my world, my prison. It held secrets locked inside its walls. I knew if the walls talked, they would say I was a complainer who dwelt too much on insecure thoughts. Kahuna's letter brought comfort; it brought warmth and joy to know he still loved me. I wished Kahuna and I were still at the ROTC ball, dancing.

Mom brought my soup and informed me of a neurology appointment downtown for a second opinion on why my brain was unable to send correct messages to my legs. Her smile stretched when she told me Dax had called and wanted to be there for moral support.

Dax came to my appointment, and we sat together in the waiting room. My head drooped, making me feel ugly. He, on the other hand, looked dashingly handsome in his sky-blue oxford shirt and nice pair of jeans.

I mustered the strength to look at him. "How did you get here? Are you ditching school?" My head dropped while I listened.

"Yes, I ditched and rode my bike. It's only fifteen miles from home."

They called me back, and humiliation set in from walking down a hallway so the neurologist could scrutinize me. Each step sent electric waves down my legs, and I walked on the tips of my toes to dim the pain. My knees wouldn't straighten, and when I tried, it hurt.

I returned to the waiting room, and Grandmother was sitting near Dax. I inched myself in Dax's direction, hoping he didn't see my imperfections as clearly as the doctor did. Once again, Grandmother was showing her true colors as an intrusive, nosy person who stuck her nose into everyone's life. The nurse called my mother to come speak to the doctor. Grandmother looked at my mother, as if expecting an invitation to go with her. Mother smiled and walked toward the door, and, yes, Grandmother did follow.

Dax and I didn't talk much, but the love between us was transparent. With effort, I turn to get a view of Dax. Once our eyes connected, the pain that lingered in my arms and legs subsided. I soaked up his presence as if I were a dried sponge wanting to absorb any type of liquid. Peace surrounded us. I craved to hug him and express my gratitude for the support I desperately needed, but the pain won over. Instead I gave an invisible hug with a smile attached. When he returned the smile, we connected in ways I never believed possible. I thought of the letter I had read days before from Kahuna about our physical problems that were leading us to moral sin. I wished Kahuna and I had a spotless relationship, like I had with Dax.

Months had passed since my visit with Dax in the waiting room, and I had adapted to the new, still-sick me, even though I missed school, concert choir, and cross-country.

Kahuna came to see me for the first time since I'd been diagnosed with Guillain Barre. He sat beside me and gave a tender smile.

I smiled and slurred, "I miss our Saturday-night dances together."

His eyes had hope in them, and I captured that hope and stored it in my heart. His smile faded. Had he lost interest in me? Maybe he didn't want to be my boyfriend anymore, because I wasn't the same girl he fell in love with. Kahuna grabbed my hands. "Rose, I want to say a prayer. Will you join me?"

I said, "Sure."

Kahuna slipped off his shoes and knelt next to my bed. He rested his arms on my desk chair and bowed his head.

His voice rang with both urgency and gratitude. "Dear Heavenly Father, I feel blessed for Rose and our relationship. I feel blessed to visit with her this day. I come before thee with a humble heart, asking that you will heal Rose from this awful sickness and allow her to walk normally and go back to high school. Please bless Rose and me that we can have a healthy, virtuous relationship and control our physical desires. We love you, Heavenly Father, and feel blessed for bringing us together. Bless our families, and please heal Rose."

Kahuna finished with tears in his eyes, and I cried. I was grateful that he could look past my deformed blind eye and present infirmities.

In the days that followed, my health plunged further in the wrong direction. I was unable to call a friend or sit on my bedroom floor and read the letters from my Liberty Box. I prayed with faith, and I hoped this illness would disappear.

Finally, after two months of being bedridden, my hands and legs stopped aching, and I was strong enough to dress and bathe myself. Being confined to a bed taught me that I shouldn't take my arms and legs for granted. I thought about Bobby, my brother in the Philippines, and hoped he knew I'd won the battle.

Dax called often, even during school when he was in journalism class, but Kahuna vanished and never contacted me after his first visit. After weeks of physical therapy, I recovered.

Summer arrived, and Dax's birthday was right around the corner. He wrote me often, even when I went to girls camp.

June 1, 1981

Rose:

> *(I am writing this very late at night and I am so tired, so if it's messy, please excuse.) Hello! How are you doing? Are you a cabin mom yet? I thought so! (Just kidding) So what is it like being on JS? Mucho responsibility? You can handle it.*

Have you heard from Kahuna yet? Neither have I. What are we going to do with him?

Nobody besides Rose had better be reading this letter; I have the "Invasion of Privacy Act" (AZ St. 107) memorized! And I know how to use it. I think embarrassing the girls by reading their mail is utterly childish, and very irresponsible. Besides all of this, I get mad very easily!

I hope that stopped an idiot from reading this—besides you, Rose. Getting back to Kahuna: I think your idea of just the three of us going out would be fine except Kahuna and I don't communicate well with you around. Nothing personal! It's just that he gets so uncomfortable. Remember how uncomfortable it was when we went to the mall with Kahuna? If we could—both of us, together—break into him, we could easily work things out. But that won't be easy.

You may find him less physical as the summer progresses; remember how I said that exercise would help relieve the tension and anxiety that make him that way? Well, it's gonna be hard to beat the exercise he'll be getting as a lifeguard.

Question: Isn't the main reason you didn't want him to be a lifeguard is because he'd be always around scantily clothed, cute girls?

Have you written and told him that you got a job? Remember everything he said to you when you chewed him out for becoming a lifeguard. You can use it against him when he blows up. Now we're gonna see just how he likes it.

Work is going fine, and so am I. I'm still thinking about moving out, but I don't know. Remember, I love you, and so does Kahuna. Keep us always in mind. Write your family, especially Bobby, and keep smiling.

You had better write me!!!

The next letter you get will be at home the day you get back. I'm getting a haircut tomorrow. Take care. Say your prayers.

Love, Dax

P.S. Tell Kahuna I miss him!

P.P.S. This is the 2nd longest letter I've ever written. I hope you're happy.

P.P.P.S Only 16 Days till "18!"

I prayed for weeks that Kahuna would call, and he did.

30
GRANDMOTHER'S VISIT

February 1982

The whip of the tongue can break the heart.

While helping Dad with the dishes, I gazed out our kitchen window at our mulberry tree dancing with the wind. "Oh, no, Dad—look who's outside."

Dad rinsed his hands, and I darted to my bedroom. As soon as I'd closed my door, the doorbell rang. Poor Dad was stuck opening the door for Grandmother to make her grand entrance. I sat on my bed and pictured her, with shoulders back, head held high with a sway of her beautiful, wavy, light-blond hair. All that she ever brought with her was her downpour of empty love.

"Sweetie, your mother is here," Dad called.

Mom moaned when she tottered down our hallway. I envisioned my mom, hunched over and head down, seated across the living room from Grandmother. Rocking her foot, heel to toe, against the floor, causing her wheelchair to move back in forth in a rhythmic tempo between each word my grandmother spoke. How she stayed in the same spot was a mystery to me.

Had someone in the hospital switched Mother with another baby? Because Mother had brown, curly hair, and Grandmother's was naturally white.

I sat on the edge of my bed and tried to get the courage to go rescue Mom. The lawnmower wailed, and I knew then that Dad had found a shield from Grandmother. Now Mom needed me to be her shield from Grandmother's hurtful arrows.

"Rose, can you come here, please?" Mom yelled.

I tried to get off the bed, but it had a hold on me and wouldn't let me go. I hollered at Mom, "OK, just a minute."

I hesitated as I inched myself down our narrow hallway to see my emotional yo-yo Grandmother.

I prayed as I moved toward the living room that she wouldn't say, "Rosie, you are a spoiled brat!"

Those words lingered as I tried to mentally shield myself, hoping to safeguard my emotions from her soul-piercing sword. Entering the living room, I felt the usual coldness hit me, with Grandmother seated on our blue recliner.

"Hi there, Rosie."

I wasn't sure that it would do any good, but I tried to convey love and tenderness in the way I hugged her, hoping that might influence her response.

"Hi, Grandmother. How are you?"

"Oh, not good."

I knew immediately that she'd already stabbed Mom with her usual swords and that she was ready to use other daggers as well.

"Are you sick, Grandmother?"

"Oh, no."

Here it came, a dagger with guilt. The room grew silent, and I couldn't respond to her. I sat near Mom on the couch, biting my tongue while Grandmother said to my mom, "If you were a paper doll, I would rip you up and throw you in the trash." Each time Grandmother said something like that, I wanted to change the course of the dagger's path, but I was not capable of stopping the harsh words that found their way out of Grandmother's mouth.

Grandmother scowled at Mom. "Why haven't you been over to see me?"

"Well, Mother, the car hasn't been running very well, and I'm not sure it would make it."

"What's wrong with your husband? Can't he fix the car?"

Mom adjusted her glasses, which were held together with yellow duct tape. "Mother, we haven't had the money to replace the radiator."

Grandmother shifted deeper into the chair. "I would think your church could help you. Why haven't you asked for help?"

"We want to figure that out on our own, Mother."

With each question or comment that came out of Grandmother's mouth, Mom's wheelchair rolled faster back and forth.

"Rosie, don't you think your church should help your parents?"

Silence filled the room, and Grandmother threw a dagger in my direction. "Rosie, when I ask you a question, you'd better answer me."

Grandmother moved to the edge of the recliner and gave one quick hand movement to her hair, fluffing it as if she owned the world.

"I'll tell you one thing: your church should be helping you so that you can come over and see me." She paused, looked around the living room, and then attacked Mom with a callous expression of hatred. "Your family are white trash. Do you hear me? White trash!"

The tempo of Mom's wheelchair increased. She may not have spoken, but the rhythm of her wheelchair showed the intensity of her distress. Mom repeated the same sentences: "Yes, Mother. I don't know, Mother," and I didn't see any tears in her eyes. When Grandmother spoke against my Dad, Mom answered, "You're right, Mother, but we'll find a way to do what we need to do."

Grandmother held her chin high, pushed herself out of the recliner, and then waltzed herself out our living-room door. My mom rolled to the comfort of her bedroom walls.

After Grandmother's visit, Mom called Dad the minute he walked in the back door.

"Honey, can you come here, please?"

Dad shook his head and strolled into their room.

Mom's voice escalated. "What do you think of what my mother said to me?"

"It's horrible, Sweetie."

I sat in the living room and pictured Mom rolling her wheelchair less as Dad validated that Grandmother was wrong. Dad must have had his hand on the crown of his head. With each pick, he'd tear skin from his scalp, causing blood to dye his white hair red. His frustration was visible hours later, when fresh blood kept re-surfacing from his sores. Grandmother's daggers and swords toward my mother left no visible signs or scars—only frustration.

Grandmother's visit made me understand why Mom recorded conversations with Grandmother. It had to be justification of her pain. Mom's boxes, stacked in the corner of her room, contained hundreds of conversations over the years, tangible proof of rejection. Each cassette tape carried invisible hurt that was as real as the blood on my father's head.

31
WASHINGTON, DC

April 1982

To love life is to witness all its potential.

The airplane door shut, and my throat closed, likewise. I was sitting on the right side of the plane, in row 14, seat B, between my high school friend Kevra and Kahuna.

As the plane climbed toward the sky, gravity pulled me in the opposite direction.

My stomach turned, and I prayed. I feared that our plane would crash like the airplane that, a few weeks earlier, had hit Washington, DC's 14th Street bridge and crashed into the Potomac River's icy water. The accident killed 78 people, including four motorists on the bridge.

Kahuna pointed at the wing vibrating. "Look, Rose! The wing is going to fall off."

I leaned closer to Kahuna and watched the wing.

Kahuna spoke. "It's common for the wings to move. You know we are in the safest spot on the plane. Do you want to switch seats so you have a better view?"

I moved back in my seat. "No, that's okay. I've never been on a plane before, so I'll stay right here."

Kevra, with her cute, round face and dimple on the right cheek, focused on a book. Her beautiful hair was a bonus to her radiance, and I wished I looked like her. What helped me to cope with her being so pretty was that I had Kahuna. I was bothered, though, that they shared the same birthday, but, thankfully, they'd been born in different years. Kevra was my height, with the perfect figure. My skinny, long body and flat chest didn't seem normal for girls my age.

Mr. Pullet, my history teacher, stood out with his bright-blue eyes and blond hair. He kept a constant watch on us from across the aisle; I guess that was his responsibility as our chaperone for the weeklong stay in Washington, DC. Everyone loved his comedian personality that had a political side to it.

I grabbed Kahuna's hand and closed my eyes as the plane landed in St. Louis. During this brief layover, Kahuna and I decided to get off. I wanted to see what another airport looked like. Kevra stayed aboard and read. We decided to go to the front entrance and look outside. There was a train going down a railway, and there was a river not far away. I marveled at how different it looked compared to home. No cacti, no palm trees, no mesquite trees.

I was startled when my name echoed over the loudspeakers. Kahuna looked at his watch and clenched his teeth while taking in a gasp of air. "We'd better go, Rose."

We ran and weaved around people as if we were in a race through a forest. When we entered the plane, I noticed a look of relief on Mr. Pullet's face.

As the plane made a quick turn, flying sideways, I got a clear view of the damage to the Potomac River bridge that had been inflicted by the airplane crash.

Our plane rumbled when it hit the Ronald Reagan Washington National Airport tarmac.

We stayed in Silver Spring, Maryland, at the Sheraton Hotel. Kevra and I stayed on the fourth floor, and Kahuna was on the fifth. It was great to have two other roommates from Colorado. Cassie had light-blond hair and beautiful blue eyes. Angie was a quiet girl, with the olive complexion that all girls desired.

That evening we attended a formal dinner and orientation, filled with information about our schedule, about government events, and how our country is run in Washington, DC.

I didn't care about the United States Senate or to watch the Ninety-Seventh Congress on the floor as they tried to find ways to make efficient decisions on bills, resolutions, and other matters that required action by the senators. I did have a bit of interest in the qualifications to become a senator, because I knew Kahuna wanted to study political science and maybe become one.

My first morning in Washington, DC, was heavenly, with the pink flowers—and their wonderful aroma—that covered the trees. We visited the Library of Congress and learned it provided numerous services that benefited all Americans. It was awe-inspiring to see the Thomas Jefferson Memorial as it looked across the Tidal Basin and at the Washington Monument.

The next day, I got to see the long reflecting pool in front of the Lincoln Memorial. When I looked out at the shimmering water and saw the Jefferson Memorial and Washington Monument, I marveled how the placement of these monuments brought all three of these remarkable leaders together with a triangle. My favorite was the Jefferson Memorial, because of the oversized statue.

We strolled beneath the trees blooming with red, pink, and purple flowers near the Capitol Building. The Japanese cherry blossoms and tulips caught my eye. Never in my life had I seen a tulip planted in the ground. I wished I had a magical bag so that I could take the flowers home. Dad would have loved them.

Kahuna begged me the day we arrived to go and visit with Senator Barry Goldwater at his office. On our fourth day there, we studied the map and rode the metro to visit him. Kahuna carried on a governmental conversation with Mr. Goldwater, and I sat amidst the Native-American-style decorations and listened to them chat. When we left his office, we both agreed it was the highlight of our trip. At least it was for Kahuna.

Our group attended a play called *Gypsy Rose Lee* at a restaurant near Washington, DC. When we walked in, we saw generously proportioned black velvet drapes covering the wall opposite the entrance. The tablecloths matched the red carpet. Booths, with elegant settings of cream plates, lighted small candles in the center, and glass salt and pepper shakers, faced the stage. Colossal white carved columns were scattered throughout the restaurant. Kahuna and I found a booth near the stage with a spectacular view. Two other teenagers joined us. We ordered spaghetti and garlic bread. Moments after I took my first bite, the lights dimmed to the point I couldn't see across the table. Then, a man in '40s-style clothes stood on the stage and talked to all of us teenagers.

"Welcome, ladies and gentlemen to the best play ever shown. Please stay seated during the show, because we don't want anyone to break a leg while the lights are down."

Everyone clapped and whistled. Gypsy Rose came out onto the stage, and the lights dimmed to the point you couldn't even see the person next to you. There were lights attached to her outfit that were suggestive and obviously meant to entice the audience.

Kahuna leaned closer to me and spoke over the music. "I think we need to leave, Rose, don't you?"

I grabbed his arm. "Look at her dance in those scanty clothes. Yes, let's leave."

We were in a situation neither one of us wanted to be in.

Kahuna grabbed my hand. "Rose, let's go; let's leave now."

"Okay, but will we get in trouble for leaving?"

Kahuna brought his mouth closer to my ear. "Doesn't matter. We need to leave now!"

Kahuna held my hand and led me out. We both kept focused on the red-lighted exit sign above the door and I tried not to bump into others. Several times people yelled at us to move. Mr. Pullet grabbed my arm when we were near the exit. I could barely see the outline of his face.

"Where are you two going?" he asked with a firm tone.

Kahuna shouted, "Mr. Pullet, I have no desire to watch such a show as this, and neither does Rose."

Mr. Pullet stood closer to us as he spoke. "Okay, but you will have to wait in the bus for about two hours."

"Sounds fine with me. How about you, Rose?"

"I'm fine with it."

A cold chill hit my face when we stepped outside. I put my sweater on and prayed the bus driver would let us in. We reached the bus and heard music from inside. Kahuna tapped hard on the door. The bus driver turned down his music and opened the door.

Kahuna walked up the steps of the bus. "Can we get on, please?" The driver had a questioning look in his eyes as he asked Kahuna,

"Was it worth seeing?"

Kahuna responded. "No, it wasn't. Can we get on the bus?"

The bus driver arched his back. "Sure, that's fine."

We walked to the back and found our seats.

I moved closer to Kahuna. "I think we made the right choice in leaving."

"I think we did, too."

"You know, Kahuna, we made choices to never smoke, drink, or take drugs, and I'm glad I made the choice not to watch such a show. I guess the weakness we have is getting too physically close."

Kahuna wrapped his arm around me. "You know it's hard to avoid not kissing and hugging you. I crave to be close to you. Don't you want to hug me and kiss me?"

"I do. There are times I wish we were together all the time."

Kahuna smiled. "Someday, Rose, we will be together forever."

Right after his tender kiss, I whispered, "I like that idea of us together forever."

32
PROM NIGHT
May 1982

When you freely share your love it can either hinder your relationship or make it stronger.

My heart beat as if an untamed bird lived in my chest as I studied Kahuna's handsome profile as he drove. The sun's rays touched Kahuna's lips and made me crave to have my lips touch his, too.

Streetlights came and went as we drove in his parents' navy-blue Toyota camper to the Arizona Biltmore for our senior prom. I marveled at the large, majestic building near Camelback Mountain. A young man dressed in a tailored suit approached Kahuna and asked if he would like valet parking. He said "Yes," and another young man, also in a tailored suit, opened my door.

We walked hand in hand through two electronic sliding doors and caught the aroma from the fresh-picked flowers in the center of a round antique table. My long, pleated dress made me feel as if I belonged. Kahuna's fingers interlocked with mine as he guided me to our booth. The quietness of the restaurant made us want to whisper when we ordered our meals. They brought our steaks and set them on a fold-out table.

After Kahuna and I ate, we strolled about the first floor until we found the sign that said: "High School Prom Second Floor." We walked up the freestanding staircase. When we arrived on the second floor, we glanced over at the high school prom dance and then looked at each other.

"Let's take a walk out on the balcony, Rose."

I smiled. "I like that idea."

I grabbed the balcony rail and drank in the beauty of the tall palm trees with the moon gleaming on one side of them. Kahuna wrapped his arms around my waist.

"I love you, Kahuna, and I'm glad we're together. I wish the night would never end."

Kahuna pulled me closer; he looked into my eyes, and his tender lips connected with mine. His welcoming kiss stirred a thirst for more, but his words "I love you" kept me hydrated.

After several kisses, we re-entered the dance area. The song "Wishing on a Star" seemed more memorable tonight. The instant we walked onto the dance floor, we wrapped our arms around each other. After we danced, we greeted friends, but neither Kahuna nor I had a desire to be at the prom, so we left.

Kahuna handed the valet a small ticket, and the valet retrieved the truck. Kahuna opened my door, and I slid in. We drove off, and silence sat between us.

We both had been taught the dangers of being alone with someone of the opposite sex. But I didn't care; I loved him, desired to be with him, and wanted him with me always. In my head, I retold myself over and over, "You are both eighteen."

I studied Kahuna and memorized his small eyes, manly nose, and full lips each time a streetlight found him. We drove through town, and I relived the memories from the places we had been to over the years, places I hoped we would go to in years to come.

Kahuna spoke. "Rose, you want to stop somewhere before I take you home?"

I squeezed his hand. "Sure."

We pulled into a shopping center parking lot and chatted.

"Kahuna, I'm sure going to miss you when you leave for college."

Kahuna leaned over and pressed his lips on mine. When we stopped, I gazed at his face.

"I don't want the night to end."

Kahuna caressed my shoulder.

"I hope our relationship never ends, Rose."

I kissed him.

"Rose, let's go sit on the back of the truck bed."

Would that be such a clever idea?

"Sure."

We sat with our legs dangling over the edge of the tailgate. His cream-colored tuxedo enhanced his physique, and I felt like the luckiest girl on Earth. Vehicles passed by, but I didn't hear them. Here we were in the same situation we were in two weeks before, after we'd had our ROTC ball pictures retaken. Now I searched his deep-brown eyes and thought of that first encounter.

Kahuna leaned in closer with a twinkle in his eyes. Our lips linked, and Kahuna's eyes sent a sensation coursing through my bloodstream. Our lips were warm; he moved his lips down my neck. We paused and looked back at the dark, empty area of the truck camper. Silence was shared. We scooted further into the bed of the truck. This was wrong, but I hungered to share my love with him. To fill my empty world. A world of rejection, doubt, and fear. We let the dam break so that our love could run free when we became connected as one.

Within seconds, he moved away. We looked at each other, unsure of what to do or say next. No words could take back our actions. We got out of the truck bed as quickly as we had entered it, got back into the cab, and drove off. My mind kept repeating the same sentence: *What was I thinking?* Kahuna held tight to the steering wheel, and it brought back memories of my father clinging to the steering wheel when he had to tell my mom that Pepe was gone. Now Kahuna would have to tell his mother our deep, dark secret, which I wanted to keep only between us. I crossed my legs and wished I had a relationship with my mother like Kahuna had with his. I bit my lower lip and tried to fight the tears, knowing my mom couldn't be the mother I needed. Kahuna told his mother everything. Now I would have dreams shattered because of those seconds we shared—connected in a way we were told to wait for until married. What would become of me? Ugly, used, and worthless, and his mother would agree.

We stopped in front of my home, a home that held even deeper secrets than the one Kahuna and I had developed—secrets like the one Kahuna had and which only I knew about. Kahuna kept the truck idling, reached over, pulled me closer, and kissed me.

When the tail lights of his truck vanished down the road, so did the warmth of his hug that he had given me.

33
YEARBOOK SIGNING

May 1982

Rejection from a loved one stops the heart
and brings fear of more rejection.

The school cafeteria looked as hollow as I was feeling. All the chairs that were usually occupied by boisterous students at lunchtime now sat empty. I cleared my throat and made my way to find Dax. A wave of anxiety stirred in me when I found him standing behind the yearbook table, taking money from a student. Dax stood tall, like he had last month when he watched me from the back of the auditorium as I sang my solo in the choir concert. I was shocked when he came to see me perform, and Kahuna didn't even attend the concert. As I neared Dax, I sent him a smile. He caught it and lifted his eyebrows with a grin. I waited for him to finish.

Dax scanned the cafeteria before he spoke. "Is Kahuna here?"

I looked around the cafeteria and back at Dax before I cleared my throat again. I wished Dax could read my mind. Then he'd know that I felt like I had become an object in Kahuna's eyes, like Dax had become years before. I knew I wasn't like Dax, driving Kahuna crazy with affectionate hugs and overwhelming phone calls. Kahuna declared often that Dax seemed to smother him.

Kahuna had pushed us both out of his life when we needed him. He had to have looked at us as pathetic human beings. But I believed that the truth was that we'd exposed the real feelings he had hidden deep in his soul. Kahuna didn't want us anymore. The same frustration resurfaced as when my foster mother had fed me zucchini, squash, and white hominy mixed together, and I wanted to tell her how much I hated it. I swallowed hard and tried to hold back from spilling out the words I had on the tip of my tongue. Kahuna had forced me to keep our secret from Dax, in the same manner as I was forced to keep my secret about how much I hated the foods placed before me when living in foster care. I wanted to hug Dax and whisper in his ear, "Help me, Dax; help Kahuna and me." I held back the tears, bit at my tongue, and told myself, *Don't, Rose—don't say anything that could risk your relationship with Kahuna forever.*

I answered him, "I don't know if Kahuna is coming."

Dax glanced over my shoulder at the entrance. "Kahuna should be here, I'd think."

I stood closer to Dax, so no one else could hear us. "Well, he might be busy with family stuff tonight. Can I buy a yearbook?"

Dax handed me a yearbook. "They are ten dollars and fifty cents."

"Here you go. Can you sign my book right now, please? I'm going to leave soon. My father is out in the parking lot waiting for me."

Dax walked around the table and guided me with his arm over to the chairs near the entrance.

He sat and reached for my book. "Can I use my own pen?"

I sat next to him. "Sure."

I looked intently at the double doors while he wrote in my yearbook and hoped with each passing minute that Kahuna would come.

Dax closed the book and slipped his pen clip on his collar.

"Rose, please wait until you get home to read what I wrote."

I hugged Dax, wanting to hold on to him forever. "I will wait."

At home, I read what Dax had written.

Rose,

> *So, it's almost over . . . high school, that is. I don't really know what to say. What can I say? I'll miss ya a lot while I'm gone, and I hope you write. I will. I knew that I haven't been the friend you want, but I've tried, and will try to do better in the future. You're a special spirit, and many great blessings are in store for you. Life won't always be as hard as it has been. Remember the things the three of us have learned . . . it may help later on. Take care of Kahuna for me, at least till he leaves, and you'd better always take care of you. Best wishes always. Stay true to what you know is true. Love, Dax*

I cringed, squeezing the yearbook knowing nothing between Dax and I would ever be the same. His Christmas gift of pierced earrings that had swarovski crystals in them would be the first and last time I would ever receive a gift from him.

Maybe I wouldn't ever have to inform him that Kahuna and I might become parents in nine months. Maybe what the doctor said after my surgery last year, about my uterus being tipped and deformed from the Congenital Rubella Syndrome, would be enough protection as birth control. I can still hear the doctor, with his firm voice, giving me the lowdown on how I might never be able to have children.

34

TEST

June 1982

**Hold close those who love you;
hold closer those who despise you.**

I ran my hands over my face and then down my neck to my tummy. Was there a life inside me that would call me "Mommy" and Kahuna "Daddy"? I hoped a part of Kahuna was in me because I wanted a permanent attachment to him, a bond that could never be broken by anyone. I wanted the new life in me, carrying his genes, to be free and never feel rejected like I did. I wanted my baby to love whoever he or she wanted to love and to be loved in return.

A raw bleakness enveloped me, and hope didn't seem achievable. My emotions rushed forth as fast as Niagara Falls. I pushed my pillow into my face and spoke out loud: "A pregnancy test is for a married woman, who has a husband and a home—not for me, who needs to finish high school and journey out into the world."

Perfect Rose Cracked Vase

The armor I wore during my grandmother's visits wasn't available while I was pinned between Kahuna and his mother in the cab of their small truck. Topics I had never heard discussed between Kahuna and his mother traveled back and forth, as if I weren't present—no, as if I had no thoughts, opinions, or concerns to contribute.

I had crossed the line from child to woman, and still Kahuna and his mother treated me as if I were a little girl who had no say about my own body and future. I wondered why his mom thought she had a right to take over my life and Kahuna's. We were eighteen and, by law, adults. I wanted to climb over Kahuna and jump out. Was it enough that Kahuna's mom had persuaded me not to tell my parents that I might be pregnant? I hoped Kahuna's mother could imagine how painful this was for me. The loneliness in my soul deepened. I felt a need to have my mom there, if only to assure me that everything was going to be fine. *Who would protect me?* She protected Kahuna at the expense of hurting me. *Was he a failure for loving me?*

Kahuna's mom asked, "Kahuna, how are you going to take care of a baby?"

Kahuna held my hand and squeezed it. "I'll get a full-time job."

"Kahuna, are you going to marry Rose?"

He moved his head forward to look at her. "Of course, Mom, of course. I love her."

The air thickened in the cab, and I needed oxygen while I continued to be the topic of their conversation.

His mother glanced over at us and then looked back at the road. "Let's figure out when the baby would be due."

"I figure it would be around February. I went back three months and then forward two weeks and around then would be the due date."

"Are you sure, Kahuna, that it would be February?"

I knew that, next February, Kahuna should be in college, not working full time with a baby. I turned my head as far as I could to the right to get a partial look at Kahuna's handsome face. I wished at that moment I had vision in my right eye. To be able to study his face would have helped me interpret his thoughts. Here I was, a large thorn, and his mother wanted to pluck me out of her son's life.

In Kahuna's past letters, he'd expressed his desire to obey his mother, and today was no different. He honored any advice she gave about our relationship. Tension grew with each question and answer that was thrown across the cab, and there I was, sandwiched between them. Kahuna's mom's voice rang loud and clear. I was "that girl" who prevented Kahuna from achieving his full potential. I had destroyed his reputation of a "good, upstanding boy with his peers and siblings."

Eager to escape that toxic environment, I sighed in relief as we drove into the parking lot.

Kahuna's mom didn't want to go in with us to Planned Parenthood and mingle with pregnant teenagers in the waiting room; instead, she went to the Tupperware dealership to pick up an order and then to the grocery store. I looked around the waiting room at the other girls my age and older while Kahuna went to pay for the pregnancy test. His 5'6" body was perfect, and I was completely attracted to every part of him. I loved him, cherished him, and hoped not to lose him. I rubbed my blind eye and knew I wasn't perfect, with the deformities I had.

Time slipped, my heart ached, and my love for Kahuna was alive when I watched him hand a ten-dollar bill to the receptionist. After he paid, he sat with me. I hoped he would grab my hand and give some type of affection to show others in the waiting room that he loved me.

Soon, a skinny lady with dark long hair called my name so loud I knew the people in the parking lot could hear. "Rose, Rose, could you come this way, please?"

I could hear Kahuna's footsteps as I followed her. I was glad he was behind me. I sat down in "The Chair." I observed various kinds of glass tubes with different-colored caps. There were posters saying safe sex is the best way to go. "Which arm do you want me to draw the blood from?"

I rolled my sleeve up. "Let's try my left arm."

Perfect Rose Cracked Vase

She wrapped a band around my arm, constricting it tightly. I thought of Kahuna's mom and how she was constricting our love. Kahuna held my right hand while the woman extracted blood out of my vein and into a small tube.

Kahuna looked at me and then at the woman. "When will the test results be in?"

"In three days, and we will call Rose with the results. Have either of you thought of birth control if there is no pregnancy?"

I squeezed Kahuna's hand and then looked at the woman. "Mm . . . hum mm . . . we aren't going to have a physical relationship anymore."

She pushed the cap on the tube of blood. "Well if you two would like, I can still give you some birth-control pills."

I looked at her. "That's all right. No, thank you."

I pulled my sleeve over my bandage and grabbed Kahuna's hand. "I'll call you with the results."

I glimpsed at the tube of blood with my name on it. She touched my shoulder. "Are you all right?"

I walked toward the door. "Yes, I'm fine. Thanks for asking."

Kahuna and I walked outside to face the harsh sun and sat under a palm tree that offered no shade.

I squeezed Kahuna's hand. "I appreciate you coming with me."

Kahuna wiggled his hand out of mine. "You're welcome."

I grinned. "When do you think your mother will be here?"

Kahuna looked down, avoiding eye contact. "I hope soon; it's hot."

He said little but stared at the desert scenery and man-made lake.

After a few minutes of silence, he glared at me and grabbed my hand. "Rose, you will call me, right?"

I smiled. "Of course, I'll call you. You know, Kahuna, I wouldn't have gotten into this situation with just anyone, because you're the one I love."

The firmness of his grip was gone, as though his hand had no life left in it. Our hands separated when Kahuna's mother drove into the parking lot. I walked behind Kahuna and dreaded getting back into the truck between Kahuna and his mother. Each time I reached over to hold his hand, he moved. Silence filled the cab, and no words ever surfaced from his mother's lips. When I got out of the truck, Kahuna's mom's smile looked plastic, like one you would see on a mannequin.

"Bye, Rose."

I bent down so I could see Kahuna's mother. "Bye, Mrs. Pali. Thank you for helping Kahuna and me."

Kahuna held on to the handle of the truck. "Mom, I'm going to walk Rose to the door."

She put the truck in park and turned it off. "Hurry, Kahuna, so we can get the food home."

We walked side by side, with a solid invisible wall between us, but as we got to the door, he did touch his lips to my cheek.

"I'll call you."

Kahuna smiled. "I love you, Rose."

"I love you, too, Kahuna."

I watched him sprint to the truck. I opened the door and went to my room. I checked my bandage. When I entered the kitchen, Mom was eating. "Where did you go with Kahuna?"

I reached into the cabinet to get a cup and tried to get my emotions under control before I spoke. "We rode with his mother to a warehouse for some products she sells."

My lips trembled at the shame of lying, but Kahuna's mom didn't want me to tell my parents.

I cringed at the thought that I had to stay within arm's length of the phone for the next three days. I couldn't have anyone answer the phone and hear the woman say, "This is Planned Parenthood. Is Rose there?"

I sat on one of the yellow dining chairs and placed my cup of milk on the table. "What have you been doing this morning?" I asked.

Mom rubbed the edge of the table. "Oh, the usual, with putting a load of laundry in."

The swipe of her napkin across her mouth covered the lower part of her face, so I couldn't read her expression. Did she know I'd lied?

I focused on the wall behind my mom and wanted to tell Mother the truth; I wanted to heave this serious burden off my back.

Perfect Rose Cracked Vase

I huddled over the phone for three days.

"Hello."

"Hello. Is Rose there?"

The receiver was heavier to hold as the woman spoke. "Yes, this is Rose."

"Hi. This is Marsha, with Planned Parenthood, with your results."

I sat down on the telephone chair, and my hands shook.

"Your test came back negative, so you aren't pregnant."

A gush of relief came as I spoke quietly into the phone. "Thank you, oh, thank you, for calling me."

I sat at the telephone chair, knowing I needed to call Kahuna. But I thought, *If he can make me feel so discarded, then why should I be anxious to call and save him from the torture of knowing he could be a father?* I thought, *One more day for him to hear the results of my test won't hurt him or his sweet, loving mother.* It gave me some sense of control to prolong the rejection I knew I would hear at the other end of the line when I told him the results.

That night, I prayed for strength to endure this call I knew I needed to make. I prayed for faith that our relationship wouldn't be erased merely because of his mother. I prayed for forgiveness because I'd lied to my parents to save Kahuna from humiliation.

The pregnancy test was my physical test, but the spiritual test of being honest with my loved ones was the real test. The most difficult test would be learning to love myself. I counted to sixty each time I watched my alarm clock change numbers. I thought of the lies and secrecy of the past weeks and how it had worn me out to the point I was dying inside. I lied even to Dax.

I sat on the telephone chair and stared at the phone while my heart sprinted a million miles. It was a perfect time to call Kahuna, with my parents still in bed. My finger dialed, and my tears fell too fast for me to catch them. I prayed that an angel would be with me and that Kahuna would answer the phone.

His voice came through the phone. "Hello."

I swallowed before I spoke and squeezed the phone tight, as if that were the only way I could hold on to Kahuna. "Kahuna, the pregnancy results came back negative."

His voice went three scales down in notes. "Thanks for letting me know."

I gripped the phone tighter, with a prayer that he could feel my grip. His three bitter words, "Call you later," ended the so-called "conversation" after he knew the results. He didn't ask me if I was okay; maybe he would have if I'd been pregnant with his child. I shook my head and assumed he had discarded me like a torn paper doll ready to be thrown in the trash—just like my grandmother would have loved to do to my mother. I spoke out loud, as though it were the only way to relieve the hurt. "I don't matter to him anymore." Kahuna's mom had won the war by convincing Kahuna that I was a one-eyed freak that could never measure up to what his mother thought he needed in a wife or even a friend.

The special memories of his kiss, hug, and words made me sulk around the house as though death had entered my life. My internal organs crumbled, unable to function; grief entered my soul.

I sat in my usual spot at the kitchen table and stared at my mother. These last four days of emptiness were more than I could cope with. I begged God for strength to open my mouth and share my trials with my mother. The pain boiled inside me, like a hot kettle of water. My sister-in-law Lisa, who'd married my brother Bobby three months earlier, was seated on the opposite side of the table. Envy of her put a barrier between us—a barrier of disbelief that, even though she was only a month older than me, she could love the one she wanted, and I couldn't.

My mother looked over at me after she took a bite of her toast, spread with a substantial layer of butter. "Rose, aren't you hungry?"

I set my elbows on the table and rested my cheekbones on my fists. I tried not to cry. "No, I'm not hungry."

She put her toast down and looked at me. "Rose, what is the matter?"

The kettle of water in me wanted to burst. I anchored myself down, and, with hesitation, I opened my mouth. "Mom, I could have been pregnant, but I'm not."

Mom backed away from table and screamed. I looked at the ceiling and knew the roof was going to cave in on us.

Mom glared. "What do you mean, 'you could have been pregnant'?"

My brother stormed in and interrupted my next sentence. I guess he'd heard Mom scream from the bedroom he and his wife were renting from my parents.

He yelled so loud the neighbors had to think someone was being murdered. "What's going on?"

Tears streamed down my face, and my body quivered.

My mother stared at my brother and pointed over at me. "Rose could have been pregnant."

At that moment, I searched for strength.

My brother yelled over and over. "What . . . what? That boy Kahuna has a lot to answer for."

I sat with relief, glad the lie I'd been holding captive was free. My brother walked back and forth between the kitchen sink and table with anger in his eyes. He spoke with a firm voice as he combed his hair with his fingers.

"I want to talk to Kahuna. Now."

His wife hurried to hide their car keys. Mother talked with a firm voice, and my brother responded with anger. Words exchanged between them made me feel like it was about them and not me. My torment deepened with each word from my mother. Aches and soreness grew in me while I sat there and watched my family flare out of control over what Kahuna and I had done.

To control the pain, I focused at our brown curtains and remembered an experience I'd had at thirteen with my grandmother. I pictured myself rolled in that curtain, trying to protect myself, when Grandmother had come after me with a knife. I wished at that moment I could wrap myself in the curtain and have Grandmother stab me. I wanted a refuge; I wanted my heart to stop aching. All along my grandmother had been a culprit, and now I was the culprit.

I didn't want my brother to talk with Kahuna. I didn't want Kahuna to hurt like I did.

35
MOVING ON

June 1982

Trust your instincts, and never let love be consumed by pride.

My heart beat simultaneously with the clock hanging on the wall directly above me while I sat on the telephone-chair desk. I peeked every few minutes to see if the hands had both reached the 12, and when they did, my heart pounded as if a drummer were inside my chest.

Not often did Kahuna and I call each other at midnight, but this was a special occasion. I was thrilled when he'd called me two days before, while his mother was out shopping, to arrange to talk at midnight. The moment the phone rang, I answered it.

"Hi, Kahuna. I was worried you wouldn't call me." I sprang up and looked down the hallway. "Just a second, Kahuna." I took the receiver away from my ear and listened. "I'm back. I wanted to check to make sure my parents or brother didn't wake up. I am so glad you called. I have missed you."

Kahuna cleared this throat before he spoke. "I have missed you."

I leaned back to rest my head against the wall. "I wish you weren't leaving. Why is your mother having you leave tomorrow and not in a month, like you had planned?"

"I guess she believes it will give me a fresh start, and I will have more options for a job."

Before I answered him, I rubbed my fingers over my eyes. "Well, I feel like it's too soon. I want to see you before you go. Where will you live when you get there?"

"I will stay with my uncle and aunt near the university campus, but it will be only until the dorms open in August. Hold on a second, Rose." His receiver dropped to the floor.

"That was a close one. My sister Mollie was in the kitchen getting a drink of water. I prayed as I hid behind the family-room wall that she wouldn't notice the long telephone cord stretched across the kitchen and into the family room. I'm glad she didn't hear the phone drop. I knew there was a reason for me to sit in the dark. I know she would have told on me. Well, I probably shouldn't stay on here long; I don't want to get in trouble. I know this is going to be a challenge for us to be apart and not able to talk daily on the phone. It's been difficult on me not to be able to call you these last three weeks, but my mom grounded me from communicating with you. Every day, I have had a desire to call you, and I'm glad that at least we can talk tonight. I am going to miss you."

My tears flowed as I spoke just loud enough for only me to hear. "I imagine you will have a wonderful time. I just hope you don't forget about me. Are you coming back before Dax leaves?"

I could hear him move the receiver closer to his mouth. "I don't think so; I won't have money for the trip."

I used my nightgown to wipe my tears. "I never dreamed you would leave." I couldn't say anything else.

"Rose, I'll be back. I'd better go and get some sleep. I have a little more packing to do."

I sniffled. "Remember always that I love and care about you."

"Rose, you can still be my girlfriend."

I squeezed my eyes tight to control my tears. "I would like that. I'm just afraid you will find someone better." He tapped something against the floor.

"I would never find someone better. Well, I need to go. I love you and always will. I'll send you a letter in a couple of days. Bye."

I looked at the clock before I spoke and believed my heart would stop the minute our conversation ended. "I love you, too. I'll wait for a letter. Goodbye."

He hung up, and I wasn't sure he'd heard me.

The next three days, I ate, slept, and showered, and on the fourth day after Kahuna left, I received my first letter from him. I sat on the front porch beneath the black mailbox, leaned against the house, and soaked up each word he'd written as if I were a dried-up flower that thirsted for water.

Dear Rose,

> *Thank you for the letter. Yours was the first and only letter I've received here. I can tell you how glad I was to get it. I'm still in love with you, Rose. I still don't relish the idea of going to one of the many activities where I might be expected to get involved with the girls. Any girl who might like me puts me on the offensive.*
>
> *I have a job, now. I'm starting at $3.50 an hour. Anything higher than minimum wage is rare here. Each day I try to learn something new, and I'm already ahead of some students.*
>
> *My bike is falling apart. I've called around, and I'm thinking of selling it and either buying a new bike or getting a car for the winter. Anyway, I want to save my money if I can.*

Something unpleasant happened this week. As I parked my bike in its usual place while I worked at the student government, I discovered that our church group was on campus for the youth conference. After a day of working in student government, I went outside and discovered Dax had recognized my bike and was waiting there for me. He was very forward and sarcastically blurted out, "Kahuna, don't leave!" when I left. Needless to say, he got very upset. I was even more disgusted when I found he'd found my uncle's phone number and called the house without leaving a name and asked my aunt not to tell me he'd called. I've been very worried about him since, and I realized he may still be here. His actions seem so devilish, it scares me. I won't tell you what else he pulled, and I don't trust him in the least bit. I can see he doesn't trust my feelings or patience in the least. I know he probably already told you his story.

I guess that's most of the news up here. I really appreciate your letters, and I hope you'll keep in touch. I truly hope you're happy. Some of the days are so hard, but it's what I expected, and it's something to build on. I do love you, Rose, just like family. Your heart is purer than anyone I know. When you say you love me, I know you mean it. You're true to your family and friends. The only one you're not true to might be yourself. But you can't help it.

Last night I was praying for you as usual, and I remembered how sick you sounded over the phone. I suddenly was overcome with a great deal of concern for your health.

Love Always, Kahuna

I folded his letter, and then opened the next letter.

Dearest Rose,

> *I can't help writing to you right now; I've been very worried about you and think of you often. I know you can't promise me anything, and I feel very badly about leaving when I did. Still, I feel I had to for both our sakes. The tensions are a bit heavier here, but it's for the best.*
>
> *Do you think you could write to me and let me know how you are? I would really appreciate it. I have bad memories too, and they haunt me—not ones that make me lustful, but ones that bring shame and unhappiness. We must learn to resolve our discouragements of that time and replace them with happy thoughts. Remember you're still very special and valuable.*
>
> *You have done so much for me, Rose, and all I give you is headaches. I hope you'll eventually forgive me for all I've done wrong, and I hope you can always be happy.*
>
> *No girl deserves the problems I've given you. You're a special young lady, and I'll always have a high regard for you. There were so many times that I slowed you down, halting our spiritual and social growth. I hope I never, ever hinder anybody as badly as I did you. It's my hope that you'll be able to grow freely now, without me there to get in the way. Take care of yourself, and please write if you'd like.*

Love always and forever, Kahuna

I slipped the paper in the envelope and then wiped the sweat off my forehead. He hadn't ". . . halted my growth. . . ." I was glad that he had come into my life four and half years ago. The mistakes we had made were made by both of us. I pushed my hands against the cement porch and stood facing our mailbox that had served its time holding letters meant for me. I retrieved the other envelopes out of the mailbox and placed them on the telephone chair before heading to my bedroom. Mom was in the kitchen when I walked past the entrance.

"Hey, Sweetie, do you want lunch?"

I stopped and went back to the entrance of the kitchen.

"Sure, but give me a minute. I need to put something away. Oh, the mail is on the telephone chair."

When I walked into the kitchen, Mom was seated at the table with a bag of raw potatoes.

I sat at the table and watched her peel the potatoes, and, for that moment, life seemed almost normal.

"Yummy, Mom. I love your delicious mashed potatoes."

My heart throbbed with tenderness as Mom rolled in her wheelchair. Her feet took turns pawing against the floor to move across the kitchen with her large bowl of potatoes. She reached for the faucet, but her arms were not long enough when she was sitting in the wheelchair, so she mustered the strength to stand to turn on the water. I was glad she'd remembered to put the brakes on, so her wheelchair wouldn't slip out from underneath her. When she pushed her hands against the armrest, did one section of her back hurt, or was it all over her body? With the way she sighed, it looked like a big ordeal of physical labor. Her body leaned against the counter as she swooshed her hand in the bowl.

She plopped down into the wheelchair, exhaling loudly, still holding the bowl. The next step seemed more physically challenging. She switched arms, holding the heavy bowl against her large midsection while she released each brake. She rolled, with the bowl of potatoes in her arms, for the same spot at the table.

Each movement Mom made sent waves of compassion for her toward me. Her battles of living with mental and physical illness had not only broken her spirit but had also caused pain. Her body flinched—I'm sure, due do the discs in her back breaking into more fragments. What a blessing that the doctor had ordered her a wheelchair less than a year ago. The wheelchair gave her freedom and less pain.

"Mom, would you like me to get the green pot for you?"

She looked up. "I would appreciate it if you would."

I searched in the cupboard for the green pot that had been my grandmother's favorite, but now it was my mother's favorite.

Mom seemed very grateful for the help, and I was pleased to lend a hand. I sensed my mother had something she wanted to say, so I asked her if something was bothering her.

I took a bite of raw potato slice.

"Have you received a letter from Kahuna since he left?" she said.

I wiggled in my chair. "I got a letter from him today; why do you ask?"

She used a great deal of force as she cut the potatoes. "Did he tell you he came over to visit me last Sunday?"

I had taken another bite of the raw potato—and about swallowed my mouthful without chewing it.

"Did you invite him over to the house? Where was I? Why didn't you tell me?"

Her eyes fixed on me, and she shook her knife. "Calm down, Honey. I wanted to ask him some questions regarding you two. I didn't want you to see him and get hurt any more than you already have."

I hit the table. "Mom, I would love to have seen him. I needed closure. What did you ask him, and why did you do this behind my back?"

She used more force as she cut the potato. "Well, he committed a man's act with you, and I had a right to question him."

I stood, looked down at her, and yelled, "How dare you talk to him without me? What did you ask him?"

"I asked him if he had plans to marry you, and if he was going to be a man and take responsibility for the act he'd committed with you. I told him he needed to grow up and treat you better. You know, Rose, he told me he wasn't a man and that he was just a boy. He told me he was going to college to fulfill all the goals he had set and that no one would stop him."

Perfect Rose Cracked Vase

Mom looked relieved to have him out of my life, as if she had done me the greatest favor.

I sat back down to digest what Mom had said. Why did he leave me to deal with the nightmare by myself? I lost my appetite and sensed an urge to scream at Mom. I couldn't deal much more with others, including my mother. At that moment, I understood why Romeo and Juliet wanted to die—because they already were dead when they had to part. My body was numb, and my soul was dying.

"Where was I when he came?"

She placed her hands together on the table.

"When I found out you were going to the young-adult devotional with Andrew, I had him come over after I knew you would be gone."

I walked over to her, hoping she would notice the tears streaming down my face.

"Mom, how could you do this to me, and why? I feel as if you made him leave me. You are the one who pushed him out of my life. I would have loved to see him. I *need* to see him."

She kept her hands on the table, and our eyes met.

"I had to do it, Rose. I had to find out if he really loved you. You know, he was so outraged when he left that, in his anger, he slammed the front door so forcefully that it cracked the living-room window."

I looked at her. "He loved me."

I left to see the living-room window. There it was, a crack that went from one corner to the other. My heart crumbled into a billion pieces. I darted to my bedroom. I was a cracked vase, and my relationship with Kahuna had likewise cracked. Mom hollered at me.

"Rose, please come here. We need to finish talking."

I couldn't go into the kitchen; I had to protest her action. I collapsed on my bed, which became my dark, deep hole. I examined my lamp and spoke to myself. "'Misery, Rejection' should be my real name."

Shadows of gloom swirled around me, and doubts grew as to whether he'd ever loved me, cared about me. Maybe he'd used me. I couldn't understand why Kahuna hadn't told me on the phone the night we talked.

No wonder, I thought, tossing my letter into the Liberty Box and sealing it with the lid. Neither my mom, nor my dad, my brothers, their wives, and Kahuna couldn't see me as an adult.

There was scurrying from the kitchen, the sound of a chair scraping against linoleum. I'd learned to adapt to comments about my deformed eyeball, but it was unbearable to think about trying to deal with the comments and stares because of what I'd done with Kahuna. It was a mistake that could have been avoided. Even though we'd gotten into this predicament together, I had to cope with the reactions from others alone, by myself.

I imprisoned myself in my room after Kahuna deserted me and forced myself to shower, eat, and clean the house. I was isolated in my world, and I was the only one living in it.

Time came and went, and my days and weeks had no significance to me, even when Mom knocked faintly on my bedroom door and spoke. "Rose, I would like you to come and see our visitors."

I staggered down the hallway and saw Kahuna's aunt Alana (ah-lah-nah) and his cousin, Taiana. I wiped my eyes with the bottom of my shirt and lifted my head. I greeted them with a forced smile.

I was three feet from Taiana, trying to evaluate her reason for coming.

"Hi. We came over to visit with you and your mother."

Kahuna's aunt sat on our white couch, the one where Kahuna and I had kissed, and Taiana sat next to her. Mom was in her wheelchair, and I stood.

Kahuna's aunt looked at my mother. "What happened between Kahuna and Rose? My sister won't tell me but heard it was serious. Did Rose get a pregnancy test?"

My mother rolled closer to her and looked at me with eyes of deep concern. Then she looked over at Kahuna's aunt. My chest burned as I listened to them struggle through halting sentences and stiff smiles. Did my face turn several shades of red? I recognized an expression often seen in Kahuna's mom's face in his aunt's face that gave me a clammy, cold feeling in my heart. I wanted to leave, but at the same time, the bitter pain of letting the secret out thrilled me. Mom pulled my hand. I bent down, my ear closer to her mouth.

"Rose, I want you and Taiana to go to your bedroom."

Kahuna's cousin gave me a half smile. She motioned with her head toward our hallway.

Taiana sat on the edge of my bed and talked about her summer plans. I sat next to her and rested my back against the wall. Taiana crossed her legs, with her back straight, and I envisioned a book balanced on her head. She looked wholesome, both physically and mentally, like I wanted to be.

Did she think less of me, as if I were a simple catch with any guy? Did she know I loved Kahuna? Did she know how much I wanted her to be my friend? Did she know Kahuna's letters lived underneath my bed in the Liberty Box? Each time she talked, I bit my tongue. The continuous cool air from the evaporative cooler brought a pleasant, rhythmic sound, a resonance I'd hear each summer as the temperatures soared into the hundreds. It helped lessen the strain of tension.

A knock on my door brought reprieve from my nervousness and broke the anxiety. I envied her perfectness that had no imperfection; even the beauty of her face was flawless. Her dark, wavy hair complemented her Polynesian face and tiny nose. I loved her ruby-red lips, with the firmness and sweetness they had.

Taiana stood and smiled. "See you later, Rose. It's been good to talk with you."

I moved myself to the edge of my bed and stood to give her a hug. "Thanks, Taiana, for visiting with me."

I endured three weeks of endless crying myself to sleep after Taiana and her mother visited. Kahuna's letters came, but they were excruciating to read. Kahuna had moved on; even though he stated he loved me, it didn't relieve the ache. Dax called often, and his questions—"How's Kahuna?" "Have you heard from him?"—pierced my heart. I wanted to tell Dax the truth, but I knew it would demolish the excellent image that Dax had of Kahuna.

I rested in bed and thought how "hope" was no longer part of my vocabulary. Food became no source of comfort, and water was an afterthought. Tenderness formed in my heart. Every thought of Kahuna was unbearable. I sank into despair. All this was due to the mistake of getting too physically close to Kahuna and for loving him.

36
MOM'S WONDERFUL TRICK

July 1982

**My faith was seeing light with my heart,
even when my eye saw only darkness.**

When Mom visited my room, I glared at her as her words traveled in the air but never registered. This time, she rolled to the edge of my bed.

"Rose, Dad has made lunch. Would you like to come eat with us?"

"No, Mom. I can't eat."

"Honey, you haven't eaten in days, and you really need to."

If anyone understood my depression, it was Mom. She lived with it, and I had watched her muddle through with the pain, but she never went without eating. Food was her way to cover the anguish. Mine was to live without it. I couldn't decide which was better—to overeat or go without.

I raised my hand. "Mom, I'm not hungry."

Mom patted my leg. "Rose, I made an appointment for you to see the doctor today. You need to be seen because you haven't eaten or gotten out of bed for days."

"Mom, I don't need to see a doctor."

I watched her rub her upper arms, creating a soothing sound. She wheeled closer to the head of my bed.

"I'm going to eat with Dad. We would love for you to eat with us."

I sat in my bed. "I'll consider it, Mom."

Her feet touched the floor one step at a time while she moved along in her chair. The weight of her body pushed the sides of the chair outward and rubbed against the wheels. Once she got to my door, she spoke.

"Well, there is enough food for you, too."

Silence filled the air, and my bedroom door closed.

I focused on a book on my nightstand called *Self-esteem for Women* that Lillie had given me a couple of weeks ago. Lillie was a dear lady who'd attended my church. She was assigned to visit my mother once a month, and in her doing so, I got to know her. I felt a need to read the note she'd written in the book.

Rose,

I love you for who you are, and I feel that you have the power within you to accomplish your desires. The Lord has blessed you with talents, gifts, and trials that no other woman can claim as her own. You have the power within you to reach your greatest potential.

Love, Eternal friend, Lillie

What potential do I have? No words of encouragement could erase the past mistakes I had made.

I rested on my bed; sleep took over, and hours passed.

I awoke to the sound of Mom's squeaky wheelchair.

"Rose, we need to leave for the doctor. Do you want to take a bath?"

"Yes, I do, Mom."

She lifted her hand. "Then you need to get out of bed."

I submerged myself in the warm water and used my legs to turn the water off and on. After soaking, my fingers were like dried prunes, yet, I didn't feel any cleaner. No bar of soap—not even my favorite type—could erase the dirt that lingered in me from the awful act I had committed with Kahuna.

I rubbed my flat tummy, remembering how I could have been pregnant. I wept as I reached through the cloud of steam for my stiff towel that had dried out on the umbrella clothesline. I wrapped the scratchy towel around me and discreetly walked to my room. I dressed and brushed my hair into a ponytail.

Mom said from the other side of my door, "Are you ready to go, Rose?"

"I guess so; just a minute."

I opened my Liberty Box of letters filled with his thoughts, wishes, and dreams that had stolen my heart. Each letter was a puzzle piece, and I hoped more pieces would fill my box. In time, my Liberty Box would hold a complete, broad, beautiful picture. I pulled an envelope out of the pile and gave it freedom to speak to me.

> *Dearest Rose,*
>
> *How have you been lately? I've still been thinking about you quite often. Yesterday, I took out your picture, and I got a strange feeling, of belonging, as if you belonged in my life. It makes me wonder how much happier things would have been if I'd done things right from the start.*
>
> *I've enjoyed the weekend and seen some of my cousins. They are nice to be around.*
>
> *I've still been feeling the pressure, too. It's like having a headache all day, but trying to function anyway. Sometimes it gets lonely, too, with no one my age to associate with. In some ways, I wish you were here, but I know you can't be. I still miss you.*
>
> *Love always, Kahuna*

His words sheltered me from my storms of trouble. Priceless words God knew I needed. Letters that mended my broken heart from the life

I hated. I dug deep inside my soul, put the lid on my treasure of letters, and pushed the brown box under my bed. I listened as the box slid on the linoleum tile and hit the wall.

I stood from kneeling and had an urge to pray, but I didn't. I grabbed my purse, and, as I walked past the kitchen entrance, my sister-in-law waved goodbye. Outside, a wave of heat circled around me as if I had been thrown into an oven.

Mom and Dad rolled their windows down, inviting the summer air into the car while Dad drove down McDowell Road. My ponytail danced in the wind and several times blocked my good eye, but the warm air dried my hair. The constant gust of air made it impossible to hear my parents. Instead, I reminisced about places I had been with Dax and Kahuna, but the memory of driving down this road with Kahuna and his mom for the pregnancy test made those blissful memories evaporate.

Dad drove to a large, white building. My emotions were so torn from the memories of Kahuna and Dax, I hadn't paid attention to where we were going. I glanced at the building. "Mom, this isn't the doctor's office."

Mom rolled up her window. "They have moved here."

"Oh, really?"

I opened the car door, slung my purse over my shoulder, and closed the door. I stood next to the car and watched Dad lift Mom's brown wheelchair out of the trunk. Mom opened the passenger-side door and swung her legs out.

"Honey, hurry! It's hot."

"Give me a minute. I need to latch the feet on your wheelchair."

I recognized Dad's irritation with Mom, and it seemed he worked even slower as he pulled her wheelchair out of the trunk. Poor, overworked Dad. Mom had anchored a trial in his life, of hauling her wheelchair in and out of the trunk. Dad looked physically exhausted as the sweat dripped down his face. I noticed as he pushed the wheelchair over to Mom, he moved as if he had all the time in the world. He locked the brakes, put her purse on the back handles, and stood tall, stretched his back, and groaned.

"Can you get the cushion, please?"

Dad limped to the trunk, pulled the cushion out, and slowly returned and placed the cushion on the wheelchair seat. He straightened, sighed, and walked back to close the trunk. This wasn't the first time I'd observed this routine.

It took the force of his body to push Mom up the ramp. He walked at the speed of a turtle, while Mom wanted to be as fast as a rabbit.

"It's hot. Can't you push faster?"

He grumbled, pulled his head back, and pushed slower. I followed and observed each step my father took. His toes pushed against the sidewalk to give him leverage to move her forward. I sensed Dad didn't seem pleased about where we were headed.

I dragged behind my parents through sliding electric doors and noticed it wasn't the doctor's office. It didn't even smell like a doctor's office; it had a weird odor, like the kitchen cleaner my mom used to clean the countertops. A woman walked past me, talking to herself. I stared at the glass wall on the other side of the main entrance filled with people. Doctors' offices had fish aquariums, and this place had an aquarium of people displayed for others to gawk at.

A lady dressed in hospital scrubs tapped my shoulder and spoke. "Step over here, Rose." She read a clipboard with my birthday, address, and full name on it.

I was baffled that my parents didn't stop her from talking to me.

"You need to take off your jewelry, watch, and ponytail holder. Do you have any safety pins on your clothing?"

I answered her, and I stared at Dad, who had his fingers deep in the crown of his head. I knew then that he didn't agree with Mom.

My anger was rising. "No, I don't."

Mom talked with a receptionist, and I tried to figure out what they were saying, but the nurse waved her hand in front of my face. "Rose, do you hear me? I need you to give me your purse and hold your hands in the air."

A chill went down my back as this woman knelt and rubbed her hands up and down my legs, and she didn't stop at my thighs. She then proceeded to rub my back and chest area. I wanted to scream, "I'm not a criminal, and get your hands off me!" but I sensed that would be wrong.

I hollered, "Mom, where are we?"

She wheeled closer. "Rose, Dad and I believed you needed some help, so we brought you to Camelback Mental Hospital."

My eyes watered. I glared at Mom. "How could you deceive me? You lied to me."

"We knew you needed help."

Dad didn't speak a word, and I looked in his direction, but he didn't look back.

I stomped closer to my mother. "How could you do this to me?"

Mom folded some papers in half and rubbed the crease again and again. "Rose, you need to stay and get help."

The nurse who touched my entire body looked at my mother with a firm face, like a baboon ready to attack. "Papers have been signed, and you are free to leave now."

I spoke with determination and fear. "Mom, you can't leave me."

Father was still digging at his head as they left. I knew he wanted to hug me and was disappointed with Mom.

Mom smiled, and then her face went still. "I need to leave; you'll be fine here. Later, Dad and I will bring some clothes for you."

The nurse stopped Mom as she pushed herself toward the door and handed her my purse.

"Oh, Rose won't be able to have any items until after the twenty-four-hour suicide watch. We will call you when those twenty-four hours are done."

I cupped my hands around my mouth and yelled, "Mom, please. I beg you—don't leave me here."

I squeezed my upper arms and watched my mother leave through the double doors. The nurse touched my shoulder.

"Come this way."

I knew I wasn't mentally ill. I knew I wasn't suicidal. I knew I needed to watch each movement I made—one unethical behavior, and they would label me "psychotic." I followed her down the well-lit hallway that had white floors. I turned my head toward each vacant room we passed. At the end of the hallway, on the left side, was a scale.

The nurse tapped the scale. "Take your flip-flops off, and let's get your weight. So, how long have you wanted to kill yourself?"

It was a question often asked of my mother but never to me.

I moved back. "I don't want to stand on that scale, and I don't want to be here."

She cradled her hand on my shoulder. "You must be weighed."

As always, I gave in and stood on the scale without saying a word.

"One hundred pounds. Now let's see how tall you are."

She pulled out the ruler attached to the back of the scale and placed the L-shaped part on my head.

"You are five feet, four inches."

"Why do you have to weigh me?"

While she wrote, she spoke as if she owned the world. "Just in case the doctor prescribes medication for you. He needs your weight and height for accurate dosage."

I stepped off the scale. "I don't think medication will help."

She moved toward a door and gestured for me to enter. "Come in here. This is your room for the night."

I stepped into a cave. Even with its bright white walls, my new cavern was dark. Did the sun's warmth ever visit? A white blanket and sheet dressed the hospital bed that had an empty nightstand next to it.

The nurse opened the door next to the entrance. "You have your own restroom. Shower times are posted on the back of the bathroom door. We will need someone to sit in the room while you shower."

This empty world surrounded me. A fire inside me flared, and I was engulfed by angry thoughts centered on my mom.

The nurse flowed over to the window, which was fixed firmly shut with long, strong screws. "Dinner will be in about an hour. You can either stay in here or wander around the halls until it is time for dinner. We meet in the front entrance, so we can walk as a group to the dining hall. Do you have any questions?"

I sat on the edge of the bed, focusing on the wall behind her. "No."

As she walked to exit my cave, she spoke with a softer tone. "My name is Holland; if you need anything, let me know."

The nurse left, and I glanced out the door while I sat on the firm bed. I knew that, this time, Kahuna and Dax would not be able to comfort me like when I had *Guillain Barre* Syndrome. Was Kahuna dating pretty ladies? Did he even think about me? My head drooped at the thought that there would be no Kahuna, no Dax, no phone, no pictures, and no possessions of mine on the nightstand. Again, I had been put in a displacement I experienced with my past foster-home visits. But, in this unusual abandonment by Kahuna, Dax, and now my parents, sorrow pierced my soul. Rejection was just one negativity that lingered. I was not just physically alone—I was mentally alone.

The sound of footsteps grew potent with each second. A different nurse in bright orange scrubs and long brown hair stood at the doorway.

"Rose, it's time for dinner. Could you come with me?"

When I entered, it seemed lifeless, even though it was full of strange people. Tears formed, and fear followed. I did not desire to step farther into the cafeteria, but I had to go through the line to receive food. A young man, about twenty, stood behind the counter and served. I stared at his white-and-blue college football jersey. I froze, unsure of how to cope with the fact he attended the same university Kahuna had escaped to. I sat by myself and tried to hold back the tears, but they continued to pour out.

A lady at the next table constantly picked at her facial sores. I ate and made a break for the exit.

I dashed out into the hallway and rested against the wall, trying to remember the way back to my room. A nurse helped me. When I entered my room, I rested on a stiff white pillow that I covered with tears. I talked to the moon showing its face in the window. I hoped the moon would relay a message to Kahuna that I loved him. I was mesmerized by the stars that dressed the sky, stars that danced freely. Before I drifted off to sleep, I wished on the brightest star that Kahuna still loved me.

I awoke to a bleak speck of sun and rolled my body out of bed to use the restroom. With each stroke of the toothbrush against my teeth, I prayed for someone to rescue me. I brushed my hair with the bargain-basement style brush they had provided. I splashed water on my face to remove the tears that I'd shed the night before. I shut the bathroom door and leisurely walked back to the bed. I waited for what seemed hours for the nurse to appear. I stared out the doorway into the vacant hallway. I closed my eyes, and words welled through my lips.

Heavenly Father, please help me cope. Please give me strength to pull through this. I'm trapped in a well and unable to pull myself out. Lower a rope to pull me up. Please let the doctors see I'm not suicidal. Know, Heavenly Father, that my mother is the one that thought I was suicidal, not me. Never would I destroy something you created.

Peace entered, with reassurance that I would leave this place. I tried to pull the bitterness toward my mother out of me, but the anger that stirred with each moment that passed made it hard.

When I opened my eyes, a nurse was at the door, smiling.

"You're moving to another room and will have a roommate. Come."

"You missed breakfast, but lunch will be served in fifteen minutes. So, once I show you your room, you can go eat."

The room looked like a four-star hotel room, with a southwestern lamp resting on a nightstand sandwiched between two twin beds. A woman with brown, shoulder-length hair was seated on her bed; gum wrappers covered her bed, along with a gum-wrapper chain. I sighed with relief when I was given the bed closest to the door.

The nurse looked at my new roommate. "Margo, this is your new roommate, Rose."

Margo glared and went back to her gum wrappers. "Hi, Rose."

The nurse opened the door. "I think you'll be happier in this room."

"I hope so."

Right after the nurse left, I sat on the edge of the bed and watched my roommate work her hundred-plus-piece-long gum-wrapper chain. I touched the phone on the nightstand and thought of hearing Kahuna's voice on the other end of the line.

My roommate kept her head down while she explained the schedule and the therapy groups we were to attend. I wasn't getting it. I wasn't feeling the thrill of excitement she demonstrated. Each activity she rattled on about made me desperately want to leave.

I stood near the door and focused on Margo connecting the wrappers. "How long have you been working on that chain?"

Margo's cold demeanor thawed before she gave me a glimpse of eye contact. She rubbed part of the chain. "Oh, since I first arrived here. It's easy to make, if you want me to show you how."

I stared at the chain and said nothing, but I listened to her.

"All you do is . . ."—she opened the chewing-gum wrapper—"make sure to use printed wrappers because they make interesting chains."

She creased the middle and tore it in half along the length. Then she wet the crease with her tongue. "This helps it when I wet it, but it's not necessary."

Then she folded the wrapper in half lengthwise, opened and folded the edge of the wrapper in, toward the center fold line, and then held it for me to look at.

"See how it's coming together?"

She went on in detail, explaining the next fold. After those long-winded instructions, I interrupted her. "Excuse me. I need to use the restroom."

She chattered while I was in the restroom and when I left the bathroom. "Margo, I'm hungry, and I'm going to the dining hall."

She continued to fold her gum wrappers. "Okay. Enjoy your lunch."

I entered the dining hall and was face to face with the young man who had worn the university shirt in the food line the day before. Lunch was good, but not as tasty as my hot dog on a fork cooked over a gas burner.

I returned to my room and brushed my teeth. Then Margo informed me we had a therapy session to attend in the main room of the building. I cringed at the thought of sitting by unstable people, like when I visited my mother in the state hospital. I held my head high when I entered the room. I gazed around; I tried to decide who looked normal and wouldn't go crazy. Margo came in right behind me and took a seat before I could decide.

The counselor walked around, outside of the circle. I sat between an old man and a girl a few years older than me.

"Let those who are new to the group introduce themselves," the counselor said and pointed at me.

"Why don't we start with you with the red shirt on?"

I touched my chest. "My name is Rose."

The counselor then pointed to a woman on the other side of the circle. Once she said her name, the counselor sat in the last empty chair. Everyone stared at him as if they were the animals and he was the circus ringmaster. "I hope I can help each of you, through these group therapies, learn to prevent chronic stress while promoting relaxation. Would any of you like to say how your day has gone?"

A hospital-gowned gentleman in his late sixties spoke with tears in his eyes.

"I have never had to ask anybody for anything, and now—" his throat moved like a ball was stuck in his neck— "I'm, umm, old, and I can't get to the bathroom on time."

He dropped his head and sobbed. "My family has their own life, and I don't want to be a burden on them."

He took his glasses off, folded them, and held them in his hand. "I guess I have to drag alongside them and try to be flexible that way."

He rubbed his bald head and spoke. "I don't know. I'm confused. I don't even know what my body is telling me—if the pain I feel is something to worry about or not. I'm uncertain about what is going to happen next." Tears began to stream down his face as he continued to speak.

"I used to be a guy who helped others all the time. My satisfaction would be in helping others. Now I'm at a hollow door. I opened it, and there is nothing out there."

The counselor crossed his legs and focused on this man. "I am happy with what you shared. I hope you will be able to continue to share your struggles with us." Then the counselor uncrossed his legs and looked around. "Does anyone else have anything they would like to say?"

I had to be the youngest person in the circle and the only one who didn't want to be there.

As I was leaving the room, a nurse approached me with a brown paper bag. "Here are some clothes your parents dropped off for you."

When I got to my room, I opened the bag and saw pants and shirts. No bra.

I rested on the bed. *How am I going to escape from this mental jail that I have spent three miserable days in with yucky food and down-in-the-dumps group sessions that were a waste of time?* I closed my eyes and dreamed someone would save me. I jumped when the phone rang.

Margo lifted the receiver. "Hello."

She stared at me and held out the receiver. "It's for you."

"Really, the phone is for me?" I took the receiver and sat on the floor.

"Hello, Rose. This is Lillie."

"Hi, Lillie. You don't know how good it is to hear your voice."

"Rose, I don't think you belong in a mental hospital. Would you like me to come get you?"

I wrapped my arm around my knees and held back my tears. "I would love that, Lillie, but what about my mom?"

Tension stirred in me, thinking of Mom.

"Don't worry about your mom. Let's get you out of there."

I looked at Margo, who was listening in on my conversation. I searched for a piece of paper and pen but couldn't find one. The only thing on the nightstand was a Bible. So, I had to remember what Lillie was about to say.

"What do I need to do to get out of here?"

"You are eighteen and are legally able to sign yourself out. You need to speak with the head counselor at the hospital and tell him you want to be discharged. They will give you papers to fill out and sign. Then you will be free to go."

I stood next to the nightstand, and my legs wobbled more than even after a long run. My hand trembled while I held the phone to my ear.

Somewhere inside of me, I needed to find the courage to follow through with what Lillie said.

"Lillie, will you come get me?"

I could hear her little boy in the background.

"Yes, just call me when you can leave. We can meet in the lobby."

"Thanks so much for the help."

"No problem, Rose."

Those three words let me know that God had indeed heard my prayer three days ago.

I grabbed my paper bag and walked over to the head office.

I approached the secretary's desk. "Hi, my name is Rose, and I would like to speak to the head counselor about leaving."

The secretary stood. "Wait right here."

I moved closer to the counter. "Okay, I'll wait."

Minutes later, a man came toward me. "Hi. Are you Rose?"

I held out my right hand to greet him. "Yes."

He gave me a firm handshake. "Well, then follow me."

We walked down a long, narrow hallway.

He stood at the doorway with his hair in a ponytail and motioned. "Step in and have a seat." I sat on a maroon leathered chair and placed my bag near my feet. Unique as he was, with the name "Freddie Willpie" on his desk made me wonder, *Would he help me?*

He leaned back in his seat and placed his hands behind his head. "Why do you want to leave?"

I folded my arms. "I don't belong here. I want be discharged today."

He spread his fingers out on the desk. "Are you suicidal?"

I raised my hands above my shoulders. "Why is everyone accusing me of being suicidal? No, I never was suicidal, and I never will be. It's just my boyfriend dumped me after a five-year relationship."

I locked my hands in my lap and looked at him. "Haven't you ever had your heart broken?"

He picked up the papers in front of him and pointed to some words. "Why does it say on your paperwork that you are suicidal?"

I pushed my hands against the chair to lift my bottom off the seat and then sat down.

"I told you. My mother exaggerates. Those are my mother's words, not mine. If I were suicidal, I would have taken my life weeks ago."

He rolled his chair closer to his desk, and then he bent forward, as if he were going to tell me a secret.

"Can you seek help outside of here to deal with the breakup?"

I moved to the edge of the seat. "I'm sure I can."

He spun in his chair and bent toward me a second time; I got a whiff of his cologne.

"I'll get the paperwork, and you can leave today, if you promise to get help."

I crossed my legs. "If it means I can leave, I will get help."

He wrote on a paper and spoke. "Do you have items in the room you need to get?"

"No." I leaned back in my chair.

"Then have a seat in the lobby, and we'll call you when the papers are ready."

He stood, pushed his chair in, and walked over to the door. He motioned for me to walk out.

After I called Lillie, I sat on a cold metal chair near the reception desk. I held tight to the brown paper bag and went over in my mind the best way to greet my mother. *Should I be angry? Should I be sad? Should I be polite and beg for mercy so she'll let me stay? Will she believe I'm not suicidal?*

Freddie Willpie walked toward me and broke my meditation. I stood as he approached me.

"Rose, here are your discharge papers, and I included a list of counselors located near your home. Please get help with how to cope with what you have been through."

I dropped my brown paper bag on the chair and took the papers. "Thanks, Mr. Willpie, for helping me."

His smile showed a mouthful of teeth and a dimple on his cheek. "You are certainly welcome. Is someone coming to get you?"

"Yes. I called right after I left your office for a ride. She should be here soon."

He slipped his hand in his pocket. "Take care, and if your ride doesn't show in the next hour, let me know."

"I will. Thanks again for your help."

He took several steps back before he pulled his hand out of his pocket and waved it a little. "No problem."

I turned each time the electric door opened and hoped it would be Lillie. When she walked in, with her short, brown, wavy hair and affectionate smile, peace came with her.

Lillie's car was a warm welcome, not because of the summer heat but the comfort of knowing this nightmare was over. When Lillie drove out of the parking lot, Kahuna's and my favorite song came on the radio: "Wishing on a Star." I needed more than one star to have my life the way it was months ago. I focused on the words as I held my brown bag. The warmth of the sun penetrating through the window was welcome after I'd been stuck inside for three days.

Lillie came to a stoplight and touched my arm. "Did you call your mother to let her know you were coming home?"

I waited until the light turned green before I responded.

"No, Lillie. I haven't. I wanted to surprise her."

Lillie was fashionable, and I loved her response. "Yeah, I think you are right. Give her a surprise that will last a lifetime. How are you? I heard the breakup with Kahuna has been difficult. Do you miss him?"

My emotions wanted to burst. "Umm, I do miss him and wish we were together, like years ago."

Lillie looked at me while we were sitting at another red light and patted my hand. "Years from now, you will look back on this whole situation and see how it has helped you grow."

I studied her profile and spoke firmly. "I sure hope so."

Lillie turned the volume on the radio up and began to sing along with Elton John, a song called "Sorry Seems to Be the Hardest Word." I listened as she sang along, and, even though it had never been a favorite song of mine, some lyrics spoke to my heart. One part that got me was, *"What do*

I have to do to make you love me?/ What do I have to do to make you care?/ Why can't we talk it over?"

My relationship with Kahuna was like broken glass. If you touched it, it could cut you. Better to throw it out than try to glue it back together. But I wanted to try, even though I knew I could get hurt.

My home looked no different than it had three days before, only this time it seemed vacant, even from the outside. Lillie pulled into the driveway behind my parents' car.

"Do you want me to come in with you?"

I squeezed her arm. "I think I will be okay. I appreciate all you have done for me." The moment I opened the car door, heat intruded in.

"I will call you later to see how you are. Please promise me that, if you need anything, you will call me."

I bent so I could see her after getting out of the car. "I will; thanks a million for the support."

I swallowed to relieve the frog in my throat before opening the front door. The moment I turned the doorknob, my dog Minnie barked.

Dad shouted from the bedroom. "Who is it?"

I took small steps and decided, with the frog still stuck in my throat, I'd wait until I reached their room.

Mom jumped out of her bed. "How did you get home?"

I leaned against the doorframe and dropped my bag on the floor. "I got a ride from Lillie. Are you not happy to see me?"

Dad smiled. "Oh, Rose, I have missed you."

Dad walked over to me and gave a long-awaited hug.

I picked up my bag. "I think I'll take a shower, if that is OK with you."

Dad tilted his head and smiled. "Sure, Honey."

Mom chimed in. "When you're done with your shower, Dad and I want to talk to you."

I smiled. "Sure, Mom."

37
TATTERED BAG—TATTERED HEART
July 1982

Never underestimate the power of prayer,
because it will carry you through.

I dropped the tattered brown paper bag on the desk and collapsed on my bed, relieved to be out of the mental institution. I studied the tattered brown bag and recalled the many brown bags I had used at foster homes. None had deteriorated that badly; my soul was just as tattered. Unbelievable. Both were once smooth, strong, and new. The bag contains items, I contain burdens . . . some thrust upon me and some by choice. This baggage consumed me. I wished to be a bag and flip upside down and let it out, but it wasn't possible. I decided the next best thing would be a shower.

After my shower, I dropped my dirty clothes in the white plastic laundry basket that Kahuna had given me on my seventeenth birthday, another reminder of him.

In the kitchen, my parents were sitting around the table. Dad was comfortable with a bowl of Cracked Wheat, and mom had her usual—a peanut-butter-and-jelly sandwich. I sat near my mother across the table from my father. Both had red, swollen eyes. I focused on the refrigerator, to avoid eye contact with my mother, and waited for my parents to speak.

Yet, when Mom did speak, my thoughts were of Kahuna.

One sentence hit hard: "Rose, Kahuna doesn't love you."

Could she be right?

At that moment I wanted the house to crumble and end the pain. I prayed Dad would take my side, but he didn't. Mom gazed at me with tenderness, sadness, and love. I wanted to respond to her, but words wouldn't come. I sighed and internalized that sentence, *"Rose, Kahuna doesn't love you."* I felt that each word she spoke separated me from my mom. Mom rolled near me, and her eyes met mine. "Do you think Kahuna loves you? Do you think he cares about your feelings? Do you think he will ever return to be with you again?" She lowered her head and rolled her wheelchair out of the room.

Dad's blue eyes looked in my direction with no words attached. I realized then that I hadn't responded to Mom's questions. I hurt her, but I couldn't answer her. Dad left me alone.

I sat on the yellow dining-room chair and pondered. My life, a disaster, spiraled into a dark hole and crumbled. I had memories of Dax and me munching on fresh pineapple wrapped in ham and watching Kahuna slap dance in his sarong at a family Luau. To even think about Kahuna dancing made my heart pulsate faster. Kahuna abandoned me and shattered my life. His rejection hit me harder than living in foster homes and being shipped to one house with Bobby and then separated from Bobby to another. I felt like a piece of furniture, mismatched with any home décor.

The slow-cooker contained a yummy dinner that I couldn't smell. The swamp cooler pushed a cool breeze through the vents that I could not feel. I was numb. Kahuna's meaningless letters still came in my black mailbox—words I could not hold on to or digest. How could I make it without Kahuna and Dax in my life? I hungered to have them near, feel the breeze of their words, and treasure their wisdom. Why did my two best friends discard me?

38
Letter of Love

August 1982

Mothers nurture with love,
even when their hearts are broken, too.

Summer should have picnics in the park, late-night strolls through the neighborhood, and dates that you wished would never end. For me, there were no picnics, walks, or dates ending with a goodnight kiss. It was a summer of a long, drawn-out nightmare, not one I hoped to relive or one I would wish upon my worst enemy.

My heart ached every second, minute, and hour of each day as Kahuna continued to alienate me from his new world. Kahuna's letters came, and I read them, but emptiness was all that filled those pages. One letter I received a week after I'd returned home from the mental hospital was from my mother, who had placed it on my pillow while I was in the shower.

Dearest Rose,

I went into your room at 4:00 a.m. this morning. You were asleep on your stomach; there you lay as sweet and innocent as a little child. I longed to brush the hair from your face and touch you. I was afraid you would wake up. I looked at you and felt all the love a mother can feel for her daughter. You are my daughter. The little life I carried for 9 months, gave birth to, and fed at my side. I'm so happy you survived through the rubella-German measles. You will someday know the joy of a child of your own.

I know you feel I have let you down by not talking with you. I do think you do miss Kahuna and the long talks you two had. I wish I could take his place and fill the emptiness you feel. I can't. I know you miss him and the loss is so painful. In time the emptiness will be filled and, although you will never forget your times with Kahuna, it will become less painful.

So many times, you became angry with me when we talked, and you would say, "I don't want to talk about it." I felt frustrated and at a loss, so I guess I just walked away. Next week you will be getting back into school. It will help to be with other friends and be busy. It has been a hard summer stuck here day after day. I hope you understand someday why I put you in the hospital.

If we had a car, or if I was not so sick, we could have taken the bus around. It will get cooler, school will start, and with the holidays time will pass more quickly. I know Kahuna will be here this Christmas. Then you can see him.

I want to help you learn to drive. You said your friend Zane was taking you Tuesday for your learner's permit. How exciting! Let's really study so you can pass. If you could drive, it would be nice for all of us.

Today let's try to get some cleaning done. I know you don't feel really good. I don't too much myself. If we could just get the dishes done up and clean the floor and vacuum, it would make me feel better. If you can just mop the floor, I would appreciate it.

Saturday, I would like you and me to go shopping together. We can look for school clothes and maybe we can go out to eat. I saw something advertised in the paper at Skaggs that you might like. It's a surprise. Okay?

I love you dear Rose, my daughter. I want you to have my wedding rings when I die. You can give them to your daughter. I don't have much in the way of material things to leave you or give you. I do have much love, deep and bursting, for you. No one could love a daughter more. If you think giving them a car or beautiful presents proves love, that is wrong. Yes, we show love by giving material things, but real love comes from within.

I know you came into my room last night to ask me if I was asleep. I was asleep and woke up when you came in. How I wanted to get up and come to you. I was just too tired. My days are so full with so many things to think about, worry about, and take care of. I am exhausted at night. Forgive me for not getting up. I still love you. No one can ever take your place within my heart.

I am getting hungry so I guess I will go to the kitchen and eat!! That's all I seem to do!

Have a Happy Day!!!

Love, Mom

Stillness settled in my heart because of the loved-filled words she'd written. I crawled underneath my bed and reached for my Liberty Box. Moving around in the darkness under my bed stirred thoughts of how Kahuna's letters were distinct-size hooks connected to a fishing line that reeled me in toward him. Each letter scarred, ripped, and damaged me from the inside out.

Laughter from my brother and his wife stretched across the hallway. I was a tad jealous of my sister-in-law, who was a month older than me and had everything I wanted. I stared at my box—the only connection to Kahuna. My brother's wife could have a relationship with the one she loved. I, on the other hand, was like Juliet—unable to love. My brother, who I missed while he was away, had changed in ways I couldn't describe or come close to understanding. I missed him, but I knew how much his wife loved him. He adored her, cherished her and gave her the attention the same way I wanted Kahuna to give me.

I covered my ears and prayed God would find it in his heart to ease the memories of that horrific mental institution. That place held people who had no desire to live—people like my mother, who struggled to survive. Poor mother lived a life of back pain, stomach upset, or problems with mental illness.

Mom's mental illness built a wall between us, a wall that taught me how to leave her alone. Never was it feasible for me to share my personal problems, even though I wanted to last night when I entered her bedroom to talk.

I placed mom's letter in my Liberty Box, and I thought of how Mom's letter was filled with more warmth than any I had received from Kahuna. I loved her letter, but I knew the words she had written about going shopping would never be fulfilled. Kahuna's letters were filled with empty promises, too. Mother is not capable of being the mother I dreamed of, but at least she chose to keep me and raise me herself rather than putting me in an institution to rot away.

A month after the mental-hospital experience, life took a turn. I was given a different view of life when I witnessed Dax at the church pulpit, in his crisp black suit. He stood tall, with no flaws or noticeable signs of rejection from Kahuna. As Dax spoke, my thoughts turned to memories of the three of us together. My empty arms craved to embrace him, and, once the meeting finished, I greeted him with a smile. Words filled with denial escaped my lips and the words of rejection, anguish, and loss couldn't be freed. Not even to my dear friend Dax, whom I had grown to love as much as I loved Kahuna.

Dax was gone, school had started, and the contention between Mom and me elevated higher than the Empire State Building.

I guess it was Mom's inabilities, more than anything else, that made me accept Kahuna's mom's invitation to stay at their home when school started. I had no idea why his mother offered, but I needed time away from Mother. Now, sleeping in Kahuna's bed, I sniffed in the faint smell of his cologne that lingered on his pillow. I stared at the desk that was built into the wall, a desk that had served its purpose by offering a solid surface for Kahuna to write me letters.

Thinking about the letters made me think of home and the negative feelings I had when I left. Mom's focus was on my brothers and on my brother's wives. Bobby's wife always seemed more important to my mother than me. At least that is what I accepted as true. She wasn't a cracked vase like me.

Kahuna's sisters Mollie and Susie's beds were lined up parallel to mine like I would imagine them to be in an orphanage. But Kahuna's home was nothing like an orphanage. Kahuna's mom's words drilled deeper into my head—things I knew she meant for me to hear. "Kahuna has new friends." I clenched my teeth to keep from responding to her at the dinner table.

With those thoughts returning that morning, I rubbed my hands and bowed my head. *"Please, Heavenly Father, don't let me feel like garbage."* When I finished my prayer, I opened my eyes and stared at the ceiling. Kahuna had to have stared at it many times over the years. Why did Kahuna's mom let me stay at their house? Was it guilt for what her son had done? Maybe she pitied me; maybe it was her way of correcting her son's mistake.

Why am I in his home? Why was he put in my life? Why was this nightmare so real? I wanted to go home.

When I entered my home, it was quiet and empty, because Bobby and his wife had moved out. Mother had left mail from Kahuna on my bed. I didn't know he had written. Why didn't he mail them to his house when I was staying there?

> Dear Rose,
>
> How are you doing? Mom says your health is again failing. I'd hoped it wouldn't be as bad as it was before. I also hope that it doesn't slow down your schooling. If it does, though, don't worry. There must be a reason for you to miss school, if the Lord makes it that way. I'd been wondering why you haven't written, and I see you've got very good reasons. It bothers me that you must suffer like that. It's beyond me why you have to go through so much pain. But the Lord will bless you for your burden.
>
> Please don't think you're being punished for something. Heavenly Father doesn't work that way. Undoubtedly, your problems must be some test to see if you endure or to see if you can deal with them and solve them.
>
> I just got called to a new position in church, this morning. I have the duty of reporting a summary of the weekly world news events at every Sunday meeting. The bishopric thought it might assist me in my studies in international relations and would appreciate my background.
>
> I've been very blessed here, at school. I'm doing well in my classes and especially enjoy my classes in Russian and international politics. I always sit front and center, and the instructors like me. I work hard, and it pays off. I'm still very busy in student government. My vice president is very good to me, and I enjoy it very much. My finances are also something to behold. Whenever I need money, I pray and think, and money just comes to me.
>
> Love Always, Kahuna

Another letter tossed in my Liberty Box filled with words—words that make me feel in a different world from him. He is learning and experiencing life, and I'm lost in a world of no hope.

December 1982
Mom placed a Christmas card on my nightstand.

Dearest Rose,

> *I know it has been a very, very, hard year. I am proud of the way you have handled all the problems. Be sweet, and let the light of the Gospel shine from your soul. Let all men see the beauty within you as you reach out and touch someone with love. Love all your brothers and sisters. They are your friends and you can be with them for eternity. Never let bitterness twist your soul and mind.*
>
> *Rose, go out and mingle with others. Isn't Tyli's brother Floy coming home from his mission next month? He seems like a nice young fellow. There are people out in the world waiting to be your friend.*
>
> *You are a beautiful girl; you have a lot to offer. Remember beauty of the body is only skin deep, but the true beauty of the soul must be cultivated like a beautiful garden. You can grow that garden with flowers or thorns.*
> *Love, Mom*

39

GRADUATION

May 1983

Shake off the rejection. The longer you let it linger, the more it will paralyze you.

"A day late and a dollar short," is a quote Grandmother often used. I took one last look in the mirror and told myself, "It's okay that I am graduating a year late." I positioned my graduation cap—specially ordered to fit my small head—gently over my curled blond hair and then grabbed my lip gloss.

When I entered the living room, Mom was seated near the front door.

I approached her. "Aren't you coming to my graduation?"

Mom rolled her wheelchair closer to me. "Rose, my back hurts, and it's just not feasible for me to come."

I held back the tears. "I understand, Mom."

Dad's keys jingled in his pocket as he walked down the hallway toward Mom. He was wearing his dress slacks and plaid shirt. "Ready to go, Rose?"

"Yes, I'm ready . . . I wish Mom was coming."

Dad kissed Mom and opened the door without another word. I sat in the front seat of the car, unsure if Dad would stay for my graduation ceremony. When we arrived at my high school, Dad drove into the drop-off parking area. "Good luck, sweetie." And then he drove off.

When I entered the gymnasium, I took my place in line between two guys. One had long red hair and a beard. The other never stopped talking. His conversation seemed superficial as he told the girl in front of him what party he was going to after the graduation ceremony. I looked at my white sandals and black-purple dress that Lillie had helped me pick out at the store. She was the one who rescued me. She was the one who always gave encouraging words like, "Rose, you are a valuable human being." I rubbed the front of my purple sash that formed a large bow in the back and told myself, *Don't be nervous. Don't be disappointed. Be happy with your accomplishments, and think of the reassuring words that Lillie told you.*

I was pleased that I had not followed the advice from the counselor at my previous high school, who told me the best thing I could do is drop out of high school and get a GED. I spoke aloud, "I'm glad I stuck it out and finished." The boy in front of me turned quickly around. "What did you say?" I rocked my feet back and forth. "Oh, I didn't say anything." I was surprised he'd even heard me with his mouth going a mile a minute.

A teacher stood near the double doors and instructed us to walk outside in the order we were standing. Before I entered the field, an emotional ache, a raw pain came. I blinked back the tears, seeing Kahuna for the first time since the pregnancy test a year ago. Tears fell with the thought that this should be a joyous day, not one of rejection. I squeezed my hand while looking at his hand that once held mine, while he spoke to his sister. The graduation march started, and the line moved forward. Within a few minutes, I was closer to Kahuna. I smiled at him and hoped he'd smile back.

The ceremony was drawn out, but when I threw my cap in the air, it brought gratification. After I found my cap, I focused on the bleachers, scanning for Kahuna, before a friend, Carla, who'd graduated the year before with Kahuna and Dax, called my name. I turned and hugged her. She was with Floy, my friend Tyli's brother. While we talked, I caught a view of my dad. Sudden warmth emanated from my heart at knowing that my dad had stayed for the ceremony. I rushed to him. My brother Bobby and his wife were also there, and he handed me a beautiful gold necklace while we stood out on the field. My other brother, Kevin, was in Colorado working, but his wife, Natalie, and my nephew came. I noticed my father's tears when he handed me a bouquet of flowers. We hugged, and he sweetly whispered in my ear, "Congratulations."

I squeezed him tight, and I responded with, "Oh, Dad, I love you to the moon and back. Thank you."

When I released myself from my dad's hug, I noticed the dark circles under his eyes. He stood hunched over as though he were going to collapse. "Dad, I need to return my gown to the gymnasium. Can you wait for me?" Carla looked at my dad and then back at me. "Floy can give you a ride home."

I grabbed Dad's hand and studied his sky-blue eyes. "Dad, Floy can bring me home, so you won't have to stay."

Dad lifted his foot. "Are you sure you're able to get a ride home?"

Floy spoke with assurance. "I would be glad to give Rose a ride."

Dad squeezed me. "I'm proud of you, and I'll see you at home."

"Thanks, Dad."

My family left with my dad after they congratulated and hugged me goodbye.

Carla, Floy, and I were walking, and someone called my name. I stopped and turned around, and there was my woodshop teacher in front of me, with a warm, friendly smile.

"Hi, Rose. Congratulations. I want to know if you would go on a date with me now that you are officially out of high school."

I wiped my hair away from my eyes and studied his short stature. It hit me right at that moment why he had reminded me throughout the semester that he was only five years older than me.

"No, I, uh, don't think that would be a wise idea, Mr. Carpenter."

He nodded and looked at Carla and Floy.

"I guess it would be awkward, but if you change your mind, call me at the school number, and I will return your call."

He gave me a hug and strolled away.

When Carla, Floy, and I left the football field, I scanned the empty bleachers and told myself, *At least I saw Kahuna.*

40
CAMP GERONIMO

May 26, 1983

Living off someone else's dream does nothing but destroy your own destiny.

Two days after graduation, I slipped out of bed and put on my running shoes after a slice of sunlight came through my window. A long-needed jog was a must to shake off the mountain of rejection. Before heading out the door, I went into the kitchen to get a drink of water.

Dad was seated at the table with toast. "Good morning."

I reached for a cup in the cabinet. "Good morning to you."

Dad swallowed. "Looks like you're going for a run."

"I thought I would go for a short run before helping you with the floors. Do you mind?"

"No problem, sweetie."

I closed the living room door, hoping I wouldn't wake Mom. I peeked inside the mailbox with a wish that Kahuna had written. I sighed and closed the lid to the mailbox.

I stretched to touch my toes and spoke out: "Be rational. Set them free."

I leaned against the house and played over in my mind the past year's trials: The loss of Kahuna, Kevin and Bobby getting married, and Dax blinded by what had happened. I had sent Dax letters filled with empty words and sent him packages with useless objects. Lies were buried in all that I had given Dax.

I ran down our single carport and headed for the park. I tried to pace each step and tell myself that summer marked a fresh start for me, one that wouldn't take me back to the horrible mental hospital.

My run was cut short when the sun poured down more heat than I could deal with. I never made it to the park. I staggered home and noticed that none of the neighbors were outside.

When I opened our living-room door, the swamp cooler gave relief. I showered, put on comfy clothes, and then greeted my parents at their bedroom door. Dad was seated on the edge of the bed, reading his scriptures, and mom was changing out of her nightgown.

Mom showed me a flyer once she had her muumuu on. "Rose, have you signed up to attend the young-adult retreat at Camp Geronimo?"

I removed the towel from my head and combed my fingers through my wet hair. "I was thinking about going so I could see what the Boy Scout camp looked like. Do you think I should go?"

Dad closed his scriptures and cleared his throat. "I think it would be a wonderful way for you to meet new people. I think Mom would agree it would be good for you."

Here, a year later, they want me to leave again, just like they did last summer, when they whisked me off to the mental hospital.

I folded my towel, set it on the foot of their bed, and then took the flyer from Mom. "I guess it would be good for me to go."

Mom smiled.

I had the jitters the morning I packed for the retreat. Maybe it was because of the insecure emptiness, now that Kahuna was gone. To get my mind off him, I made it a habit to keep myself busy with my chores. This morning, it was no different. As I placed items in my suitcase, I questioned myself as to who else might come to the retreat. I strolled out of my room to retrieve something from the bathroom, and, on the way, I sneaked into Mom's room to observe her. The TV was on, but her eyes were closed, and her leg was still.

The clatter of dishes clanked. Dad must be in the kitchen.

Back in my room, I read my list of things I would need for my three-day retreat. I wasn't sure how warm or cold it would be in the mountains, so I packed winter and summer clothes. I took one last look at the list and made sure, as I hovered over my travel case, that everything I needed was there. Once completed, I struggled with all my might, with every ounce of my weight, by sitting on it—to close the jaws of my suitcase.

I lugged my luggage out of my bedroom and took one last peek into Mom's room. Her legs had moved, either because she'd woken up or was nervous about something. Often, when she shook her leg, it was a physical sign of frustration or anxiety.

My scrawny arms dragged the suitcase down the hallway to the front door. After several stops, I finally made it and then walked into the kitchen. Leaning against the kitchen wall, I took a visual picture of Dad in my heart as he stood near the stove with a spatula in his hand.

"Hi. How are you this morning, Dad?"

"Hi, Sweetie. Ready for your trip? I'm so pleased you're going. It will be good for you to meet new people and put some previous friendships to rest."

"Yes, I suppose you're right, but it's still difficult for me to let those two best friends go."

"I can't imagine how tough it's been on you this past year. I know you loved Kahuna . . . uh . . . when will your ride be here?"

I walked closer to my dad. "In about ten minutes."

"Have you said goodbye to Mom yet?"

"No, I've, uh, been in your room twice to see if she was awake. Each time she was asleep. I didn't want to wake her."

Dad placed the spatula on the counter, turned down the gas stove, faced me, and gave me his full attention. "I think she would be hurt if you didn't say goodbye. I'm almost done with her breakfast. Why don't you go talk with her?"

"Okay. Do you want me to tell her anything?"

"Just let her know breakfast is almost ready and that you're leaving."

"I will."

I walked down the hallway and knew that, if these walls could talk, we would have discussions of the past events that still haunt me. We'd talk about both pleasant and dreadful memories. For one, I still recall leaning my back against the wall as Kahuna hugged and kissed me, pushing his body deeper into mine. The warmth of his embrace seemed present even then. To break the memory, I thought of the time when Grandmother yelled at me in the same spot in the hallway and told me I should change my underwear more than once a day. That experience was humiliating because Tyli, a dear friend of mine, heard each word Grandmother spoke when she shook her finger at me. At least Grandmother didn't slap me in front of Tyli, like she usually did.

I knocked on my parents' bedroom door. "Mom, I'm leaving now for the retreat."

Mom moved her hospital bed to the upright position. I was sad she had no control over her life, but the control of her hospital-bed remote served as an immense strength to her, and that made me happy.

"Turn the light on, so I can see you."

With the light on and the sun making its way in the window, her face spoke of loneliness.

"How do I look?" I asked.

"I like your hair draped around your face. Did you curl it?"

"Yes, I used my pink sponge curlers. I'm glad you like it."

"When are they coming to get you?"

"Any time now. Oh, Dad wanted you to know he is almost done with breakfast."

"Rose, have a fabulous time."

I bent down to kiss her cheek. The last thing she'd said occupied my thoughts. I doubted I'd have a pleasurable time without Kahuna, who had vanished from my existence. I thought of the letter Mom wrote last summer of encouragement and moving on after Kahuna.

"I love you, Mom."

"I love you, too."

Mom's leg was rolling back and forth, a dead giveaway. I took one last glimpse at Mother, who had raised and nurtured me the most excellent way she knew. Tears of tenderness formed in my eyes, as I reflected on her labors of love—the comfort she tried to give me last summer with her trick of admitting me into a mental hospital, hoping I'd overcome my desire to be with Kahuna. I was livid with her last year for lying to me, but now I knew she did it out of love. It wasn't to impair me but to help me manage the anguish of losing Kahuna. Secretly, vacancy and sorrow filled my heart.

A knock on the front door startled me from the thoughts that caused the tears to form.

Mom pointed to the door. "Your ride must be here."

"I think you are right. So, I guess I'd better go. Bye!" I gave her one last hug.

"Bye, Honey."

I covered my heart and told myself I was not horrible for leaving her. I wished I could take the stress and misery out of her room, her mind, and her life. I walked down the hallway and rubbed my fingers over the large pictures of my brothers that I had pinned up with thumbtacks and which my mother treasured. I kept my eyes focused on Dad, near the front door, handing my suitcase to Floy. I caught a wink from Floy.

"See you later." I placed my arms around Dad and gave him a hug. His hug made me feel incredible, and I didn't want it to end.

"Okay, take care." I looked in his eyes, mesmerized by the soft blueness that calmed my soul. I knew he wouldn't abandon my mother like Kahuna had me. He would be there to facilitate and console her.

Dad held the door open and watched us walk to the red-and-white VW van parked in our driveway. Dad waved with a smile, and a special kindheartedness traveled between us.

I hopped into the white bench seat behind Carla, Orem, and Tori. Carla's red hair radiated with curls, and I knew she would never need my pink sponge curlers. Carla turned around after Orem took his arm off her shoulder.

"Hi, Rose. Are you excited about the retreat?"

"I guess I am. It should be fun."

Orem turned and looked at me. "It will be extremely enjoyable."

I liked how Orem always was positive and never seemed to talk without a smile.

When Floy drove out of my driveway, Carla and Orem turned back to face forward and whispered into each other's ears. I knew soon a wedding date would be planned. I watched them, and it made me miss those moments with Kahuna. Carla and Orem seemed to have a love that would never fail, like mine and Kahuna's.

About an hour later, we left Maricopa County and began to travel toward the Mogollon Rim. Tori, who sat next to Carla, flirted with Floy while he drove. I was amused with her comments and taps on his shoulder. Floy's sister, Heidi, dressed in blue overalls, sat in the front passenger seat. How pitiful it was to watch Tori, because she had waited for Floy these last two years while he served a church mission. It was obvious she dreamed of marrying Floy. Tori paid no attention to the lovebirds because her eyes were fixed on Floy's every move. Floy was not a bit interested in her, from what I could observe. Poor Tori was as brokenhearted as I had been, deserted and rejected by her one true love. I hoped this retreat would bring Tori and Floy closer together, because I had no interest in Floy, even though I caught him peeking at me through the rearview mirror.

The van slowed down. Then, after another half mile, it lost power, and a final pop in the engine made it evident that we would be stranded on the side of the road. There wasn't a building in sight. Orem opened the side van door to let in some fresh warm air. I looked out the framed window at a landscape of cacti and desert plants engulfed by brown dirt.

Three hours later, the weather cooled to about 90 degrees, and the sun began to set, pulling the full moon in our direction. I took on an odor that made my earlier shower useless. Everyone in the van was in the same boat, with sweat dripping off them. I think we put an inch of sweat on the floor of the van.

My hair clung to my face and neck. I opened my suitcase. I just had to have my pink sponge curlers to hold up my hair. I unbuckled the right buckle and then the left. I expected my belongings to jump out and go flying in all directions. I knew if I opened it all the way, I would never get it closed, so I used my left hand to hold my suitcase partly closed while my right hand moved to locate the bag of sponge curlers. Once I found it, I pulled them out of the small opening and prayed I could complete this task. I positioned all my upper weight on my suitcase and leaned my body toward the buckles. Miraculously, it closed. I promised myself I would go without anything else in the suitcase until we got to the cabin.

We waited for hours before a policeman stopped. Through the window, I listened to the conversation between Floy and the policeman.

"Could you call my dad and tell him I need this part for the van?" Floy handed him a piece of paper.

"Sure, I can do that. Is your dad's phone number on here, too?"

Floy pointed. "Yes, it's on the bottom."

The police officer wiped the sweat from his forehead. "Will you guys be fine waiting here?"

I thought to myself, *Maybe fine, but hot and sweaty.*

"We'll be okay," Floy said.

The police officer walked to his car and drove away.

Cars, trucks, and vans drove by, stirring the still, warm air, swaying the van like we were on a boat. When Floy's Dad arrived, he helped Floy work on the motor. A couple of hours later, we were back on the road.

When we arrived, it was midnight, and the camp seemed empty, even though there were cars and vans parked in front of the cabins. It was hard to see the numbers on the cabins. Floy moved the van toward the signs to use the headlights to see. I found the cabin with the number "4" on it, pulled my suitcase out of the van, and dragged it on the gravel to the cabin. I tried not to make noise, but I did. Entering the cabin, young-adult girls' bodies shadowed by the moon rustled in their beds.

"Hi, Rose. We wondered if you were going to make it."

I pulled my flashlight out to see where I was going and whispered so I wouldn't wake everyone.

"We were stuck on the side of the road for hours."

I could see the outline of Caroline's body as she was sitting on her bed. "Why do you have curlers in your hair?"

Just as I was about to answer, Tori walked in. She turned on the light and moaned while she dragged her suitcase across the room, acting like a drama queen.

Heidi followed Tori and took the bed next to her. They had been best friends for years and had plans of being sisters-in-law. I had been assigned to a cabin with girls I'd never hung out with, while they had all been friends for several years. I knew it was my fault for never making the effort to have girlfriends, but Dax and Kahuna had been the only friends I thought I needed. I walked to the bathroom and dressed for bed. When I returned to my cot, I rolled out my sleeping bag, knelt by the side of my cot, said a prayer, and crawled into bed. I pulled my bag over my shoulders and glanced at Caroline. She was looking over at me with excitement in her voice.

"Rose, are you going to sleep?"

I scooted down in my sleeping bag and sunk my head onto my pillow. My sponge curlers poked me, but I was too lazy to take them out.

I spoke in her direction. "Yes, I'm tired. Aren't you?"

"Yes, but I'm also excited about being here. Okay, I'll talk with you in the morning."

Early the next morning, I awoke to birds chirping outside the cabin window, and the sun brought in enough light for me to tiptoe to the bathroom. I swiftly entered the small, square shower stall, even though the cool air brought goose bumps. I wanted to shave my legs, though I knew I'd wear pants. I shivered under the cold water and spoke, out loud, "My mother never taught me the right way to shave."

I dressed in my favorite cream-colored blouse with my brown Ditto pants. I tied a thin, brown ribbon underneath my collar to add more fashion to my outfit. I walked in front of the mirror over the sink and took my sponge curlers out. I noticed my deformed right eye as it involuntarily drifted upward. Was I unattractive? How different would I look if my eyes were the same?

When I opened the door, I was surprised by Caroline, who was standing right beside the door.

"Rose, I thought you would never come out."

I knew if I hadn't cut my leg shaving, I would have been out sooner.

Caroline offered to walk with me to breakfast.

When we came through the double doors, I stood planted in one spot and scanned the dining hall. Floy pointed at his table for me to sit with him and his friends. A high school friend I hadn't seen in more than a year waved, too. I waved back. Caroline had attended a different high school and wanted to sit with her friends. We separated, but I hoped to see her later. After breakfast, we attended classes that were held all over the campground. In the evening, all the young adults gathered together under a large ramada to watch a movie.

I arrived late and found an empty spot next to Landon. "Do you mind if I sit by you?"

Landon moved over a little. "No, that—that's fine."

Right after I sat down, his big blue eyes caught me off guard. He was tall and slender, like Dax. I was comfortable sitting next to Landon, because Kahuna had introduced me to him four years before.

The sun had already set, and all I could see was the outline of Landon's face. "How have you been, Landon?"

He rubbed his shaking, nervous hand over his leg. "Good, just busy with work and college."

The exhilaration of the movie stirred lots of "oohs," "aahs," and other weird noises, but I wasn't too interested. I'd hoped for a romantic movie, but, instead, it was packed with adventures of a man climbing some steep, rocky mountain.

Halfway through the movie, they had an intermission for those who needed to use the restroom or get a blanket. I was glad I had brought a warm jacket. When the ramada lights came on, there was Kahuna. His dark, curly hair and smile were the same. I squeezed my eyes tight and then opened them to see if I were dreaming.

His piercing eyes turned dark and unreadable. His lifeless expression froze, and he looked away as if he didn't know me. My heart twisted into knots, and my body craved to be near him—to kiss him, hug him, and talk to him was all I could think of. Empty vibes passed between us as though we had never shared an intimate moment. My life shattered in dreamless hopes of ever being with him again. Each time I glanced at him, the shadows of the movie brought outlines of the face I had waited to see for a year. Kahuna became my movie. I knew I still loved him, even though he'd told me last November that he didn't love me anymore. I wished I understood why I still had deep feelings for Kahuna. Even after all the counseling to help me cope with the rejection, I still wanted him. *Why?* I asked myself. Once the movie was over, he vanished. Landon was friendly but embarrassed to start a conversation. I guess he belonged to a club called "Too Frightened to Communicate."

"Thanks for letting me sit with you, Landon. Did you like the movie?"

Landon turned his legs toward me. "Yeah, it was a good one, but I don't think I would see it again."

I stood before I responded. "I didn't like it. Well, I'd better find my roommates. I'll see you tomorrow."

Landon stood. "Yes. See you tomorrow. Maybe we'll be in some classes together."

"Well, if you see me, save me a spot next to you."

Landon tilted his head and smiled. "Sounds great. Bye."

When I left the ramada, Floy approached me. "Hi, Rose. Would you go on a walk with me tomorrow?"

Noticing my roommates, I answered him quickly. "Sure, I guess."

The next morning, I searched the dining hall for Kahuna, like a hunter looking for prey. I found him across the dining hall with his cousins. I sat four tables away from him, where I had a full view of him. When our eyes met, warmth flowed through every part of my body. His face put on the same mask he had at my graduation.

Stewart waved his hand in front of me. "Did you hear me, Rose?"

"Hear what, Stewart?"

He sat next to me. "If you liked the movie last night."

I pushed my plate forward. "It was okay, Stewart. Did you like it?"

Stewart scooped eggs on his fork. "I liked it, especially when that guy climbing the mountain almost slipped."

I took a sip of my milk. "That part made me nervous. I was so terrified he'd fall and die. Well, Stewart, I need to go. My first class is on the other side of camp."

Stewart pointed to my food. "Aren't you going to finish breakfast?"

I grabbed my plate and said, "I'm not hungry."

His eyes got big. "How can you not be hungry?"

I stood and faced him. "I'm not hungry."

Stewart grabbed my hand. "You're kidding me, right?"

"I can't talk right now, Stewart. Maybe later."

I took a quick look at Kahuna as he stood.

"I'll talk to you later and explain everything to you."

Stewart tapped the table. "Okay—bye."

I grabbed my tray of untouched food and patted his shoulder before I left. "Bye."

Caroline waved for to me to come over to her, but I just couldn't lose this opportunity to talk with Kahuna. Taiana's sister yelled, "Rose, come here." I waved and then pointed at Kahuna. She knew everything about Kahuna and me because their moms were sisters.

I followed Kahuna out the double doors. As soon as he noticed me, he bolted faster than I had ever seen him run. I tried to catch up to him.

He hustled up the mountain, farther and farther away from me. He was out of reach, and I had lost strength. I wanted to yell his name, but, instead, whispered it. I followed Kahuna with my eyes as he darted through the thick forest and disappeared from my view. I looked at the sky and pleaded with God to take away the anguish. I stood alone, surrounded by pine trees, and no one to turn to. Others passed by, said, "Hi," and even motioned for me to come with them. I thought of Stewart and how amiable he'd been at breakfast. As the shadows of the pine trees moved, I knew I needed to move, too. I didn't know how much time had passed before I left that hopeless spot. Why did I have strong desires to be with Kahuna?

Once in my cabin, I glanced at Heidi, Tori, and Anna near the bathroom, and a silence stood between us. I collapsed on my cot and buried my face in my strawberry pillowcase. It was obvious the whispers exchanged between them were about me. They had to have noticed that I'd been crying. It was no secret about Kahuna. Did they know about the pregnancy test? Gossip is a sick disease that can do more damage to the soul than any other illness. Heidi, Anna, and Tori tried to avoid me, because they didn't want to hurt me. A cold breeze entered as the door opened. Moments later, my cot drooped down on one side. I peeked and saw Caroline seated next to me.

"Rose, class is in fifteen minutes. Are you coming?"

I turned so she could hear me. "No." I pushed my face in my pillow, and tears came. A cool breeze announced itself when the door opened, and Heidi, Tori, and Anna said goodbye as they left.

Caroline rubbed my back. "Well, then, what can I do to help you?"

The warmth of her words made me feel better, and I wanted to talk to her, but I was terrified of what she would think. I lifted my head to speak. "I appreciate your concern for me."

Her hand left my back. "Mm . . . hmmm. If I can help, let me know. Are you sure you don't want to walk with me to class?"

I rolled over, and my tears rolled down my cheek, too. "I will rest and leave soon." If counselors couldn't help me, how could Caroline? The counselors told me that I had experienced a death and a divorce all in one with Kahuna.

When Caroline got up, my cot didn't gravitate to one side anymore.

She rested her hand on her hip. "I'll go and save you a seat, OK?" Caroline's feet clapped against the wood floor. The next sound was the click of the door. I rolled into the fetal position; my body gave in, and I fell asleep.

Caroline, with her brown, wavy hair and blue eyes, tapped me on my shoulder, which awoke me from my deep slumber.

"It's lunchtime. You need to get up."

I rolled onto my back. "Thanks, I must have missed some good classes, and I was supposed to meet Floy after class."

"Yes, you did, and Floy asked me where you were."

I sat on the edge of my cot. "I sure missed out."

Caroline sat on Anna's cot, next to mine. "Are you sick?"

I pulled my hair away from my face. "No, just disappointed."

Caroline spoke with a happy tone in her voice. "Let's go to lunch."

I smiled. "Well, I need to brush my hair."

She stood and looked at me. "Would you like me to wait for you?"

I dropped my head. "No, that's all right."

Caroline touched my shoulder. "I don't mind waiting while you brush your hair. I can tell you what happened at class."

Caroline leaned against the bathroom door and talked nonstop. "You would have loved this one class we had on faith. Anna said that, if she remains faithful, Mr. Right will find her. What do you think?"

I stopped brushing my hair before I spoke. "Faith is hard to live by, and when difficult trials come that weren't anticipated, you lose hope."

Caroline looked at her watch. "We'd better leave before prayer is said."

Caroline was out the door before I dropped my brush on my cot. She waited for me on the wood deck. I walked toward the door and contemplated why Kahuna had ignored me, with a hope my blind eye wasn't the reason he didn't want me anymore. When I got to the doorway, I smelled an odor I'd often smelled at girls camp—a skunk was near.

"Caroline, do you smell the skunk?" I looked down in between the wood gaps in the deck to see if the skunk was near.

Caroline shrugged. "I think the skunk is gone, and we don't need to worry."

I stepped off the deck, trusting Caroline's judgment. As we passed my hopeless spot that no longer had shadows of pine trees, I wished Kahuna would have let me say a few words to him. When we entered the dining hall, cheerful young-adult chatter occupied the room. Caroline and I filled our plates. The moment I finished the food line, I saw that Caroline was sitting at the same table as Kahuna. Caroline beckoned me, and I stood glued in one spot, holding my tray. I couldn't tell if Kahuna noticed what she was doing because his back was toward me. I waved back to her and then pointed over to Stewart. I had to pass on Caroline's invitation.

Tori broke my thoughts as she bumped me. "Hi, Rose. Heidi told me you are sitting in the passenger seat on the way home. Is that true?"

I glanced at Floy and then over at Kahuna. "I guess it's true. I don't know. Why are you asking me?"

"Well, I have a deal to make with you, then. If you let me sit in the front passenger seat, I will let you listen all the way home to my Michael Jackson cassette tape."

I lost my focus on Kahuna when I heard her say "Michael Jackson." "Tori, I'll take that deal in a heartbeat. I don't have any reason to sit in the front passenger seat. I take it you like Floy?"

Tori's smile grew when I asked her that question. "Yes, I have liked him for a long time."

I moved forward, hoping to give her a hint I wanted to sit down. "Well, then, I'll grant your wish."

I sat and focused on the back of Kahuna's head. It stirred thoughts of my Liberty Box that held my hundred and eighty-six love letters that he wrote, proclaiming he would love me always and forever. I took a bite of my sandwich to fill my empty tummy and stared at Kahuna, and this time, I thought about how his letters testified that I was a part of him and that he loved me. Were we the only two young adults in the room who had shared a physical and mental union? I searched the room for others like me and knew nobody had pain lingering deep within them, to the point of believing they were worthless and unwanted—tortured by a lack of affection from their one true love as I had been. Not even Kahuna. Me, a cracked vase unable to contain a rose.

After I finished, I left alone . . . and sat on the steps outside the building. The pine trees whistled as the wind danced around them and made them give up their pine scent. Today I would go home. I spoke as if the trees could understand me. "If only I could capture this forest in a bottle and take it with me."

Floy sat down next to me. "What did you say?"

I pointed to the trees. "Aren't those trees pretty to look at?"

Floy moved a little closer. "I guess. Do you want to go for a walk down to the stream with me?"

I stood. "Sure. I would like that."

Water flowed over the rocks with ease, and birds sang along to the wind. Floy and I took pictures of each other near the stream until we realized the time. We knew we needed to pack and leave before three.

The journey home was entertaining seated in the back seat of the van. Orem and Carla were seated right in front of me, and I counted how many times they kissed. Heidi drove home with Caroline, so Tori took her spot in the front passenger seat, while I sang along to Michael Jackson in the back seat.

I watched Tori keep her eyes on Floy, and Floy kept his eyes on the road and then on me through the rearview mirror. Did Tori have any clue? Did she catch him winking at me? Did he see me as a one-eyed freak? I believe I got the better end of the deal. *Good luck with Floy, Tori.* Oh, boy—I hope Floy doesn't think I like him because I went to his homecoming party, when he returned home from the Dominican Republic and gave me a ride home after the party.

41
DANCE, DANCE, DANCE
June 1983

Give me peace so I can see the real me.
Give me joy so I can smile once again.

Give me faith so I can hold on to what
I dream of always having, and that is you.

Lack of confidence stirred inside me as I stood in the dim dance hall near a large black speaker and sang along. Young adults strolled in the double doors and anticipated meeting their one true love. I took a panoramic view of everyone; some tapped their feet to the rhythm of the song or moved their hips to the beat. Was it their way to indicate that they wanted to dance? Did they struggle to be noticed? My struggles weren't the same. Why, you ask? Because I wanted to be accepted by Kahuna, Dax, and no one else.

Prayer was my survival and my life jacket that I wrapped around me with faith that Kahuna would come to his senses. I pictured Kahuna entering the hall, walking over to me, and showering me with love. I dreamed of his arms around me with his lips against mine.

When a young man with light-brown hair asked me to dance, I tried to focus on him while we danced. But halfway into the dance, Kahuna came through the double doors in his navy-blue button-up shirt.

Once the song ended, I thanked the nameless guy and walked to the double doors. The dimly lit room made it hard to see. I stood on my tiptoes near the entrance and searched for Kahuna through two more songs and even turned some guys down. I hoped Kahuna noticed. I decided to walk around to see if I could find him. I wanted to call out his name, but I resisted.

Finally, there he was. I waved with a smile, only to find hatred connected to a scalpel. Our eyes connected, and then he darted in the opposite direction. I remained in that same spot and wished he knew how difficult this experience had been for me. My lips trembled, and I was swept into a current of all that I had lost. I wanted one more second, minute, or hour with him. I kept my eye focused on him as I followed his footsteps. He turned and looked at me before he reached for the door handle and exited.

The door shut. I stood numb and unable to move.

Memories of the pronounced click of the phone last November finally registered—the last phone call I'd had with Kahuna after he'd broken his collarbone. The last conversation we had turned hardhearted when he told me he didn't love me anymore. I grabbed my necklace. Would Kahuna strangle me like my mother did, but not stop?

The rest of the night was a blur of confusion, even though there was a hole inside of me—an emptiness that would not leave me. I was shocked that I'd said "Yes" to Floy and John, who both asked me out on a date.

I knew my love for Kahuna would live forever—even after I died.

That night, I wrote in my journal . . .

Friends come and go as fast as a breeze that goes right through you.

Sometimes you wish that breeze would continue.

And other times you wish it would vanish.

Pamela L. Reynolds

To take in the fresh air from a breeze you never dreamed of smelling
or to inhale a scent you wish never entered your nose.
Friends can leave a good scent of warmth and compassion
And other times can leave an odor that makes it difficult to breathe.
Trying to grasp, connect, and hold that sweet breeze,
that you wish would never, ever leave, especially on a hot summer day.

42
BLIND LOVE

August 1983

When light seeped into darkness,
it filled the emptiness of my soul.

I sat next to Floy on a cold, gray, mental chair in the far-right corner of the chapel at Kahuna's church, camouflaged by families of every age. I looked at the high, brown-beamed ceiling and then back to eye level assessing the rows of pews where people had firmly planted themselves. Like rows of roses in a garden, they sat organized and silent—roses of red, pink, white, yellow, in bouquets of different fragrances and moods. They had all been watered, fertilized, and given sun to help them maintain a balanced life to produce to their full potential—and then there was me. Inside, perfect and whole, but, with the cracked vase that was my Rubella body and my life's situation, I'd never had a chance to bloom. I was a wilted, off-colored rose compared to the healthy ones around me.

Moving my hair away from my left eye, I also wanted to remove the name of the young lady listed on the program to sing. When the young lady stood in her light-green dress and hit the first note perfectly, my wilted rose petals detached off my dry, crooked stem.

Perfect Rose Cracked Vase

The phone call with Kahuna resurfaced with each note that she sang. His voice drowned out hers as I replayed our conversation.

"Rose, I want to invite you to hear me speak before I leave."

I think I answered with a soft tone. "When is it?"

"It's August tenth, at four. Do you think you can come?"

"Um . . . Can I get back with you on that? I would love to come."

A high note from this unknown singer pierced my ears and destroyed the memory of that phone call. Heartbreaking tears swelled in my eyes with puddles of disbelief that he had even called me. I lowered my head to hide the torturous rainstorm that overflowed and fell into my lap.

I trusted Kahuna more than I trusted myself. I'd opened my heart and shared my deepest secrets with him, with a belief he would help me and be a forever friend. I gave him the freedom to love me and see deep into my heart. I studied the beam above me and wished our relationship was as strong. But instead he took the beam and threw it at me—with not a care that the splinters would enter my soul. I'd relied on him for survival, and now I had to bury my unfathomable love, my hope of survival, in a deep, dark hole, where no one could see it, and I could forget it. Apparently, I hadn't shoveled deep enough, because Kahuna's relationship rematerialized in my mind as I sat amongst the congregation.

My drooping head sprang when a familiar voice resonated through the speakers. Kahuna's voice loosened my grip on the invisible large shovel. A sentence that echoed from his last phone call unearthed itself and rose above the last shovelful of dirt.

"I know you will be married before I come home."

I struggled to hold myself up, to straighten my stem, and feel like a premium rose in a suitable vase. But that statement Kahuna had made on the phone haunted me. Try as I might, I couldn't feel comfort in those words he spoke.

All that was left of my weak rose seemed to be the thorns that grew on my stem—thorns that I didn't even want but came unbidden.

Why am I so different? Why did I trust him, and why did he leave me more cracked and broken than ever?

Even as I sat questioning, comforting words came from his lips:

"God loves me, and He loves you. He cares about your salvation and mine. Prayer is the key for receiving strength in keeping yourself free from things that aren't good for your body and spirit."

I tried to concentrate on what he was saying, but the screaming toddler behind me made it difficult. A mix of confusion stirred inside me, the lilt of love for Kahuna and the heavy darkness of betrayal. I shifted in my seat and tried to control my fragile emotions . . .

Numbness made it easy to fade into doubt. Dax had asked a question in a recent letter from Europe: "How is Kahuna? Why don't I hear from him?" Those questions invaded my mind and inhibited my attentiveness on Kahuna's talk. Dax's voice flooded my head with questions I couldn't answer.

Water and air was what I needed, but love from Kahuna was all I longed to consume. Kahuna finished his talk, and the small child behind me became silent, but Dax's questions—and mine—stayed with me throughout the rest of the meeting.

After the closing song, I turned to Floy. "I'm going to congratulate Kahuna, and I'll be right back."

Floy pointed to the foyer. "I'll wait for you over there."

I stood five feet away and waited my turn to wish Kahuna well. I recalled the first time he'd embraced me with a kiss that sealed our love. Overcome with a storm of conflicting feelings of hope, guilt, yearning, panic, and love invaded me. There was so much I wanted to say to him, so many things. The threads on his dark-colored suit were woven together perfectly. And was our relationship woven together just the same? But, then maybe he saw how I was cracked—not capable of being that perfect thread to blend with his. I kept focused on his back and listened to him say "Thank you" to those who greeted him. Then, it happened. He turned 180 degrees, toward me.

Don't droop like a weak rose, Rose, I internally coached myself.

My right hand moved toward him. I searched for some type of expression, but there was only emptiness in his face, with no attachment or noticeable feeling at all. He could have easily been wearing a cloak and carrying a dagger with him. A flash of memories resurfaced in my mind of sharing our life trials together. Part of me wanted to throw myself into his arms and say "Sorry" for all the pain I caused. I pulled at my dress, trying to fight off how self-conscious I was in front of him.

Then, just as quickly as he had turned toward me, he made a 180-degree turn away from me. My mouth hung open to say, "Congratulations" and "Good luck," but I could only stare silently at his back. The hand I had extended to shake his froze in the air like a statue. My arm dropped. Somehow, I found the strength to move my arms back and forth, like a pendulum on a clock, and it gave me the momentum to move my body away from him.

Walking away, I could feel the thread between us slowly unraveling out of the woven material that we had sewn together. When I got to the double doors, I paused and turned to take one last glance at Kahuna. I spoke out loud, hoping God could hear me. "I hurt him, God, and now I'm hurting. I drove him away. This is wrong, and I love him."

A ghostlike memory of a year and a half ago ran in front of me, with scenes of our last moments when we were physically together as one. That fateful moment we had shared had shattered our dreams, even though I thought it would strengthen them. This experience we'd shared was a confidential secret, one that had left the same skeleton in both our lives. How he could hide it was a mystery to me, but I knew each skeleton bone brought new insights to what really mattered. He took the liberty to wave his magic wand and evaporate me from his life. I took his Liberty Box of letters and captured them.

Would Dax be the next to disappear from Kahuna's world? Stepping out the double doors, I hoped it wasn't a sign of stepping away from Dax and from everything I had loved thus far.

Floy stood on the other side of the foyer in his gray suit, ready to take me home. It was hard for me to believe that, at the age of nine, I'd lived in his home as a foster child. Over the years, he'd bailed me and his sister Tyli from getting caught toilet-papering someone's house. I studied his sky-blue eyes as I walked toward him. He gave me a smirk that I had often seen on the dates we'd had over the last six months, but when he asked me to marry him last June, I'd stopped dating him. Whatever happened between Floy and Gail? I couldn't ask Gail because she wouldn't talk to me anymore. In high school, I promised Gail I would never date or take Floy away from her, because I had Kahuna. Today was an exception, because I needed a ride to hear Kahuna speak. I couldn't pass up this opportunity, so I gave in and came with Floy. Did Floy love me . . . more than Kahuna ever did? I told myself to walk tall and banish all the negative thoughts that my schoolmate, my mom, my grandmother, and now Kahuna had placed in my life. I told myself not to feel bad for dating Floy. Someday, I hoped, Gail would be my friend again.

My body was a cracked vase that could never hold a perfect rose, even with the imperfections I knew my perfect rose had. Was my personality, my very soul, as cracked as the vase that held it?

When I got in Floy's car and buckled up, peace entered with me—a peace that God had given me to help me cope as a fetus, a baby, and a young child. He helped me to handle the growing-up years and all the turmoil passed down through my grandmother, to my mom, and then to me. He helped me deal with teenage struggles.

My thoughts of gratitude continued while we drove out of the parking lot and across the street to Kahuna's house, where we went in to talk briefly with others gathered there and get some important papers Kahuna had of mine. I sat frozen on a brown chair, unable to feel any type of pain or joy. How long we stayed is a mystery, but I didn't once see Kahuna or get my important papers.

When Floy and I left, I had a strong awareness that Heavenly Father loved me, even with my physical disabilities from the Rubella. I knew He would never abandon me, like Kahuna had. While we drove out of Kahuna's neighborhood, I focused on the road ahead and captured the raw emotions that reminded me that yes, I'm not perfect. Reassurance came from knowing God knew me and would always love me. He stood with me while I lived in foster homes, he guided me while I was blind, and he comforted me when I was forced to walk away from Kahuna. Thanks, Heavenly Father, for taking my hand.

43
CIRCLE OF SURVIVAL

June 17, 2006

The horrible experiences of our past
do not have to dictate our future journey.

Who Am I?

Not the person you see and know. I am an actor,
choosing my parts carefully.

Bright, friendly, happy are the characters I play,

Your world is my stage, and it is so easy
to play my roles, deny the real me.

I have an impregnable wall
behind which I hide myself.

Sadness, despair, and hate raise their ugly heads
and parade my inadequacy to the world.

Some actors are fulfilled; someday I hope to be.
I'm not yet sure what that real self will be.
~ Rose ~
(written at age 18)

Perfect Rose Cracked Vase

After I dried my eyes and wiped my nose with my shirt, I reached for the scattered journals and stacked them next to the trunk. My fingers were shaky from this journey through my past. Soon the sun would rise, and my husband, Floy, and my five children would wake from their night's rest. Tranquility and warmth surrounded me and brought peace to my soul as I knelt over the trunk to put my journals back in their original spot. I have heard it's not good to live in the past, but, for me, it helped, even with rocks thrown in my path, potholes in the road, and large mountains too hard to climb. A sensation engulfed me. *My life is a ray of sunshine compared to my mother's.*

Now my youngest child copes daily with autism. He lives in a world with social impairments, communication difficulties, and restricted, repetitive, and stereotyped patterns of behavior. I wish I could take him out of that world, but I needed to adapt to his world until he became verbal, able to share his ideas and wants. I wanted a Fairy Godmother to wave her magic wand and remove the behaviors of banging his head on the floor, running out into heavy traffic, and hitting us when he couldn't speak. My mother must have had the same desires as I have for my son to help us be as typical as any other child. I didn't bang my head on the floor or run into the street, but I was physically unable to function like other children. It was the only world I knew, and now my son lives in the only world he knows how to live in.

I needed water. I quickly, but carefully, put the boxes back in the closet. After I had put the last box away, I froze in one spot and patted my cheeks. Nestled in between two boxes near me was my Liberty Box. "That's got to be my imagination."

Thirst for water wasn't a desire anymore. Instead, I thirsted to read my love letters from Kahuna, to read again the words that had been meant for me, preserved in this box for years. There were the words of love, the hundreds of written promises, the kind words and flattery I had believed in wholeheartedly.

A match flared a spark of past eventful memories deep in the core of my heart. Some of the memories I wasn't proud of, and others were moments I wished had never ended. I scooped up the box.

I pinched the bridge of my nose, while seated on the floor with my back resting against the stack of boxes, and rubbed my middle-aged hands over the lid. Unleashed words came. "Oh, Kahuna, why did things go so terribly wrong? Why, when you pledged your undying love, why did you betray me and our future?"

I detached the lid and spoke. This time, the words were for me, not Kahuna. They were words I knew needed to come. The age-old questions spewed forth. "Why did I trust him? Why did I put more confidence in him than in myself? Why did I believe in him even after he quit believing in me?"

Tears escaped. Did Kahuna think about me and the years we'd spent together or marvel at what we'd shared? *Do I remain alive in his mind, like he has in mine?* I could picture his handsome smile. *"Whatever happened to Dax?"*

Tissue brought assistance, so I could read Kahuna's letters. The written words made my throat tighten, and a strong, bitter taste filled my mouth. Callous anger mixed with sadness churned in me. The pain resurfaced—all the emptiness of losing Kahuna, all the disappointment of discovering that my dreams had been only mirages and broken promises.

Dearest Rose,

> *Right now, all I can feel is love for you. I can't get my mind off of you. The Lord has truly blessed me. When I asked you that sacred question, I really thought that the Lord was punishing me by taking you away and giving you to Dax. It seemed you two were perfect for each other. I felt like dying. All the things you said about how rotten our relationship is began to wear on my mind. It was painful.*

You can imagine how surprised I am to hear that you really, truly, honestly believe we'll make it. After all your complaining about us. You'd never really felt that way. Does that mean no matter how rotten our relationship gets, we'll still make it at the end? I still worry about other guys stealing you away from me. You noticed I need security. If you can show me that going steady means having a commitment, and you can show me you won't be asking to break it, I might ask you to go steady. Sounds chauvinistic, but it's up to you, too.

I want so badly for us to agree on decisions as one. The Lord wants us to work as one individual, and because our desire is so great, we will be able to do it. We just must keep hoping and prove we want it.

I also believe I'm not using you. I'm abusing you. I don't quite see how, but that's what you really mean, isn't it?

I love you,

Love forever, Kahuna

P.S. if this letter is hard to understand, it's because I don't want people snooping.

Why was my faith in an adolescent boyfriend and not in God? Before I put the lid on the box, I touched the pile of letters to let all the anger run out of my heart and into that box—the anger of believing that no one would want me with my deformed eye and living with Congenital Rubella Syndrome. Those teenage years were filled with annoyance that my friends would complain about a pimple on their face and not wanting to go out in public with it, but I, on the other hand, would never be able to cover up or wait for my deformed eye to go away. Were these letters sealed with love? Did he mean what he wrote? Now that the years had distanced me from the experiences of my younger days, what came rushing back was not only pain and anger, but something else as well. This time I didn't want them to live anymore, but to die and remove the torture that I had ignored. I reflect often on a statement a friend made back in high school. "Rose, I feel sorry for you not being able to see out of two eyes." I pitied myself many times for not having a mother to comfort me or not having the physical abilities my friends had. Kahuna's letters served as a barrier to the pain, but now they *were* the pain that lingered.

The Liberty Box now served as a reminder that, even though I have Congenital Rubella Syndrome and I had a mother who was unable to be the mother I needed, rejection from someone you love can strengthen you even after years of pain. This Liberty Box was truly filled with liberty. I had the liberty—and took it, to cast out the ugly, dirty past that made me believe I was a cracked vase. I gave them the freedom to run out and down, miraculously filling the cracks, gluing together the holes, smoothing everything that had been rough and ugly and broken. Deep inside, the healing, the coming together of a whole piece—still fragile, but I knew I was whole—about to produce a single blooming flower—or even a bouquet.

Why carry this horrible burden? Why did Mother carry staggering burdens, too? The problems we kept locked inside seemed to travel on through generations. One link of the chain I'm pleased my mother broke was the hatred toward everything and everyone that Grandmother had.

Since the day I packed Mom's belongings and moved her from the world she knew and the home my dad took his last breath at, she was furious that I was distancing her from the environment she loved. But I had to because of the experience I had a few days before my father passed of a man holding a gun to my head in my parents' apartment parking lot. We had just returned from visiting with my Dad who was on life support in the hospital. A man who struck fear in me as he held the gun to my head while I was seated in my brother Bobby's truck and forced me to give him all the money I had. I prayed as I bent forward knowing if he was going to shoot me I would rather have him shoot me in the bottom and not in the head. When I bent down, I put my hair alongside my head so the gunman could not see that I was calling the police in my purse. I waited for what seemed hours when I know it was only minutes before it was the right time to sit up straight in the truck. For a moment I thought of my children, husband, mother and brothers while I held the phone to my ear and looking into the barrel of the gun and said, "Yes, he is holding a gun to my head." When the gunman realized I had been on the phone the whole time he took off because he didn't want to get caught. He had to have known there is only one way in the parking lot and one way out. Weeks later he was on the news and sent to prison for killing three people at a Subway across the street from my parents' home. But after having a gun held to my head outside her home days before Dad died, I had to remove her like she had me removed from our home when I was young. I guess in a way she got to experience being plucked out of an environment like my brothers and I had dealt with as kids. And I know she didn't do it intentionally, either. I guess it was just the way the path had taken both of us. I hoped the move would bring us even closer, giving more opportunities to pay her back for the life she had given me, to build not just a mother-daughter relationship that I'd always hoped for as a child, but to have a friendship that would bind us forever. It did happen. But her last Easter, birthday, Fourth of July, Halloween, Thanksgiving, and Christmas were filled with emptiness. Stories of my father helped but never seemed to heal her broken heart.

The last Christmas season with my mother was priceless. Words of love were enclosed in each piece of Christmas decoration that I helped her pack. She actually said the words, "Oh, when I pass, you can have this for your family." Her hands slowly wrapped the baby Jesus in the paper towel and then sealed it back in the original box. Baby Jesus held my mom and my relationship intact forever. The final gift she gave me on Christmas day was a cassette tape of her talking about how much she loved me and would miss me. Now a month later, she is resting peacefully, with no oxygen connected to her nose. And she always said, "Rose, I'm a dog on a leash with the oxygen tube." Her baby Jesus is still wrapped in the box where she placed it. The box holds not just an object but also a memory I will cherish.

My friends might have had quantity of love and support, but in my mother's last year of life, she gave me quality of love. She helped me to see how blessed I am to see out of one eye and cope with living with Congenital Rubella Syndrome. My mother gave me a priceless poem on my birthday years before her death that I will treasure. Her words capture not just my struggles but hers, too.

The Soul of Our Daughter

She was a pleasant, sweet child—but from the beginning, our daughter grew against odds that would have stopped those of less faith.

Long before anyone dreamed of the woman she was destined to be, you knew she would survive.

What was within her soul? What intangible substance sustained her as she climbed upward on her quest to succeed?

Often there was a glimmer, a hint of fire that kindled deep within. It shone from her eyes, it came from her lips, you saw it in her creative talents.

She stood tall and straight, her eyes looking ahead; her hair glistened as though a halo were about it.

You knew her life would be hard, that she would shed tears for those who could not understand.

Yet you knew this soul had the courage and strength that would survive the pain.

She had come, our courageous daughter upon the Earth, knowing this opposition.

She would overcome, and, as she did, they would respect her and gain strength and courage themselves as she fought the odds.

She loved the Lord. He knew, and we loved her, too. She was one of His chosen few.

A soul that was to teach others the meaning of strength.

When she leaves this earthly home, to dwell with her Heavenly Father, she would wear a crown of glory.

Perfect Rose Cracked Vase

By Mom
Dedicated to our Daughter Rose
From Mom and Dad 1986

When I helped my daughter put white slippers on my mother's cold, motionless feet, I realized even mothers do make mistakes, but never on purpose. All mothers struggle with their own trials, and Mom sure had them. The chill of remembering her glassy eyes looking into mine while her hands were wrapped around my neck was one of the many secrets between us, a trial I couldn't comprehend. I studied her closed eyelids that concealed the eyes that would be unable to connect with mine ever again and told her, "I forgive you, Mom."

Maybe, I will find answers through her box of cassettes of conversations with my grandmother. Answers to why she struggled to be a daughter, sister, wife, mother, and friend. Dressing her in her white dress to be reunited with Dad, her sweetheart in heaven, brought thoughts about how she couldn't cope with rejection or feel like she mattered. Those days have passed, those horrible days of agony of not understanding what caused her to feel like she didn't matter. She might have not been able to give me what I believed I needed, but God did know. One struggle she won was not giving up on me. It was a gift from her heart that I carry with me. When I struggle with my vision, hearing, or just managing life, I think of my parents. Over the years, my physical deformities dragged me down, but my soul reminded me that I'm not unusual. My mother and father often told me I was a miracle. Was I?

Even though I constantly believe I'm a cracked vase, my mother always believed I was qualified to encase a beautiful bouquet of flowers. Me—who could see out of only one eye and hear out of one ear? Now, I know she was right all along. I wished I could have realized when I was young that my mother was also a Perfect Rose in a Cracked Vase. Dad knew his little girl and his wife were perfect roses. I wished Mom and I could have believed Dad. How blessed I am that my husband can see past the cracked vase to find his perfect rose.

Each one of us has dreams that shatter and give us unique perspectives on who we are and who we can become. My shattered dreams have helped me to see . . .

A journey is never ending . . . because each ending signals a new beginning. And each tribulation defines what we can achieve.

We are all perfect roses.

ACKNOWLEDGMENTS

This book was both a challenge and a wakeup call to write: a challenge because I had to relive the joys, trials, and struggles I'd lived with. My prayer is that you can relate to the characters and reflect on your own experiences that you have had in your life. It was a wake-up call because . . . well, to be honest, I realized everyone feels like a cracked vase, not just me. Each one of us lives with a struggle; each one of us dislikes something about ourselves. After working nineteen years on editing, I have come to believe we are all unique and a gift from God. We can conquer anything we set our minds to achieving.

I have been given so much and want to express my gratitude to those who have stood by my side through my life trials.

To Trent, my husband, and the man I love with every fiber of my soul. He has listened a million times to my stories and never once complained or judged me. Thank you, honey.

To my five children—Michael, Melissa, Miriam, Malachi, and Maxwell, and my daughters-in-law Haylee and Tanya and sons-in-law Bryce and Blake: You have been the greatest blessing in my life. I love each of you to the moon and beyond. Keep being the phenomenal human beings that you are. As your maternal grandparents would say, "You are my sunshine."

To my beautiful grandchildren, who have brought a fresh outlook to my life. I love you so much. Always remember: Life has challenges to make us stronger.

To Anna Arnett, my sensational friend who has stayed by my side, edited, and helped me complete this book. Thank you for being you. I am

Perfect Rose Cracked Vase

lucky to call you my best girlfriend. You have been a shining light that never goes dim. You are a remarkable writer and author.

To my two brothers. You both mean the world to me. I love you both so much. Remember always that your little sister appreciates you.

To my daughter-in-law Tanya L. Reynolds, thank you for drawing the exquisite illustration on the dedication page; it shows your deep insight into the title *Perfect Rose Cracked Vase.*

I would like to thank Brittany Petrillo owner of Swoon Salon and Boutique for using her expertise skills in styling my hair and making me feel beautiful for my book cover photo. You are sensational and talented.

To Zale Amaya Photography thank you so much for all the time and attention along with your brilliant photographic vision during my photoshoot.

To Melissa for helping me get my hair appointment and Miriam for helping me with my makeup. You both are amazing daughters. I love you both so much.

To the 1106 Design team, who have been so supportive. I've been lucky enough to work with their editor and cover and interior designers. You have been fabulous in guiding me in publishing *Perfect Rose Cracked Vase.*

To Chanda Simpler, an author and a friend who has encouraged me in ways I needed. You are a source of strength that God knew I needed.

To Richard and Linda Johnson, David and Carol Bonnell, Charles and Doreen Reynolds (my in-laws), Craig and Carolyn Black family, Vern and Anna Bingham family, Hartzog Family, Pothieres family, Mary Jane Williams, Theresa Rodebaugh, Carol Glasgow, Shirley Calhoun, and several others, who fed, clothed, and let me be a part of their families. I appreciate you and your sacrifices.

Thank you so much Erika Mendias, Barbara Stott, Lavona Richardson, Pamela Goodfellow, Patti Hulet, Kendyall Guthrie, Eve Moore, Cecily Markland, and Joyann Box. Each one of you has been a blessing in my life.

I want to thank my parents for loving me. No money in the world could ever replace you. I miss and love you.

~ Pamela ~

ABOUT THE AUTHOR

Pamela L. Reynolds was inspired to write *Perfect Rose Cracked Vase* with the hope that others would see that living with birth defects or any type of illness should not hinder opportunities to reach their goals. Pamela was born in Phoenix, Arizona, with Congenital Rubella Syndrome. The doctors told her parents that she was blind and deaf, and would not live. Congenital Rubella Syndrome gave her birth defects, and she lives with Rubella Ophthalmopathy and Microphthalmia (an eye malformation), blind in one eye due to imbedded cataract, glaucoma, heart murmur, hearing loss, and duck feet (she had to wear legs braces and corrective shoes).

Pamela has been married to her husband for 36 years, and they have been blessed with five remarkable children, daughters-in-law, sons-in-law, and grandchildren. Her hobbies include writing, reading, quilting, yoga, gardening, singing, and cooking for her family. She claims that her greatest treasures in life are her parents, husband, children, grandchildren, and brothers. She also adores her aunts, uncles, cousins, and many close friends.

PREGNANCY AND RUBELLA

Rubella is very dangerous for a pregnant woman and her developing baby. Anyone who is not vaccinated against Rubella is at risk of getting the disease. Although Rubella was declared eliminated from the U.S. in 2004, cases can occur when unvaccinated people are exposed to infected people, mostly through international travel. Women should make sure they are protected from Rubella before they get pregnant.

Infection with Rubella virus causes the most severe damage when the mother is infected early in pregnancy, especially in the first 12 weeks (first trimester). From 2005 to 2015, eight babies with CRS have been reported in the United States.

Congenital Rubella Syndrome (CRS)

Congenital Rubella Syndrome (CRS) is a condition that occurs in a developing baby in the womb whose mother is infected with the Rubella virus. Pregnant women who contract Rubella are at risk for miscarriage or stillbirth, and their developing babies are at risk for severe birth defects with devastating, lifelong consequences. CRS can affect almost everything in the developing baby's body.

The most common birth defects from CRS are:

- Deafness
- Cataracts

- Heart defects
- Intellectual disabilities
- Liver and spleen damage
- Low birth weight
- Skin rash at birth

Less-common complications from CRS are:

- Glaucoma
- Brain damage
- Thyroid and other hormone problems
- Inflammation of the lungs

During the last major rubella epidemic in the United States from 1964 to 1965, an estimated 12.5 million people got Rubella, 11,000 pregnant women lost their babies, 2,100 newborns died, and 20,000 babies were born with congenital rubella syndrome (CRS).

Content Source: Centers for Disease Control and Prevention Website
https://www.cdc.gov/rubella/pregnancy.html

www.ingramcontent.com/pod-product-compliance
Lightning Source LLC
Chambersburg PA
CBHW030431010526
44118CB00011B/586